Success in Business Calculations

Success Studybooks

Accounting and Costing
Accounting and Costing: Problems and Projects
Biology
British History 1760–1914
British History since 1914
Business Calculations
Chemistry
Commerce
Commerce: West African Edition
Economic Geography
Economics
Economics: West African Edition
Elements of Banking
European History 1815–1941
Financial Accounting
Financial Accounting: Questions and Answers
Geography: Human and Regional
Geography: Physical and Mapwork
Investment
Law
Management: Personnel
Mathematics
Nutrition
Organic Chemistry
Principles of Accounting
Principles of Accounting: Answer Book
Statistics
Twentieth Century World Affairs

Success in
BUSINESS
CALCULATIONS

Second Edition

Geoffrey Whitehead, B.Sc.(Econ.)

John Murray

Filmset in 'Monophoto' Times 9 on 11 pt. by
Richard Clay (The Chaucer Press) Ltd, Bungay, Suffolk
and printed in Hong Kong by
Wing King Tong Co Ltd

0 7195 3989 7

Foreword

Success in Business Calculations covers the basic arithmetic in use in commercial life. It takes the reader from the most elementary number processes, through decimals, fractions, ratios and proportion, percentages, and so forth, to an elementary appreciation of business statistics, charts and graphs. The simple book-keeping of receipts and payments, petty cash, depreciation and wages records are also covered.

The book meets syllabus requirements of the following: the BEC General module Business Calculations, the Business Calculations content of the Numeracy and Accounting module for BEC National, the arithmetical aspects of CSE and O-level syllabuses, the Commercial Arithmetic syllabuses of such bodies as the Royal Society of Arts and the London Chamber of Commerce, and the Business Calculations modules of the Royal Society of Arts Certificate in Basic Clerical Procedures.

For this new edition many exercises have been revised and a Unit has been added to the statistical section of the book to meet changing syllabus requirements.

G.W.

Acknowledgments

The production of this book has involved its appraisal by many teachers and lecturers active in the field of business education. I am grateful for the assistance of all those who have helped in this way, and must particularly thank Peter Roots, Graham Mead, James Taylor and Leslie Horton. My very sincere thanks go to Jean Macqueen for her indefatigable and patient work on the typescript, and to Irene Slade.

The assistance of the following organizations is gratefully acknowledged:

The Royal Society of Arts, for permission to use questions from their past
    examination papers;
Barclays Bank Group Economic Intelligence Unit;
Kalamazoo Business Systems Limited;
George Vyner Limited;
The Controller, Her Majesty's Stationery Office, for permission to use Crown
    Copyright material.

Addresses

The Royal Society of Arts,
Murray Road,
Orpington,
Kent,
BR5 3RB.

Kalamazoo Business Systems Limited,
Mill Lane,
Northfield,
Birmingham,
B31 2RW.

George Vyner Limited,
Holmfirth,
Huddersfield,
West Yorkshire,
HD7 2RP.

Contents

Contents   xi

Unit One
An Introduction to Business Calculations

1.1 What are Business Calculations?

We live in a society where our daily needs and wants are met by the activities of people working at the complex and continuous process of supplying goods and services. For instance, mass-produced goods flow from factory lines and have to be warehoused and retailed if they are to reach the final consumer. Services are provided by doctors, dentists, teachers, journalists, designers, road-sweepers, dustmen and so on. The supply of goods and services means that records have to be kept and financial transactions calculated and noted. This is the business side of the activities and it is conducted in offices, large and small.

Offices must be staffed, and staff will range from specialists who are qualified or trained—such as financial accountants, cost accountants, programmers and statisticians—to those who are untrained but able to do clerical jobs which require no specialist knowledge. Yet all these office activities have something in common: the employee—whether managing director or junior clerk—must have an ability to perform the basic skills of business calculations.

Every clerk, book-keeper or manager must be able to do addition of numbers, subtraction, multiplication and division. If you work in an office you must be able to apply these processes to money, weights and other measures. You should also know how to handle fractions, decimals, ratios, proportions and percentages, and how to calculate areas and volumes. It is helpful, too, to understand the elementary ideas of statistics.

You may be thinking, 'But I'm no good at any of these'. Don't worry. We shall cover all the ground in easy stages and give you plenty of practice. The ideas are all quite simple once you understand the principles, and it is the aim of this book to help you understand these principles.

In most offices, colleges and schools these days there are electronic aids which take much of the labour out of calculations. You must master the methods of calculation before you can use these aids with confidence. Eventually you will come to use business machines and calculators which will help you achieve speed and efficiency.

1.2 How to Study

If you are preparing for an examination your first step should be to obtain a syllabus from the relevant examining board. Compare the syllabus with the List of Contents of this book and mark the topics that you must study. If, for instance, your syllabus does not mention elementary statistics, you could omit Units 30–33 for the moment. Concentrate on those topics which are essential to you. It is also of great help to you if you obtain some of the past papers set by your examining board. You can obtain these from the board and try working through the questions before you sit your own exam.

If you are not preparing for an examination but want to improve arithmetical skills or revise knowledge of the different processes, you should work steadily through the course, using the 'Diagnostic Tests' in the early Units to help you discover your weaknesses. Concentrate on the areas in which you are least competent and merely revise sections where the work is familiar and comes easily to you. If, as you study, you find one topic difficult and don't seem to be making headway, give yourself a change and move on to something else. You can return to the difficult section later and try again.

Each Unit of study has generous sets of questions and exercises. Work through these until the processes become second nature to you.

Another important point: keep your handwriting clear and neat. When working with figures it is absolutely essential that they are in the correct position to each other, and are written distinctly so that they cannot be misread.

Unit Two

Basic Calculation Processes

2.1 The 'Four Rules'

There are four basic processes in arithmetic.

Addition is the putting together of different individual quantities to make a single larger quantity.

Subtraction is the taking away of one quantity from another, thus making it smaller.

Multiplication is a process which performs repeated additions very quickly.

Division is a process which performs repeated subtractions very quickly.

We must be familiar with the four rules of number; we must be able to add up, subtract, multiply and divide numbers quickly and easily.

2.2 Testing yourself in Business Calculations: Diagnostic Tests

You probably already have *some* basic knowledge of arithmetic, however elementary, but it is likely that you feel dissatisfied with your general level of understanding. On the other hand, you don't want to waste time on aspects you have mastered already. So we shall provide short diagnostic tests, that is, tests which try to discover your weaknesses—the exact areas in which your knowledge is poor. If you do a test, and find no real difficulties in it, skip that part of the work and proceed to the next section.

2.3 Diagnostic Test: Addition

1. Add up the following sums:

(a) 247	(b) 7 385	(c) 87 256
316	6 975	59 134
525	4 124	72 698
649	3 818	14 341

2. Add up the following:

(a) 72 + 36 + 45 =   (b) 36 + 48 + 29 =

(c) 149 + 136 + 277 =   (d) 12 721 + 13 955 + 29 727 =

3. Add up the following, putting sub-totals in on the lines shown:

(a)		(b)	
276		1 874	
325		1 395	
714		2 736	
626		4 295	
585	(sub-total)	7 126	(sub-total)
497		4 365	
281		7 216	
366		5 984	
725		2 399	
637	(sub-total)	1 675	(sub-total)
Total =		Total =	

The answers are given at the end of this Unit.

2.4 Addition of Numbers

(a) The Vocabulary of Mathematics

It is very helpful in mathematics to use the correct words, and at each stage a number of new terms must be learned. We already know that *addition* is the process of putting two or more numbers together. The result of the addition is called the *sum* or the *total* of the numbers. The word *sum* is used in everyday language to mean any piece of arithmetical work, but its mathematical meaning is the *result of an addition*.

(b) Long-totting and Cross-totting

Our number system, perhaps because we have ten fingers, is based on the number 10: it is called the *decimal system* (*decem* = Latin, ten). In this system, ten units make one ten, ten tens make one hundred, ten hundreds make one thousand, and so on.

In business we often meet addition sums, like the following:

Example

Add:

Th	H	T	U
1	8	7	6
	5	9	5
2	0	6	4
7	1	3	6
1 1	6	7	1
	1	2	2

The numbers are set down one above the other, in columns. The positions of the numbers in the columns are important. In the decimal system, a number in any column represents 10 times the same number in the column on its right, and one-tenth of the same number in the column on its left: that is, numbers have a *place value*, depending on which place they are in. Thus in the units column each number represents so many *units*: 6 means 6 units. In the tens column, each number represents *tens*, not units: 6 therefore stands for 60. Thus when we write numbers underneath each other like this, it is very important to keep the columns neat and orderly, so that every number is in its proper *place*.

Adding up sums like this is called *long-totting*, a word which comes from 'totalling'. Always start with the units column. It is a good idea to write in the 'carrying' figures, those which are to be carried into the next column. For instance, in the last example, the units total 21: the 1 is written in the answer and the carrying figure, the 2, is carried into the tens column.

Sometimes we have to add up across a line of figures, thus:

$$172 + 26 + 475 + 294 = 967$$

This is called *cross-totting*. Again we start with the units figure, saying '2 + 6 = 8, +5 = 13, +4 = 17; write down the 7 and carry the 1 into the tens column'. Continue, adding the tens in the same way: $1 + 7 = 8, +2 = 10, +7 = 17, +9 = 26$. Write down the 6 and carry the 2 into the hundreds column. Then $2 + 1 = 3, +4 = 7, +2 = 9$. The answer is thus 967.

(c) Sub-totals in addition

Sometimes a very long list of numbers has to be added. The work of checking such additions is time-consuming, and it is easy to make mistakes. The solution is to use *sub-totals*, usually every five lines, which are themselves then added to give the grand total.

Example

```
          246
          382
          721
          145
          186      1 680

          242
          362
          286
          725
          181      1 796

          492
          463
          731
          246
          512      2 444

                   5 920
```

2.5 Exercises: Long Tots and Cross Tots

1. Copy out these sums and add them up:

(a)	(b)	(c)	(d)
276	496	917	656
381	233	473	727
472	721	276	381
+ 565	+ 846	+ 384	+ 724

(e)	(f)	(g)	(h)
1 865	1 476	585 612	426 276
2 472	2 835	686 713	321 745
+ 3 613	+ 7 212	+ 947 299	+ 636 957

2. Copy out these sums and add them up across the page:
   (a) 7 + 6 + 3 + 5 + 8 =   (b) 17 + 16 + 23 + 49 =
   (c) 127 + 136 + 449 =   (d) 426 + 736 + 1 247 =
   (e) 524 + 1 237 + 5 271 =   (f) 872 + 562 + 4 275 =

3. Copy out these sums, then add them and cross-tot them as well. They are self-checking.

(a)			
274	186	475	......
386	243	263	......
172	616	724	......

(b)			
1 725	4 726	7 382	......
3 864	3 854	5 864	......
7 251	7 216	7 215	......

(c)			
14 716	16 318	18 587	......
26 312	17 216	20 326	......
17 549	14 959	17 252	......
18 216	17 636	16 313	......

(d)

Departmental sales (pounds sterling) Cheaper Supermarkets Ltd.					
Department	Furniture	Fabrics	Fashions	Beauty aids	Total
January	17 865	8 734	27 965	11 265	......
February	19 273	9 565	25 385	8 385	......
March	16 845	8 250	56 724	17 265	......
April	15 326	6 360	50 810	22 151	......
May	14 560	5 840	46 240	20 831	......
June	12 265	5 625	49 385	19 726	......
Totals					

(e)

Units of electricity supplied (thousands)			
Quarter	Standard rate	Cheap rate	Total
Spring	1 856 752	4 266 375	......
Summer	986 256	3 856 245	......
Autumn	1 973 264	5 762 595	......
Winter	2 576 264	8 319 726	......
Totals			

4. Copy out and add up these sums, using sub-totals:

(a)	(b)	(c)
272	175	1 264
256	296	7 232
381	323	6 384
721	761	7 176
462	425	4 925
581	725	6 174
492	636	7 265
294	714	3 816
731	538	7 125
656	246	4 246
426	372	4 371
523	516	3 762
611	594	5 562
728	623	7 315
594	711	8 618

(d)	2 426	(e)	8 564	(f)	7 265
	3 327		2 357		3 277
	4 516		4 162		4 166
	6 842		5 834		3 855
	5 373		7 265		2 777
	1 725		6 275		8 646
	2 362		1 384		3 585
	7 381		2 979		2 717
	4 472		1 656		3 616
	3 437		3 283		4 285
	5 268		7 362		5 276
	4 374		5 162		3 575
	5 186		7 492		1 427
	2 792		6 361		1 356
	4 134		4 371		4 472

2.6 Subtraction

Frequently in business we have to *subtract* or take away one quantity from another. For example, stock that is sold is subtracted from 'stock available' to give 'stock in hand'; similarly, 'net profit' is calculated by subtracting 'expenses' from 'gross profit'.

Again, the vocabulary is important: the result of a subtraction is called the *difference* or the *remainder*.

Before proceeding any further, test yourself in subtraction by doing the diagnostic test in Section 2.7.

2.7 Diagnostic Test: Subtraction

1. Do the following simple subtractions in your head and write down the answers:
   - (a) $7 - 2 =$
   - (b) $12 - 7 =$
   - (c) $6 - 3 =$
   - (d) $16 - 9 =$
   - (e) $9 - 5 =$
   - (f) $19 - 11 =$

2. Discover the remainders in the following subtractions:

(a)	589	(b)	694
	− 235		− 389

(c)	17 265	(d)	127 395
	− 9 318		− 38 278

The answers are given at the end of this Unit.

2.8 Subtraction of Numbers

Subtraction is taught in two ways in schools. If you are more than about eleven years old you will already have acquired habits in one or other method of subtraction and these are difficult to change. In fact there is absolutely no point in changing them, and you should continue using the method you first learned. For convenience, both methods are discussed where appropriate in the paragraphs which follow.

Stage 1. Subtracting numbers from bigger numbers, for example:

$$
\begin{array}{ccc}
8 & 7 & 3 \\
- \ 6 & - \ 4 & - \ 1 \\
\hline
2 & 3 & 2 \\
\hline
\end{array}
$$

Subtractions like these present no difficulty: '8 units less 6 units leaves 2 units' is a simple practical exercise which can even be performed on the fingers if necessary. Alternatively we can use what is called the *complementary addition* method. This does not ask the question 'what is 8 units less 6 units?' It asks instead 'what do I need to add to 6 to get 8?' The answer to both questions is 2. Use whichever method seems the simplest to you, but we will continue on the basis of asking questions like 'what is 8 units less 6 units?'

Note. The best way to check a subtraction is to add up the sum again. If the answer is added to the number which was previously subtracted, the result should be the number we started with. For instance, in the first example in this section, adding 2 + 6 = 8 proves that we have not made an error in subtraction.

Stage 2. Subtracting numbers involving tens, for example:

$$
\begin{array}{cc}
14 & 27 \\
- \ 6 & - \ 9 \\
\hline
8 & 18 \\
\hline
\end{array}
$$

In the first subtraction we find that when we try to take 6 from 4 we cannot do it: 6 is larger than 4. We have therefore to go to a higher rank of numbers, in the tens row, and use this ten to help us carry out the subtraction. We can now use one of two thought processes.

Thought process 1. I have borrowed this ten to help me do the subtraction. Put the ten with the 4, making 14. What is 14 units less 6 units? Answer: 8 units.

Alternative thought process 2. I have borrowed this ten to help me do the subtraction. Take the 6 from the ten. This leaves 4. Now put the 4 with the other 4. Answer: 8.

Whichever thought process we use we reach the same answer.

The second subtraction $(27 - 9)$ is done in the same way, but this time there are some tens left to be considered. We can say:

Thought process 1. $7 - 9$ we cannot do; give it a ten. $17 - 9 = 8$. Of the original two tens only one ten is left. The answer is therefore $10 + 8 = 18$.

Other readers will have learned the same process as follows: $7 - 9$ we cannot do; give it a ten. $17 - 9 = 8$. Pay back the ten we borrowed to the bottom row of the subtraction: 1 ten from 2 tens leaves 1 ten. Therefore the answer is $10 + 8 = 18$.

Thought process 2. $7 - 9$ we cannot do; borrow a ten. $10 - 9 = 1$. Add 7 which we had already: $1 + 7 = 8$. There is one of the original tens left, so the answer is $10 + 8 = 18$.

Other readers will say: $7 - 9$ we cannot do; borrow a ten. $10 - 9 = 1$. Add 7 which we had already: $1 + 7 = 8$. Pay back the ten we borrowed to the bottom row: 1 ten from 2 tens leaves 1 ten, so the answer is $10 + 8 = 18$.

Whichever method you have grown used to is correct for you—but you may now need plenty of practice to improve your work.

Stage 3. Using higher rank numbers in the decimal sequence, for example:

$$\begin{array}{r} 17\,258 \\ -\ \ 5\,379 \\ \hline \\ \hline \end{array}$$

We shall need, at each successive subtraction, to borrow a higher rank number in the next column to the left. We cannot take 9 from 8, so we must borrow a ten. We cannot take 7 tens from 4 tens (or 8 tens from 5 tens if you prefer it) so we borrow 10 tens, i.e. 100 from the hundreds row. Thus:

$$\begin{array}{r} 17\,258 \\ -\ \ 5\,379 \\ \hline 11\,879 \\ \hline \end{array}$$

Once again we check the correctness of our working by adding together the answer and the number subtracted. This should give us the original number in the top row.

2.9 Exercises: Subtraction

1. Perform the following subtractions in your head and write down the answers:

(a) $7 - 3 =$ (b) $9 - 5 =$

(c) $14 - 6 =$ (d) $17 - 9 =$

(e) $23 - 15 =$ (f) $26 - 7 =$

(g) $29 - 13 =$ (h) $47 - 29 =$

(i) $61 - 15 =$ (j) $49 - 19 =$

2. Copy out the following subtractions and work out the differences:

(a)	274 − 139	(b)	958 − 377	(c)	572 − 493

(d)	627 − 508	(e)	652 − 427	(f)	2 736 − 1 585

(g)	1 784 − 939	(h)	8 973 − 2 679	(i)	4 273 − 3 854

(j)	17 256 − 8 517	(k)	27 562 − 7 219	(l)	84 725 − 3 828

(m)	273 268 − 26 839	(n)	139 936 − 5 897	(o)	186 757 − 7 148

3. Copy out the following subtractions and calculate the differences:
   (a) 1 865 − 1 372 =   (b) 7 426 − 4 685 =
   (c) 15 118 − 9 893 =   (d) 16 215 − 9 384 =
   (e) 17 832 − 11 725 =   (f) 108 322 − 39 495 =
   (g) 48 617 − 27 386 =   (h) 139 489 − 46 729 =
   (i) 129 959 − 12 724 =   (j) 726 125 − 128 399 =

2.10 Multiplication

Multiplication is a shortened version of addition. Multiplications always include the word *times*, indicated by the multiply sign ×: for example, 2 × 3 is read 'two times three'.

This is a shortened way of saying 'two taken three times', that is, $2 + 2 + 2 = 6$. Similarly, 7 × 5 means 7 taken 5 times, or $7 + 7 + 7 + 7 + 7 = 35$.

Once again the vocabulary is important. The answer to a multiplication sum is called the *product*, the number being multiplied is the *multiplicand*, and the other number the *multiplier*. Thus, in the multiplication

$$27 \times 5 = 135$$

135 is the product, 27 is the multiplicand and 5 is the multiplier.

2.11 Diagnostic Test: Multiplication

1. Write down the answers to the following multiplications:
   (a) 3 × 5 =   (b) 12 × 4 =   (c) 7 × 6 =
   (d) 11 × 9 =   (e) 8 × 9 =   (f) 7 × 7 =
   (g) 5 × 12 =   (h) 6 × 8 =   (i) 7 × 11 =

2. Set down the following multiplications and work out the answers to them:
   (a) 235 × 7 =   (b) 328 × 9 =
   (c) 562 × 12 =   (d) 728 × 8 =

3. Set down the following multiplications and work out the answers to them:

    (a)   325   (b)   427
          ×   19   ×   25
          ‾‾‾‾‾   ‾‾‾‾‾

          ‾‾‾‾‾   ‾‾‾‾‾
          ═════   ═════

    (c)   1 865   (d)   2 897
          ×   39   × 194
          ‾‾‾‾‾   ‾‾‾‾‾

          ‾‾‾‾‾   ‾‾‾‾‾
          ═════   ═════

The answers are given at the end of this Unit.

2.12 Multiplication Tables

You may have learned your multiplication tables at school, at least up to '12 times' or even '13 times'. If you did, you will have no problem now. If you didn't, you will have to work at learning them off by heart. Without the ability to make an instant calculation based on your 'memory bank' of tables, you will be handicapped and find yourself struggling needlessly at a simple, elementary level. It is worth spending some time each day repeating one or more to yourself until you know them. You can say them as you walk along the street, wait for a train or bus, or do any simple job that liberates your thoughts for a bit. They are given in Table 2.1, on pages 14–15. Copy them out on small cards and keep them in your pocket or handbag. Remember that the 0 times table and the 1 times table are as important as the others. Some people find difficulty in their calculations because they have never learned the 0 times table. They find it hard to realize, for example, that 0 × 12 = 0.

2.13 Simple Multiplications

A simple multiplication uses the individual parts of the multiplication tables, or *multiplication bonds*, learned in Section 2.12. For example:

$$
\begin{array}{r}
1\,273 \\
\times \quad 7 \\
\hline
8\,911 \\
\hline
1\,52
\end{array}
$$

In a multiplication like this one, figures have to be carried from one column into the next. For example, in the units column we have $7 \times 3 = 21$. The 1 is written into the units column, and the two tens are carried into the tens column. You can either remember them in your head, or write them in under the tens column as shown here.

When multiplying by larger numbers two methods are available. Both are correct: stick to the method which comes easiest to you in the examples below.

Notice that when multiplying by a tens figure there will be no units in that line of the answer. A zero is put in the units place and the multiplication continues as before, with simple multiplication, but with the answer one place to the left all the way across. Similarly, when multiplying by a hundreds figure, there are no units and no tens, so that two zeros are required before the multiplication can continue.

Example

Calculate $1\,275 \times 195$

Method 1

$$
\begin{array}{r}
1\,275 \\
\times \quad 195 \\
\hline
6\,375 \\
114\,750 \\
127\,500 \\
\hline
248\,625
\end{array}
$$

multiply by 5
multiply by 90   } add
multiply by 100

Method 2

$$
\begin{array}{r}
1\,275 \\
\times \quad 195 \\
\hline
127\,500 \\
114\,750 \\
6\,375 \\
\hline
248\,625
\end{array}
$$

multiply by 100
multiply by 90   } add
multiply by 5

Table 2.1 The Multiplication Tables

$0 \times 0 = 0$		$0 \times 1 = 0$
$1 \times 0 = 0$		$1 \times 1 = 1$
$2 \times 0 = 0$		$2 \times 1 = 2$
$3 \times 0 = 0$		$3 \times 1 = 3$
$4 \times 0 = 0$		$4 \times 1 = 4$
$5 \times 0 = 0$		$5 \times 1 = 5$
$6 \times 0 = 0$		$6 \times 1 = 6$
$7 \times 0 = 0$		$7 \times 1 = 7$
$8 \times 0 = 0$		$8 \times 1 = 8$
$9 \times 0 = 0$		$9 \times 1 = 9$
$10 \times 0 = 0$		$10 \times 1 = 10$
$11 \times 0 = 0$		$11 \times 1 = 11$
$12 \times 0 = 0$		$12 \times 1 = 12$

$0 \times 2 = 0$	$0 \times 3 = 0$	$0 \times 4 = 0$
$1 \times 2 = 2$	$1 \times 3 = 3$	$1 \times 4 = 4$
$2 \times 2 = 4$	$2 \times 3 = 6$	$2 \times 4 = 8$
$3 \times 2 = 6$	$3 \times 3 = 9$	$3 \times 4 = 12$
$4 \times 2 = 8$	$4 \times 3 = 12$	$4 \times 4 = 16$
$5 \times 2 = 10$	$5 \times 3 = 15$	$5 \times 4 = 20$
$6 \times 2 = 12$	$6 \times 3 = 18$	$6 \times 4 = 24$
$7 \times 2 = 14$	$7 \times 3 = 21$	$7 \times 4 = 28$
$8 \times 2 = 16$	$8 \times 3 = 24$	$8 \times 4 = 32$
$9 \times 2 = 18$	$9 \times 3 = 27$	$9 \times 4 = 36$
$10 \times 2 = 20$	$10 \times 3 = 30$	$10 \times 4 = 40$
$11 \times 2 = 22$	$11 \times 3 = 33$	$11 \times 4 = 44$
$12 \times 2 = 24$	$12 \times 3 = 36$	$12 \times 4 = 48$

$0 \times 5 = 0$	$0 \times 6 = 0$
$1 \times 5 = 5$	$1 \times 6 = 6$
$2 \times 5 = 10$	$2 \times 6 = 12$
$3 \times 5 = 15$	$3 \times 6 = 18$
$4 \times 5 = 20$	$4 \times 6 = 24$
$5 \times 5 = 25$	$5 \times 6 = 30$
$6 \times 5 = 30$	$6 \times 6 = 36$
$7 \times 5 = 35$	$7 \times 6 = 42$
$8 \times 5 = 40$	$8 \times 6 = 48$
$9 \times 5 = 45$	$9 \times 6 = 54$
$10 \times 5 = 50$	$10 \times 6 = 60$
$11 \times 5 = 55$	$11 \times 6 = 66$
$12 \times 5 = 60$	$12 \times 6 = 72$

```
 0 × 7 =  0          0 × 8 =  0
 1 × 7 =  7          1 × 8 =  8
 2 × 7 = 14          2 × 8 = 16
 3 × 7 = 21          3 × 8 = 24
 4 × 7 = 28          4 × 8 = 32
 5 × 7 = 35          5 × 8 = 40
 6 × 7 = 42          6 × 8 = 48
 7 × 7 = 49          7 × 8 = 56
 8 × 7 = 56          8 × 8 = 64
 9 × 7 = 63          9 × 8 = 72
10 × 7 = 70         10 × 8 = 80
11 × 7 = 77         11 × 8 = 88
12 × 7 = 84         12 × 8 = 96
```

```
 0 × 9 =   0       0 × 10 =   0         0 × 11 =   0
 1 × 9 =   9       1 × 10 =  10         1 × 11 =  11
 2 × 9 =  18       2 × 10 =  20         2 × 11 =  22
 3 × 9 =  27       3 × 10 =  30         3 × 11 =  33
 4 × 9 =  36       4 × 10 =  40         4 × 11 =  44
 5 × 9 =  45       5 × 10 =  50         5 × 11 =  55
 6 × 9 =  54       6 × 10 =  60         6 × 11 =  66
 7 × 9 =  63       7 × 10 =  70         7 × 11 =  77
 8 × 9 =  72       8 × 10 =  80         8 × 11 =  88
 9 × 9 =  81       9 × 10 =  90         9 × 11 =  99
10 × 9 =  90      10 × 10 = 100        10 × 11 = 110
11 × 9 =  99      11 × 10 = 110        11 × 11 = 121
12 × 9 = 108      12 × 10 = 120        12 × 11 = 132
```

```
 0 × 12 =   0        0 × 13 =   0
 1 × 12 =  12        1 × 13 =  13
 2 × 12 =  24        2 × 13 =  26
 3 × 12 =  36        3 × 13 =  39
 4 × 12 =  48        4 × 13 =  52
 5 × 12 =  60        5 × 13 =  65
 6 × 12 =  72        6 × 13 =  78
 7 × 12 =  84        7 × 13 =  91
 8 × 12 =  96        8 × 13 = 104
 9 × 12 = 108        9 × 13 = 117
10 × 12 = 120       10 × 13 = 130
11 × 12 = 132       11 × 13 = 143
12 × 12 = 144       12 × 13 = 156
                    13 × 13 = 169
```

2.14 Exercises: Multiplication

1. Carry out the following multiplications:
   (a) 1 589 × 7 =   (b) 9 253 × 8 =
   (c) 1 638 × 5 =   (d) 3 686 × 12 =
   (e) 2 141 × 4 =   (f) 7 214 × 7 =
   (g) 2 476 × 19 =   (h) 1 738 × 27 =
   (i) 3 814 × 15 =   (j) 3 846 × 36 =

2. Do the following multiplications:
   (a) 3 872 × 13 =   (b) 6 519 × 29 =
   (c) 5 164 × 14 =   (d) 5 814 × 37 =
   (e) 3 817 × 18 =   (f) 6 842 × 59 =
   (g) 2 965 × 19 =   (h) 7 816 × 37 =
   (i) 7 263 × 18 =   (j) 5 127 × 29 =

3. At a book exhibition 156 visitors bought 3 books each, 272 bought 4 books each and 105 bought 5 books each. 826 visitors bought 2 books and 1 275 visitors each bought only one book. No visitor bought more than 5 books. How many books were sold altogether?

4. In a survey of milk yield 365 cows gave 25 litres each per day, 482 gave 21 litres per day and 857 gave 16 litres per day. What was the total daily milk yield?

5. A library discovers that the following issues were made: 2 785 books were issued once in the month, 7 295 were issued twice in the month, 11 565 were issued three times in the month and 854 were issued four times. No book was issued more than four times in a month. What was the total number of issues made in the month?

6. A mail-order house sells bookcases in packs which the customer fits together in his own home. In one month 2 856 people ordered a single pack, 1 527 ordered 2 packs, 856 ordered 3 packs and a library ordered 150 packs. How many packs were sold in the month?

7. At a festival 27 384 people paid for a single ticket, 15 854 paid for two persons, 11 281 paid for three persons and 1 816 group tickets for eight persons each were sold. How many seats were sold?

2.15 Division

Division is a shortened version of subtraction. If we want to know how many 2s there are in 10 we can subtract 2 from 10 (which would leave 8), then subtract 2 from 8 (which would leave 6) and so on. Eventually we would find that there were five 2s in 10. With division we do it more quickly. We ask 'how many 2s in 10?' But we know from our tables that 5 × 2 = 10, so we can say at once that the answer is 5. Division therefore becomes very easy if we know the multiplication tables.

We can write down our example, 'How many 2s in 10? Answer: 5' as $10 \div 2 = 5$ ('10 divided by 2 equals 5').

Sometimes a number will not divide exactly by another number. For instance, $11 \div 2 = 5$, and there is 1 left over at the end of the division. We answer the question 'How many 2s in 11?' by saying '5, and 1 left over'.

The vocabulary used in division is as follows:

(a) the number to be divided is called the *dividend*;

(b) the number we are dividing by is the *divisor*;

(c) the answer to a division sum is the *quotient*;

(d) a number which is left over at the end of a division is called the *remainder*.

2.16 Diagnostic Test: Division

1. Write the answers to the following divisions. Some of them will have remainders.

(a) $16 \div 4 =$ (b) $45 \div 9 =$

(c) $88 \div 11 =$ (d) $72 \div 12 =$

(e) $64 \div 4 =$ (f) $13 \div 8 =$

(g) $55 \div 6 =$ (h) $50 \div 7 =$

(i) $29 \div 9 =$ (j) $143 \div 12 =$

2. (a) $3\,784 \div 8 =$ (b) $5\,299 \div 7 =$

(c) $2\,482 \div 9 =$ (d) $3\,874 \div 12 =$

3. (a) $4\,762 \div 13 =$ (b) $59\,726 \div 15 =$

(c) $27\,387 \div 19 =$ (d) $72\,695 \div 35 =$

The answers are given at the end of this Unit.

2.17 Short Division

Whenever we divide by a number of which we know the multiplication table we can use the method of *short division*. With short division sums all the work is done in our heads and the answer can be written down straight away.

Example

Divide 2 765 by 7

We write the division ready for working thus:

$$7 \overline{)\,2\,765}$$

We can see that 7 will not go into 2 (thousands). There will not therefore be any thousand in the answer. The two thousands will have to be taken in with the next figure, which is a 7 in the hundreds column. Now 7 will go into 27 hundreds 3 times (3 × 7 = 21 and there is a remainder of 6 hundreds). We therefore put 3 into the answer row, and carry the remainder 6 into the next column, the tens column.

$$\frac{7\,)\,2\,765}{3}$$

The remainder of 6 hundreds with the 6 tens in the tens column make 66 tens altogether. We now see that 7 goes into 66 tens 9 times (9 × 7 = 63, with 3 tens over). We therefore put the 9 in the tens column of the answer and carry the 3 tens remaining into the units column. We now have 35 units, and 7 goes exactly 5 times into 35. The answer to the division is therefore 395.

$$\frac{7\,)\,2\,765}{395}$$

Example

Divide 51 763 by 9

$$\frac{9\,)\,51\,763}{5\,751 \text{ remainder } 4}$$

Work through this example for yourself, making sure that you understand how the answer was reached. It is most important to become really good at short division, since a great many business calculations come down in the end to this process.

2.18 Exercises: Short Division

1. Carry out the following divisions:
   (a) 295 ÷ 5 =   (b) 786 ÷ 3 =
   (c) 9 832 ÷ 8 =   (d) 7 275 ÷ 5 =
   (e) 4 959 ÷ 9 =   (f) 6 564 ÷ 6 =
   (g) 6 216 ÷ 7 =   (h) 7 912 ÷ 8 =
   (i) 7 326 ÷ 9 =   (j) 8 544 ÷ 12 =

2. Carry out the following divisions:
   (a) 2 796 ÷ 9 =   (b) 7 219 ÷ 3 =
   (c) 3 812 ÷ 7 =   (d) 5 872 ÷ 12 =
   (e) 7 365 ÷ 9 =   (f) 7 473 ÷ 5 =
   (g) 4 214 ÷ 4 =   (h) 9 726 ÷ 7 =
   (i) 6 875 ÷ 6 =   (j) 5 836 ÷ 9 =

2.19 Long Division

If we are required to divide by a number bigger than 12, we must usually adopt a system known as *long division*, so called because when written down it makes rather a long sum on the page. We need to use this method because we do not usually learn our tables past the 12 times table. Of course we may know the 13 times table or go on and learn the 14 times table, but it would be clearly a waste of time to carry this too far.

We usually write the division in such a way that the answer can be put at the top; the working can then be set out below, without getting in the way of the answer.

Example

Divide 27 527 by 19

```
            1 448    remainder 15
      19 ) 27 527
           19
           ‾‾‾
            8 5        4 × 19 = 76
            7 6        5 × 19 = 95
            ‾‾‾
              92
              76
             ‾‾‾
             167       19 × 8 = 152
             152       19 × 9 = 171
             ‾‾‾
              15
```

In the first part of this example we ask ourselves how many times 19 goes into 2 (actually the 2 represents 2 ten-thousands, or 20 000, but we disregard all the zeros). Clearly 19 will not go into 2, so there will be no figure in the answer above the 2. We now carry the 2 into the next column and put it with the 7, and ask how many 19s in 27? (Of course this 27 is really 27 000 but again we disregard place value.) Now 19 will go once into 27, so we write a 1 in the answer, over the top of the 7; that means the answer will have 1 thousand in it. We then write the 19 below the 27 and subtract it. We find there are 8 thousands over.

We now bring the 5 hundreds down alongside the 8 thousands making 85 hundreds, and ask how many 19s in 85? Are there 4, or 5, or what? Since we don't know the 19 times table by heart we jot down on the edge of the paper some of the number bonds from the table: 4 × 19 = 76 and 5 × 19 = 95. Clearly 19 goes 4 times into 85, and there are some over. We write 4 in the answer in the hundreds column and then subtract 4 × 19 = 76 from the 85: there are 9 hundreds left over. We bring down the 2 tens in the top row beside the 9 hundreds, and we now have 92 tens.

Now, how many 19s in 92? We already have 4 × 19 = 76 and 5 × 19 = 95. The answer is 4 again. We write 4 in the answer and 76 under the 92. When we take this away we have 16 tens left over. We bring down the 7 from the top row and write it beside the 16 tens and we have 167 units.

Next, how many 19s in 167? Again, we try it. Let's try 8: $8 \times 19 = 152$. Try 9: $9 \times 19 = 171$, and obviously this is too much. 19 goes 8 times into 167 and there will be a remainder. We write the 8 in the answer and the 152 below the 167. Subtracting, we have a remainder of 15. So the answer to our question is that $27\,527 \div 19 = 1\,448$ remainder 15.

The ability to do long division is a very good test of arithmetical aptitude. It is very important that you really understand what is happening as you divide the divisor into the dividend and find the quotient and remainder. You should do a great many of these sums until you are really confident about them.

2.20 Exercises: Long Division

1. (a) $2\,761 \div 13 =$ (b) $3\,527 \div 15 =$
   (c) $5\,846 \div 17 =$ (d) $9\,361 \div 19 =$
   (e) $16\,327 \div 16 =$ (f) $3\,726 \div 21 =$
   (g) $4\,841 \div 23 =$ (h) $13\,732 \div 25 =$
   (i) $27\,865 \div 27 =$ (j) $49\,971 \div 29 =$

2. (a) $27\,327 \div 72 =$ (b) $29\,621 \div 64 =$
   (c) $38\,850 \div 38 =$ (d) $46\,898 \div 47 =$
   (e) $95\,726 \div 24 =$ (f) $2\,786 \div 127 =$
   (g) $13\,586 \div 149 =$ (h) $27\,438 \div 174 =$
   (i) $148\,721 \div 125 =$ (j) $179\,659 \div 295 =$

3. The Working Men's Club collects a 'mountain of pennies' on its counter for the local orphanage. There prove to be 11 729 pennies in the pile, to share among 37 children. How many pennies does each child receive?

4. Because of a shortage of sugar, a grocer decides to divide his supplies equally between his 125 regular customers. In a month he receives 2 825 bags of sugar. Any remainder after sharing the bags will be sold to casual customers, a single bag to each. How many casual customers can he supply?

5. People arrive at a Safari Park in cars and coaches. 120 cars have 2 occupants each, 325 cars have 3 occupants, 162 cars have 4 occupants and 71 cars have 5 occupants. 18 coaches have 30 occupants each and each of the other coaches contains 48 visitors. If 3 190 tickets were sold, how many 48-seater coaches were there?

6. In the navy of a certain country there are 23 small vessels and 18 large vessels. The entire staff of the navy is allocated among these ships; even senior staff officers are technically members of a particular crew. The total staff numbers 27 780 men. Each small vessel has 30 men allocated to it. The large vessels are all the same size and the crews are equally divided. How many men serve each of these large ships?

2.21 Mental Arithmetic Exercises

This section is one of a number throughout this book designed to give you practice in mental arithmetic so that you can develop speed and accuracy. Write down *the answers only* to the questions in these sections.

1. (a) $12 + 9 + 15 + 13 =$
   (c) $17 + 12 + 4 + 14 =$
   (e) $163 + 273 + 159 =$
   (g) $248 - 56 =$
   (i) $327 - 25 =$

   (b) $127 \times 3 =$
   (d) $284 \times 7 =$
   (f) $2\,956 \times 5 =$
   (h) $248 \div 4 =$
   (j) $273 \div 3 =$

2. (a) $25 + 36 + 72 + 84 =$
   (c) $15 + 29 + 64 + 38 =$
   (e) $173 + 246 + 512 =$
   (g) $325 - 74 =$
   (i) $256 - 84 =$

   (b) $137 \times 4 =$
   (d) $258 \times 9 =$
   (f) $721 \times 7 =$
   (h) $816 \div 8 =$
   (j) $729 \div 6 =$

3. (a) $37 + 48 + 56 + 28 =$
   (c) $15 + 28 + 13 + 24 =$
   (e) $276 + 325 + 149 =$
   (g) $726 - 86 =$
   (i) $295 - 77 =$

   (b) $236 \times 4 =$
   (d) $381 \times 5 =$
   (f) $736 \times 8 =$
   (h) $155 \div 5 =$
   (j) $308 \div 7 =$

4. (a) Add $9 + 5 + 4 + 7 + 3$.
   (b) Add $17 + 23 + 19$.
   (c) Add $127 + 136 + 429$.
   (d) Subtract 14 from 27.
   (e) Subtract 113 from 279.
   (f) Subtract 272 from 391.
   (g) Multiply 27×9.
   (h) Multiply 136×5.

   (i) Multiply 284×12.
   (j) Divide 29 by 12.
   (k) Divide 187 by 3.
   (l) Divide 275 by 25.
   (m) What is half of 26 324?
   (n) What is twice 195?
   (o) How many seventeens in 85?

5. (a) Add $12 + 7 + 15$.
   (b) A roll of wallpaper is 12 metres long. How much paper is in 18 rolls?
   (c) Share 360 sheets of paper equally among fifteen students. How many does each get?
   (d) Multiply 135 by 12.
   (e) Divide 1 000 by 25.
   (f) What do we call the answer to a division sum?
   (g) A stallholder in a marketplace sells 37 dresses, 84 jumpers, 68 cardigans, 54 pairs of jeans and 20 T-shirts. How many garments has he sold altogether?
   (h) $625 \div 25 =$
   (i) Multiply 300×40.
   (j) Divide 1 000 000 by 200.

(k) A lottery offers a first prize of £10 000, 5 prizes of £1 000 and 200 prizes of £10 each. How much is the total prize money?

(l) 286 ÷ 13 =

(m) 48 650 ÷ 50 =

(n) Multiply 27 by 10 and add it to 38 × 5.

(o) A plantation contains 10 000 young trees. The forester decides to cut down every fifth tree to give the rest more room. How many trees left?

2.22 Answers to Diagnostic Tests

Addition (Section 2.3)

1. (a) 1 737; (b) 22 302; (c) 233 429.
2. (a) 153; (b) 113; (c) 562; (d) 56 403.
3. (a) Sub-totals 2 526 and 2 506; final total = 5 032.
   (b) Sub-totals 17 426 and 21 639; final total = 39 065.

If you made more than two mistakes in these sums you should return to Section 2.4 and work through the sections on the addition of numbers. If you did well, continue with Section 2.7, the diagnostic test on subtraction.

Subtraction (Section 2.7)

1. (a) 5; (b) 5; (c) 3; (d) 7; (e) 4; (f) 8.
2. (a) 354; (b) 305; (c) 7 947; (d) 89 117.

If you had more than two answers wrong in this section you should return to Section 2.8 and work through the sections on subtraction of numbers. If you did well on this test proceed to Section 2.11 and to the diagnostic test on multiplication.

Multiplication (Section 2.11)

1. (a) 15; (b) 48; (c) 42; (d) 99; (e) 72; (f) 49; (g) 60; (h) 48; (i) 77.
2. (a) 1 645; (b) 2 952; (c) 6 744; (d) 5 824.
3. (a) 6 175; (b) 10 675; (c) 72 735; (d) 562 018.

If you had more than two answers wrong in these multiplications you should return to Section 2.12 and work through the text on multiplication. If you did well, proceed to Section 2.16 and do the diagnostic test on division.

Division (Section 2.16)

1. (a) 4; (b) 5; (c) 8; (d) 6; (e) 16; (f) 1 remainder 5; (g) 9 remainder 1; (h) 7 remainder 1; (i) 3 remainder 2; (j) 11 remainder 11.
2. (a) 473; (b) 757; (c) 275 remainder 7; (d) 322 remainder 10.
3. (a) 366 remainder 4; (b) 3 981 remainder 11; (c) 1 441 remainder 8; (d) 2 077.

If you had more than two errors in this test, return to Section 2.17 and work through the sections on division. If you did well, proceed to Unit 3.

Unit Three

Decimal Fractions

3.1 The Decimal System

When the decimal system (see Section 2.4(*b*)) is used for parts or *fractions* of a whole number we talk about tenths, hundredths, thousandths and so on, the letters 'th' added at the end of a word indicating a part smaller than a unit. Thus when a unit is divided into ten parts each part is called *one-tenth*; if a unit is divided into a hundred parts each is called *one-hundredth*. To separate the whole numbers from the fractions we use a dot called a *decimal point*: for example, in a typical decimal number

$$127.597$$

the figure 5 represents five-tenths and the figure 9 nine-hundredths.

The great advantage of fractions like these—*decimal fractions*—is that they obey the same rules as ordinary whole numbers. When we add up 10 thousandths they make 1 hundredth, when we add up 10 hundredths they make 1 tenth, and when we add up 10 tenths they make 1 unit.

3.2 Addition and Subtraction of Decimals

When adding and subtracting numbers which have decimal fractions we always *keep the decimal points underneath one another*. This automatically brings units under units, tens under tens and hundreds under hundreds on one side of the decimal point; on the other side, the tenths will be under tenths, the hundredths under hundredths and so forth. This prevents all difficulties of place value.

Example

Add up the following numbers: 1.16, 2.75, 3.08, 4.057

$$\begin{array}{r} 1.16 \\ 2.75 \\ 3.08 \\ \underline{4.057} \\ \hline 11.047 \end{array}$$

Start to add up with the thousandths column. In this example there are only 7, so that there are not enough thousandths to make one hundredth. Write the 7 thousandths in the answer.

Now add up the hundredths column: the result is 24 hundredths. The 20 hundredths make 2 tenths: carry them into the next column. Write the 4 hundredths in the answer.

Now add the tenths column. Including the 2 tenths carried from the hundredths column they total 10 tenths, which makes exactly 1 unit. Carry this into the units column and write 0 in the answer.

The units column, including the 1 unit carried from the tenths, totals 11 altogether.

Example

Subtract 2.56 from 21.735

$$
\begin{array}{r}
21.735 \\
-\ 2.56 \\
\hline
19.175 \\
\hline
\end{array}
$$

Subtracting as in any other subtraction calculation: there are 0 thousandths to take from 5 thousandths, and the result is 5 thousandths.

Continue with the normal subtraction process, using the method you generally use (see Section 2.8).

3.3 Exercises: Addition and Subtraction of Decimals

1. Work out each of the following addition sums:
    (a) 27.75 + 14.47 + 18.69 + 24.21 =
    (b) 42.35 + 32.38 + 37.28 + 42.48 =
    (c) 94.85 + 68.52 + 40.52 + 74.37 =
    (d) 136.72 + 1.45 + 19.834 + 4.059 =
    (e) 716.35 + 27.56 + 847.25 + 827.5 =
    (f) 416.95 + 81.756 + 2 475.62 + 5.94 =
    (g) 84.359 + 276.255 + 317.628 =
    (h) 8 189.5 + 387.565 + 4.385 9 =

2. Find the remainder in each of the following subtractions:
    (a) 27.65 − 14.93 =   (b) 49.67 − 29.37 =
    (c) 74.68 − 23.25 =   (d) 31.63 − 14.95 =
    (e) 147.59 − 29.656 =   (f) 29.459 − 3.687 =
    (g) 772.563 − 258.49 =   (h) 426.32 − 28.85 =
    (i) 49.725 − 4.786 =   (j) 417.242 − 28.729 =
    (k) 38.659 − 14.984 =   (l) 646.58 − 295.635 =

3.4 Multiplication of Decimals

The simplest way of multiplying decimal fractions is to ignore the decimal points altogether until the end of the multiplication, and only then to determine the correct position of the decimal point in the result.

Example

Multiply 1.72 by 1.5

Ignore the decimal points altogether and carry out an ordinary multiplication.

$$
\begin{array}{r}
172 \\
\times\ 15 \\
\hline
860 \\
1\ 720 \\
\hline
2\ 580 \\
\hline
\end{array}
$$

The position of the decimal point is fixed as follows: count the numbers of figures after the decimal point in both the multiplier and the multiplicand; there will be the same number of figures after the decimal point in the product. In our example there is one figure after the decimal point in 1.5 and two figures after the decimal point in 1.72: that is, there are three figures after the decimal point altogether. Therefore there will be three figures after the decimal point in the product, and the result of the multiplication is 2.580. We can disregard the final 0, and give the answer as 2.58.

3.5 Exercises: Multiplication of Decimals

1. Carry out the following multiplications, taking care to place the decimal point correctly in each answer:
   (a) 7.56 × 1.5 =   (b) 8.46 × 1.8 =
   (c) 8.32 × 1.7 =   (d) 9.75 × 2.3 =
   (e) 83.7 × 2.9 =   (f) 27.3 × 3.8 =
   (g) 227.4 × 0.65 =   (h) 394.6 × 0.92 =
   (i) 386.9 × 0.32 =   (j) 257.8 × 2.9 =

2. Carry out the following multiplications, taking care to place the decimal point correctly in each answer:
   (a) 2.7 × 1.7 =   (b) 3.8 × 4.8 =
   (c) 3.85 × 3.8 =   (d) 4.98 × 6.7 =
   (e) 42.69 × 0.39 =   (f) 492.8 × 2.35 =
   (g) 7.116 × 27.2 =   (h) 876.5 × 32.6 =
   (i) 8.295 × 36.9 =   (j) 24.65 × 0.859 =

3.6 Multiplying and Dividing Decimals by Multiples of 10

Because the decimal system is a system of tens, it is possible to multiply or divide a number by 10 (or any multiple of 10) simply by changing its place value. Thus we can multiply by 10, 100, 1 000 or any other multiple of ten by moving the number physically to the left one, two, three or more places, keeping the decimal point fixed. Similarly we can divide by 10, 100 and so on, by moving the number physically to the right by one, two or more places.

Example

Here is a number:

$$227.954$$

If we multiply this number by 10 it becomes

$$2\ 279.54$$

The whole number has to be moved physically to the left one place, while the decimal point remains fixed.

If we multiply by 10 again—that is, if we multiply the original number by 100—we find the whole number again moves one place to the left, and becomes

$$22\ 795.4$$

Similarly,

$$127.52 \times 10 = 1\ 275.2$$
$$47.565 \times 100 = 4\ 756.5$$
$$2.95 \times 1\ 000 = 2\ 950$$
$$38.75 \times 1\ 000\ 000 = 38\ 750\ 000$$

Example

Here is a number:

$$38.175$$

If we divide this by 10 the result is

$$3.8175$$

and the whole number has moved one place to the right.
Similarly,

$$718.65 \div 100 = 7.186\ 5$$
$$22.954 \div 1\ 000 = 0.022\ 954$$
$$81\ 765.324 \div 1\ 000\ 000 = 0.081\ 765\ 324$$

3.7 Exercises: Multiplying and Dividing Decimals by Multiples of 10

1. Write down the products of these multiplications:

   (a) $27.65 \times 10 =$ (b) $4.275 \times 10 =$

   (c) $42.95 \times 100 =$ (d) $459.67 \times 100 =$

   (e) $3.785\ 6 \times 1\ 000 =$ (f) $4.583 \times 1\ 000 =$

   (g) $49.725 \times 100 =$ (h) $7\ 256.1 \times 100 =$

   (i) $869.7 \times 10\ 000 =$ (j) $386.56 \times 1\ 000$

2. Write down the quotients of these divisions:

   (a) $47.65 \div 10 =$ (b) $4.95 \div 10 =$

   (c) $275.84 \div 100 =$ (d) $247.65 \div 100 =$

   (e) $3.816\ 7 \div 1\ 000 =$ (f) $12.736 \div 1\ 000 =$

   (g) $297.65 \div 100 =$ (h) $1\ 896.5 \div 100 =$

   (i) $4\ 725.636 \div 10\ 000 =$ (j) $2\ 785.6 \div 1\ 000\ 000 =$

3.8 Division by Decimals

The easiest way to divide by a decimal fraction is to alter the divisor so that it becomes a whole number. For example, it is not very easy to divide by 1.5; it is simpler to remove the decimal point and divide by 15. The only way we can remove the decimal point is to multiply by 10, thus $10 \times 1.5 = 15$. But this will give us the wrong answer, unless we take some action to compensate for this change.

Example

$$4.5 \div 1.5$$

We can see at once that the answer is 3.

Suppose that, as we have suggested, we change the 1.5 to a whole number by multiplying by 10, so that it becomes 15. What shall we have to do to the 4.5 to compensate for this change so that we can get the correct answer 3? Clearly we must multiply the 4.5 by 10 as well. We then have

$$45 \div 15 = 3$$

So the rule is: *change the divisor to a whole number, then do to the dividend what you did to the divisor.*

Example

Divide 142.725 by 7.5

$$142.725 \div 7.5$$

Change the divisor to a whole number: 75

Now to do this we multiplied 7.5 by 10, so we must now multiply the dividend, 142.725, by 10. We now write the division as

$$1\ 427.25 \div 75$$

```
            19.03
75 ) 1 427.25
       75
       ──
       677
       675
       ───
         2 25
         2 25
         ────
            0
```

$$= 19.03$$

Note. It is important to place the decimal point in the answer exactly over the decimal point in the dividend.

3.9 Exercises: Division by Decimals

1. Carry out the following divisions (no remainders are involved):
   (a) $2.6 \div 1.3 =$ (b) $4.2 \div 1.4 =$
   (c) $3.52 \div 1.6 =$ (d) $82.36 \div 7.1 =$
   (e) $98.9 \div 2.3 =$ (f) $196.95 \div 6.5 =$
   (g) $244.4 \div 4.7 =$ (h) $1.989 \div 8.5 =$
   (i) $9.047 \div 8.3 =$ (j) $219.96 \div 9.4 =$

2. Carry out the following divisions:
   (a) $121.77 \div 2.7 =$ (b) $83.886 \div 8.2 =$
   (c) $45.22 \div 3.8 =$ (d) $2.592 \div 9.6 =$
   (e) $7.398 \div 0.54 =$ (f) $133.407 \div 8.1 =$
   (g) $445.5 \div 16.5 =$ (h) $3.327\ 5 \div 27.5 =$
   (i) $3\ 304.3 \div 17.3 =$ (j) $485.74 \div 32.6 =$

3.10 Divisions Which Do Not Come Out Exactly

Some divisions do not come out exactly, but the division process goes on and on. The same number, or group of numbers, may recur again and again, or there may be no clear pattern of recurrence. For example:

$100 \div 3$:   3) 100
                                 33.3333 etc.

$100 \div 9$:   9) 100
                                 11.1111 etc.

In these numbers the figures 3 and 1 recur endlessly. This type of number is known as a *recurring decimal*, and it is written 33.3̇ or 11.1̇, the dot over the decimal fraction indicating that the number repeats endlessly. These numbers are read as 'thirty-three point three recurring' and 'eleven point one recurring'. Now consider:

$100 \div 11$:

$$11 \overline{)\,100}$$
$$9.090909 \text{ etc.}$$

$100 \div 7$:

$$7 \overline{)\,100}$$
$$14.28571428571 \text{ etc.}$$

In these numbers groups of figures, 09 and 285714 respectively, go on repeating themselves. The numbers can be written 9.0̇9̇ and 14.2̇85714̇, the dots over the figures indicating that all the figures between the dots recur.

Example

$287 \div 19$

$$\begin{array}{r} 15.10526315 \\ 19 \overline{)\,287.} \\ 19 \\ \hline 97 \text{ etc.} \end{array}$$

This sum appears to go on and on and on. There is little point in continuing such a division, for the figures in the result represent smaller and smaller quantities. For instance, the figure 3 in the last example represents 3 millionths, a very small quantity indeed when compared with the whole quotient. In divisions like these an answer is usually required to a certain degree of accuracy—such as 'correct to 2 decimal places'. In this example we have:

Answer to 3 places = 15.105

Had this answer been 15.106 it would have been nearer to 15.11 than to 15.10 and we should have 'corrected up' to give the answer:

Answer = 15.11 correct to 2 places

Had the answer been 15.104 it would clearly have been closer to 15.10 than to 15.11 and we should have given the answer:

Answer = 15.10 correct to 2 places

But the answer is exactly halfway, 15.105. We can now go a further place in the division and we find that it is 15.1052. Clearly the most correct answer is therefore 15.11—because 52 ten-thousandths is more than half of a hundredth. **Note.** In cases where the answer works out to exactly halfway so that we cannot go a further place—15.105, for instance—the rule for correcting is to leave the final answer an even number, ending in 0, 2, 4, 6 or 8. So 15.105 would be corrected down to 15.10 but an answer which came to 15.755 would be corrected up to 15.76. (This rule can be quite important in statistics.)

To obtain the required degree of accuracy we must work to one decimal place more than is asked for, and use the last two figures to 'correct up'. For example, if the required degree of accuracy is 'correct to the nearest whole number' we work to one decimal place and use the figure in the tenths column to find the answer correct to the nearest whole number. For instance, an answer of 23.7 is 24 to the nearest whole number, while an answer of 23.3 is 23 to the nearest whole number. If the required degree of accuracy is 'correct to 3 places of decimals' we work to 4 places of decimals and use the fourth figure to 'correct up'.

Example

Find 385 ÷ 17 correct to 1 decimal place

$$385 \div 17$$

$$
\begin{array}{r}
22.64 \\
17 \overline{)\ 385} \\
34 \\
\hline
45 \\
34 \\
\hline
110 \\
102 \\
\hline
80 \\
68 \\
\hline
\end{array}
$$

= 22.6 correct to 1 decimal place

Note. The degree of accuracy of an answer must always be clearly specified.

3.11 Exercises: More Division of Decimals

1. Find the results of these divisions, correct to 1 decimal place:
   (a) 276.35 ÷ 29 =   (b) 714.75 ÷ 23 =
   (c) 492.65 ÷ 17 =   (d) 375.62 ÷ 25 =
   (e) 726.25 ÷ 93 =   (f) 827.54 ÷ 57 =

2. Find the results of these divisions, correct to 2 decimal places:
   (a) 37.295 ÷ 1.3 =   (b) 94.781 ÷ 2.7 =
   (c) 729.523 ÷ 1.6 =   (d) 826.395 ÷ 3.2 =
   (e) 748.817 ÷ 5.4 =   (f) 27 000 ÷ 6.1 =

3. Find the results of these divisions:

   (a) 476.25 ÷ 3.5 correct to 2 decimal places

   (b) 29.875 ÷ 0.58 correct to 1 decimal place

   (c) 3 816.4 ÷ 27.3 correct to 1 decimal place

   (d) 725.65 ÷ 32.7 correct to the nearest whole number

   (e) 138.656 ÷ 7.95 correct to 2 decimal places

   (f) 381.65 ÷ 1.75 correct to 3 decimal places.

Unit Four

Money

4.1 The Decimal Currency of the United Kingdom

The United Kingdom currency is the *pound sterling*, the symbol for which is £. The pound is divided into 100 *pence* (symbol: p) and the coinage consists of seven coins, the 50p, 20p, 10p, 5p, 2p, 1p and ½p coins. The 20p coin was introduced in June 1982 and a £1 coin is planned for April 1983.

Business calculations are largely concerned with money, which is the basis of payment for goods and services rendered, and is used as a unit of account in keeping records of indebtedness. All office records, such as book-keeping, costing and so on, require real competence in money calculations and consequently every office employee must be able to add up, subtract, multiply and divide money. Fortunately the decimal system makes these calculations very simple.

4.2 Expressing Money in Writing

Sums of money less than £1 in value may be written down in two ways. The first way is to write the number of pence, followed by a letter p, without a following full stop and without a preceding decimal point. Thus 55p, 72½p, 19p, 99½p are all correct. .55p and .99½p are incorrect.

The second way is to use the £ sign, a 0 in the £s column and a point. Thus £0.55, £0.72½, £0.19 and £0.99½ are correct, but £0.55p is incorrect—we do not use *both* £ and p symbols.

If the number of pence is less than 10 there should be a 0 in the ten-pence column to indicate that there are no ten-pence pieces involved. Thus £0.08 means the same as 8p and £0.80 means the same as 80p.

For sums of money greater than £1 the second method is always used: £132.17½ is the correct way to write one hundred and thirty-two pounds seventeen and a half pence.

If you are calling out sums of money in the office or shop it avoids confusion if you say the word 'pounds'. Thus it is better to say 'five pounds fifty' than 'five fifty' and 'one hundred and twenty-two pounds thirty-five' is better than 'one twenty-two thirty-five'.

A halfpenny is always written as a fraction ½, not as a decimal 0.005, except sometimes in calculations. For instance, in dividing a sum of money such as £212.52$\frac{1}{2}$ we may write the $\frac{1}{2}$p as £0.005 and do our calculations with £212.525.

4.3 Addition of Money

When adding up money the rule is the same as for any decimal system: *keep the decimal points under one another*, so that the pence, halfpence and pounds fall correctly into their proper columns. Begin with the right-hand column—the halfpence, if there are any, remembering that two of them make one penny, to be carried into the pence column—and then complete the addition in the usual way.

Example

Add up £2.75, £12.25$\frac{1}{2}$, £13.38$\frac{1}{2}$ and £14.72$\frac{1}{2}$

$$
\begin{array}{r}
£ \\
2.75 \\
12.25\tfrac{1}{2} \\
13.38\tfrac{1}{2} \\
14.72\tfrac{1}{2} \\
\hline
43.11\tfrac{1}{2} \\
\hline
\end{array}
$$

4.4 Exercises: Addition of Money

1. (a) Add up £2.25, £3.74$\frac{1}{2}$, £4.29, £5.65$\frac{1}{2}$.
   (b) Add up £4.56, £1.71$\frac{1}{2}$, £7.29, £13.16$\frac{1}{2}$.
   (c) Add up £7.12$\frac{1}{2}$, £7.48$\frac{1}{2}$, £17.46, £14.14$\frac{1}{2}$.
   (d) Add up £3.15, £9.32$\frac{1}{2}$, £12.25$\frac{1}{2}$, £18.29$\frac{1}{2}$.
   (e) Add up £2.16$\frac{1}{2}$, £8.64$\frac{1}{2}$, £15.38$\frac{1}{2}$, £17.17.
   (f) Add up £6.29, £6.50, £22.51$\frac{1}{2}$, £29.18.

(g) £	(h) £	(i) £	(j) £
27.36	14.29$\frac{1}{2}$	286.29$\frac{1}{2}$	49.56$\frac{1}{2}$
149.72	137.62$\frac{1}{2}$	721.34$\frac{1}{2}$	238.27$\frac{1}{2}$
156.38$\frac{1}{2}$	721.48$\frac{1}{2}$	482.56$\frac{1}{2}$	411.72$\frac{1}{2}$
721.42$\frac{1}{2}$	495.27$\frac{1}{2}$	721.72$\frac{1}{2}$	621.55$\frac{1}{2}$

2. Here are the daily takings of two departments of a greengrocery shop. Find the daily gross takings for the shop, the weekly gross takings for each department and the weekly gross takings of the shop.

Day	Vegetables £	Fruit £	Gross takings £
Monday	42.54	68.72	
Tuesday	55.63½	88.61	
Wednesday	21.72	42.54½	
Thursday	68.85½	94.82	
Friday	95.75	146.73½	
Saturday	148.65	235.64½	
Gross			

3. Here are the quarterly sales figures for five departments of a chain store. Find the totals for the year for each department and the total takings of the store for each quarter and for the whole year.

	Spring £	Summer £	Autumn £	Winter £	Totals
Dept. A	17 259	19 462	18 721	39 495	
Dept. B	14 176	16 384	17 426	19 872	
Dept. C	16 234	23 714	21 538	28 634	
Dept. D	27 589	40 965	36 724	58 856	
Dept. E	10 721	15 238	14 617	18 729	
Totals					

4.5 Subtraction of Money

In commercial life we frequently need to subtract one sum of money from another, for example, when we calculate prices involving *trade discount* or *cash discount*, or when we deduct one side of an account from another and thus discover the *outstanding balance* on the account. When subtracting money in a decimal money system, it is important to remember to *keep the decimal points underneath one another*. This will ensure that the pence and the pounds are in the correct columns and no errors should occur because of incorrect place value.

Example

A shopkeeper decides to sell goods at less than the recommended price. A bed which is recommended to sell at £45.50 is to be sold at £7.25 less than this. Find the actual selling price.

The selling price is found by subtracting £7.25 from £45.50.

$$
\begin{array}{r}
£ \\
45.50 \\
-\ 7.25 \\
\hline
38.25 \\
\hline
\end{array}
$$

4.6 Exercises: Subtraction of Money

1. (a) Subtract £4.25 from £11.75   (b) Subtract £8.32 from £64.72.
   (c) Subtract £17.64 from £138.50. (d) Subtract £18.40 from £46.95.
   (e) Subtract £27.48 from £186.50. (f) Subtract £29.25 from £128.95.

2. A firm decides to reduce the prices of articles displayed in its shop window to clear them in its forthcoming winter sale. What will be the sale prices of these items, after the reductions shown have been subtracted?
   (a) Price 95p; reduction 12p   (b) Price £1.27; reduction 13p
   (c) Price £3.72; reduction 85p   (d) Price £14.95; reduction £1.25
   (e) Price £74.25; reduction £7.50   (f) Price £100.00; reduction £12.85

3. Firms paying promptly are permitted to deduct a cash discount from their bills. What will each of the following bills amount to when the discount is deducted?
   (a) Bill £27.60; discount £1.38   (b) Bill £32.40; discount £1.62
   (c) Bill £143.60; discount £7.18   (d) Bill £196.40; discount £9.82
   (e) Bill £425.50; discount £21.27$\frac{1}{2}$ (f) Bill £2 256.30; discount £112.81$\frac{1}{2}$

4. The wages of employees are paid only after certain deductions have been made from them. Using the following table, calculate the total deductions and, by taking them from the gross wages, find the net wages payable to each employee.

Employee	Gross wage	Deductions			
		Insurance	Tax	Union	Savings
Mr A	£158.50	£12.28	£32.50	£0.48	£10.50
Mrs B	£69.60	£5.39	£11.85	£0.36	£12.00
Mr C	£84.50	£6.55	£12.25	£0.48	—
Miss D	£58.28	£4.52	£4.20	£0.24	£3.00
Mr E	£87.24	£6.76	£5.35	—	£1.00
Miss F	£73.40	£5.69	£7.20	£0.36	£2.00

4.7 Multiplication of Money

There is no difference between multiplying decimal fractions and multiplying decimal money, except where halfpennies are involved. A great many simple multiplication sums are necessary when invoicing customers for the supply of goods; for example, '5 articles at £1.87' might be a typical item on a bill. In such simple sums always ignore the decimal point and write the sum down as in an ordinary multiplication sum. Then multiply in the normal way. In the examples below, it so happens that, because there are no figures after the decimal point in the multiplier, the decimal point will automatically fall into the same place in the answer as in the top line of the calculation.

Example

What must I pay for 7 items at £3.56 each?

$$
\begin{array}{r}
£ \\
3.56 \\
\times\ 7 \\
\hline
£24.92 \\
\hline
\end{array}
$$

Example

What must I pay for 24 items at £3.35 each?

$$
\begin{array}{r}
£ \\
3.35 \\
\times\ 24 \\
\hline
13\ 40 \\
67\ 00 \\
\hline
£80.40 \\
\hline
\end{array}
$$

Example

What must I pay for 17 items at £3.56½ each?

Care is needed here, as there is a halfpenny in the price.

$$
\begin{array}{rl}
£ & \\
3.56\tfrac{1}{2} & \\
\times\ 17 & \\
\hline
24\ 95\tfrac{1}{2} & (\text{7 halfpence} = 3\tfrac{1}{2}\text{ pence}) \\
35\ 65 & (\text{10 halfpence} = 5\text{ pence}) \\
\hline
£60.60\tfrac{1}{2} & \\
\hline
\end{array}
$$

4.8 Exercises: Multiplication of Money

1. For each of the following purchases, calculate the total price which will appear on the invoice:
   (a) 4 brief cases at £27.45 each.
   (b) 12 fur collars at £31.75 each.
   (c) 6 Everbright chrome cigarette cases at £12.59½ each.
   (d) 20 corduroy jackets at £37.65 each.
   (e) 32 small women's coats at £38.50 each.
   (f) 15 waste bins at £7.78½ each.

2. A multiple shop has five branches. It pays its lowest-grade assistants £43.25 per week, its experienced assistants £59.75 per week and its floor-staff supervisors £88.90. What will be the total wage bill for each of the five shops described below?

| | Number of assistants | | |
	Lowest grade	Experienced	Supervisors
Shop A	5	2	1
Shop B	8	4	1
Shop C	12	6	2
Shop D	20	8	2
Shop E	65	12	4

3. A shipbuilder purchases 62 components for the cabins on a new ship, at £34.42½ each. Calculate the total cost.

4. 52 typewriters at £205.20 each are purchased for a typing pool. What is the total cost?

5. A plumber's mate earns £2.25 per hour for a 40-hour week. In addition he gets an increase of 37½p for each hour of overtime, plus meal allowances of £1.45. In a certain week he works 84 hours on an emergency repair, and is able to claim for 9 meals. What will his total wage be for the week?

6. A shop assistant who earns £58.75 a week is offered a post in a bank at £3 500 a year. Will it be financially advantageous for him to change jobs?

7. Calculate the total cost of the following items: 4 headlamps at £23.75 each, 2 rear quarter-lights at £21.95 each, 6 sets of lighting wiring for rebuilding cars at £14.36 per set, and 6 sets of internal lighting and switches at £15.84 per set.

8. A print shop employs 12 compositors at £163.50 per week, 12 trainee compositors at £53.25 per week and 2 foreman printers at £185.50 per week. What is the total weekly wage bill?

4.9 Division of Money

Dividing money by a number of which we know the multiplication table is exactly like dividing ordinary numbers, except that pence end at two places of decimals and after that there are only halfpence.

Example

What will it cost seven friends each to pay for a farewell sherry party for a colleague who is leaving the office, if the total cost is £39.40?

$$
\begin{array}{r}
£ \\
7\,)\,\overline{39.40} \\
\hline
5.62\tfrac{1}{2} \quad \text{remainder } 2\tfrac{1}{2} \text{ pence}
\end{array}
$$

Clearly such a remainder is less than a halfpenny each and the friends must decide how to share it.

Example

A group bonus of £185.40 is to be shared equally among 17 hotel staff. What will each receive?

$$
\begin{array}{r}
£ \\
10.90\tfrac{1}{2} \quad \text{remainder } 1\tfrac{1}{2} \text{ pence} \\
17\,)\,\overline{185.40} \\
\underline{17} \\
154 \\
\underline{153} \\
10
\end{array}
$$

The ten pence over is equal to 20 halfpence = $\tfrac{1}{2}$ penny each and a remainder of $1\tfrac{1}{2}$ pence.

4.10 Exercises: Division of Money

1. (a) Divide £27.50 by 5.   (b) Divide £138.24 by 6.
   (c) Divide £624.20 by 8.   (d) Divide £385.49 by 7.
   (e) Divide £1 528.67 by 11.   (f) Divide £3 265.29 by 9.

2. (a) £2 934.03 ÷ 17 =   (b) £1 023.60 ÷ 24 =
   (c) £2 757.66 ÷ 38 =   (d) £6 888.24 ÷ 54 =
   (e) £47 274.48 ÷ 66 =   (f) £52 218.08 ÷ 89 =

3. Twenty-seven staff members of a multiple shop organization sell £27 324 of double-glazing contracts in a special feature offer to customers. One-tenth of this total is reserved for staff bonuses. How much will each member of staff receive if the bonus is distributed equally?

4. The total value of an invoice for 15 electric typewriters is £3 112.50. What is the cost of each typewriter?

5. 77 similar electronic calculators offered as a lot at a bankruptcy sale realize £177.10. What was the price for each?

6. A mini-size accounting machine is half the price of the maxi model. A firm orders one of each, and the total cost is £8 751. What is the price of each model?

7. A plot of building land is divided into 18. There are 10 small plots and 8 large plots, each of which is twice as big as a small plot. The total cost of the land was £253 500. How much should be allocated for land value to (*a*) a small plot and (*b*) a large plot?

4.11 Mental Arithmetic Exercises

1. $27 + 46 + 146 =$
2. $327 - 239 =$
3. $457 \times 9 =$
4. $5\,816 \div 8 =$
5. £273.65 + £428.72 + £617.36 =
6. $£2\,750 \div 50 =$
7. What shall I pay altogether for 8 items at £38.00 each and 2 items at £19.00?
8. 400 items of furniture cost £28 000. How much is that each?
9. I wish to put up a straight fence of 6 panels each 2 metres long. If panels cost £8 each and posts £3 each, how much will the fence cost?
10. How many seconds in 7 minutes 35 seconds?
11. A baby was born on March 1 1953. How old was the child on October 1 1969?
12. $0.4 \times 0.05 =$
13. $2.7 + 1.325 + 19 =$
14. $44.85 \div 0.5 =$
15. £17.20 − £9.85 =

Unit Five
Vulgar Fractions

5.1 Introduction

Vulgar fractions, or *common fractions*, such as $\frac{1}{2}$, $\frac{1}{3}$ or $\frac{1}{4}$, are used to describe quantities of less than a whole unit. They were very widely used before the introduction of the metric system, and are still important in many ways. In money we still have the halfpenny, we shall continue to talk about half metres and quarter metres even after metrication is complete, and profit margins and many other calculations still often involve simple fractions. Fractions like these are part of everyday life—we shall always cut apples in half and buy half a shoulder of lamb when the family is too small to need, or too poor to afford, a whole shoulder.

All vulgar fractions have two parts, separated by a line. Look at the following examples:

$$\frac{1}{2}, \frac{1}{3}, \frac{1}{6}, \frac{1}{10}, \frac{3}{10}, \frac{7}{15}, \frac{8}{30}, \frac{121}{140}$$

The lower half of a fraction is called the *denominator*, from the Latin *nomen*, meaning a name, and it tells us the name of the things we are talking about: halves, thirds, sixths, tenths, fifteenths, thirtieths and one-hundred-and-fortieths in these examples. Each of the following examples

$$\frac{1}{5}, \frac{2}{5}, \frac{3}{5}, \frac{4}{5}, \frac{5}{5}, \frac{6}{5}, \frac{10}{5}, \frac{100}{5}$$

concerns *fifths*: one-fifth, two-fifths, three-fifths and so on. Clearly the top half of the fraction tells us the number of fifths we are dealing with: this number is called the *numerator*, from the Latin *numeralis*, a number. We therefore have:

$$\frac{4}{5} = \frac{\text{numerator}}{\text{denominator}} = \frac{\text{number of parts}}{\text{name of parts}} = \frac{\text{four}}{\text{fifths}}$$

A fraction where the numerator is smaller than the denominator is called a *proper fraction*, and one where the numerator is greater than the denominator is called a 'top-heavy' fraction, or *improper fraction*, which is greater in value than a whole unit. A number made up of whole numbers and fractions is called a *mixed number*.

$\frac{1}{3}$ and $\frac{2}{3}$ These are proper fractions.

$\frac{3}{3}$ This is equal to a whole unit, since three thirds make a whole 1.

$\frac{4}{3}, \frac{5}{3}, \frac{6}{3}$ These are 'top-heavy' or improper fractions and equal to $1\frac{1}{3}$, $1\frac{2}{3}$ and 2 whole units respectively.

$1\frac{1}{3}, 1\frac{2}{3}$ These are mixed numbers.

Cancelling down

A fraction should always be given in its simplest form. For instance, one half ($\frac{1}{2}$) is the same as two quarters ($\frac{2}{4}$) but the former is preferred because it is, in its simplest form, often called its *lowest terms*. To decide if a fraction is in its lowest terms, examine the numerator and denominator to see if they have any *common factor*, that is, to see if a number exists which will divide exactly into them both. A fraction is in its lowest terms when the numerator and denominator have no common factor other than 1. For example, 6 and 8 have a common factor, 2, so that the fraction $\frac{6}{8}$ can be written in a simpler form $\frac{3}{4}$; the 6 and 8 are said to *cancel* by 2. We indicate this by crossing them out neatly: $\frac{\cancel{6}^3}{\cancel{8}_4}$

Similarly $\frac{12}{24}$ cancels to $\frac{1}{2}$ and $\frac{240}{960}$ cancels to $\frac{1}{4}$

We must know how to add, subtract, multiply and divide fractions. The rules are relatively simple, but a good deal of practice to ensure complete mastery of the processes is necessary.

5.2 Addition of Fractions

It is easy to add together fractions where the denominators are the same, for we are adding together the same things.

Example

Add $\frac{2}{7} + \frac{3}{7} + \frac{1}{7}$

All we need to do is to add the numerators $2 + 3 + 1 = 6$

$$\frac{2}{7} + \frac{3}{7} + \frac{1}{7} = \frac{6}{7}$$

Example

Add $\frac{3}{8} + \frac{5}{8} + \frac{7}{8}$

$$\frac{3}{8} + \frac{5}{8} + \frac{7}{8} = \frac{15}{8}$$

Here the addition of the numerators gives us 15 eighths, which is an improper fraction and must be turned into a mixed number. We do this by dividing the numerator by the denominator: 8 goes into 15 once, with seven-eighths over. Thus

$$\frac{3}{8} + \frac{5}{8} + \frac{7}{8} = \frac{15}{8} = 1\frac{7}{8}$$

Similarly we could simplify $\frac{23}{8}$ by saying that 8 into 23 goes twice with seven-eighths over:

$$\frac{23}{8} = 2\frac{7}{8}$$

Example

Add $\frac{1}{2} + \frac{2}{3}$

Here we are being asked to add two unlike things, halves and thirds. We cannot add these together unless we can turn them both into the same kind of fraction, that is, unless we can find a *common denominator*. The procedure is as follows:

(a) Look at the bigger denominator—in this case 3.

(b) Will the other denominators divide into it exactly? In this case, will 2 divide into 3 exactly? No, it will not.

(c) Find a multiple of 3 that 2 will divide into exactly. We do this by going upwards through the three times table to find a number 2 will divide into. We know that $2 \times 3 = 6$, that is, 2 will divide exactly into 6. We have therefore found a common denominator.

(d) We now change $\frac{1}{2}$ into sixths, and $\frac{2}{3}$ into sixths: $\frac{1}{2} = \frac{3}{6}$ and $\frac{2}{3} = \frac{4}{6}$. Then

$$\frac{1}{2} + \frac{2}{3} = \frac{3}{6} + \frac{4}{6} = \frac{7}{6} = 1\frac{1}{6}$$

To save time we usually write:

$$\frac{1}{2} + \frac{2}{3} = \frac{3+4}{6} = \frac{7}{6} = 1\frac{1}{6}$$

Example

Add $\frac{4}{5} + \frac{7}{15} + \frac{1}{2}$

$$\frac{4}{5} + \frac{7}{15} + \frac{1}{2}$$

$$= \frac{24 + 14 + 15}{30}$$

$$= \frac{53}{30}$$

$$= 1\frac{23}{30}$$

This addition is carried out in the following stages:

(a) We first need to find a common denominator. The largest denominator is 15. Will 5 go into 15? Yes. Will 2 go into 15? No. Then 15 is not a common denominator.

(b) What is 2×15? $2 \times 15 = 30$. Will 5 go into 30? Yes. Will 2 go into 30? Yes. Then 30 is a common denominator.

(c) 5 goes 6 times into 30, so every fifth is 6 thirtieths. $4 \times 6 = 24$ thirtieths.

(d) 15 goes twice into 30. So every fifteenth is 2 thirtieths. $7 \times 2 = 14$ thirtieths.

(e) 2 goes 15 times into 30. So every half is 15 thirtieths.

(f) Add up the thirtieths: $24 + 14 + 15 = 53$ thirtieths.

(g) 53 thirtieths is a 'top-heavy' fraction and includes 1 whole unit and 23 thirtieths, or $1\frac{23}{30}$.

Example

Add $2\frac{1}{2} + 3\frac{3}{4} + 4\frac{7}{16}$

Here we have whole numbers to deal with as well as fractions. We add the whole numbers first. Then we add the fractions, as in the previous example (the common denominator this time is 16).

$$2\frac{1}{2} + 3\frac{3}{4} + 4\frac{7}{16}$$

$$= 9\frac{8 + 12 + 7}{16}$$

$$= 9\frac{27}{16} \text{ (this 'top-heavy' fraction must now be simplified)}$$

$$= 10\frac{11}{16}$$

5.3 Exercises: Addition of Fractions

1. Add the following fractions:

(a) $\frac{1}{2} + \frac{3}{4} =$ (b) $\frac{3}{4} + \frac{7}{8} =$

(c) $\frac{2}{3} + \frac{3}{4} =$ (d) $\frac{2}{3} + \frac{3}{8} =$

(e) $\frac{7}{10} + \frac{1}{2} =$ (f) $\frac{7}{10} + \frac{4}{15} =$

(g) $\frac{1}{2} + \frac{2}{3} + \frac{3}{4} =$ (h) $\frac{6}{7} + \frac{2}{3} + \frac{16}{21} =$

(i) $\frac{2}{3} + \frac{3}{8} + \frac{7}{12} =$ (j) $\frac{7}{10} + \frac{5}{8} + \frac{3}{5} =$

(k) $\frac{3}{20} + \frac{4}{5} + \frac{5}{8} =$ (l) $\frac{6}{7} + \frac{2}{3} + \frac{17}{42} =$

2. Add the following sums, which include mixed numbers:

(a) $1\frac{1}{2} + 2\frac{3}{4} + 3\frac{7}{8} =$ (b) $3\frac{1}{5} + 4\frac{11}{15} + 2\frac{2}{3} =$

(c) $4\frac{7}{10} + 1\frac{3}{5} + 7\frac{1}{2} =$ (d) $5\frac{7}{12} + 1\frac{5}{6} + 3\frac{3}{4} =$

(e) $2\frac{5}{8} + 2\frac{2}{3} + 3\frac{7}{12} =$ (f) $9\frac{1}{2} + 3\frac{7}{10} + 4\frac{2}{3} =$

(g) $3\frac{1}{7} + 5\frac{2}{3} + 3\frac{13}{21} =$ (h) $2\frac{2}{3} + 3\frac{3}{8} + 1\frac{5}{6} =$

(i) $1\frac{2}{3} + 3\frac{7}{10} + 7\frac{1}{2} =$ (j) $3\frac{7}{10} + 4\frac{2}{5} + 6\frac{3}{4} =$

(k) $2\frac{5}{8} + 2\frac{2}{3} + 3\frac{11}{12} =$ (l) $4\frac{5}{6} + 2\frac{7}{12} + 2\frac{17}{30} =$

5.4 Subtraction of Fractions

We subtract fractions by applying the same principles that we use in addition. First, we find the common denominator, and convert both fractions to this denominator. We then subtract the numerators. If possible, we then cancel the resulting fraction to its lowest terms.

Example

Subtract $\frac{7}{12}$ from $\frac{3}{4}$

$$\frac{3}{4} - \frac{7}{12}$$

$$= \frac{9 - 7}{12}$$

$$= \frac{2}{12}$$

$$= \underline{\underline{\frac{1}{6}}}$$

If mixed numbers are involved, we subtract the whole numbers first, and then convert the fractions to a common denominator. Sometimes we cannot complete the subtraction of the numerators unless we use one of the whole numbers, converting it too into a fraction with the common denominator.

Example

Subtract $2\frac{19}{24}$ from $7\frac{3}{4}$

$$7\frac{3}{4} - 2\frac{19}{24}$$

$$= 5\frac{18 - 19}{24}$$

$$= 4\frac{\overset{24}{18} - 19}{24}$$

$$= \underline{\underline{4\frac{23}{24}}}$$

Here the common denominator is 24. But we cannot take 19 twenty-fourths from 18 twenty-fourths, so to complete the subtraction of the numerators we use one of the 5 whole units. Of course a whole unit is $\frac{24}{24}$. We can then subtract the 19 from the 24 twenty-fourths, leaving 5 twenty-fourths, and these 5 are put with the 18 to make 23 twenty-fourths. The answer is therefore 4 whole units and 23 twenty-fourths.

5.5 Exercises: Subtraction of Fractions

1. Carry out the following subtractions:
   (a) $\frac{2}{3} - \frac{1}{2} =$
   (b) $\frac{3}{4} - \frac{5}{8} =$
   (c) $\frac{7}{10} - \frac{2}{5} =$
   (d) $\frac{13}{15} - \frac{3}{5} =$
   (e) $\frac{6}{7} - \frac{1}{3} =$
   (f) $\frac{11}{12} - \frac{3}{4} =$
   (g) $\frac{19}{24} - \frac{3}{8} =$
   (h) $\frac{4}{5} - \frac{17}{30} =$
   (i) $\frac{2}{3} - \frac{7}{12} =$
   (j) $\frac{14}{15} - \frac{7}{10} =$

2. Carry out the following subtractions involving mixed numbers:
   (a) $4\frac{1}{2} - 2\frac{1}{3} =$
   (b) $5\frac{3}{4} - 2\frac{7}{10} =$
   (c) $3\frac{7}{8} - 2\frac{4}{5} =$
   (d) $7\frac{11}{12} - 3\frac{3}{4} =$
   (e) $8\frac{2}{3} - 4\frac{7}{10} =$
   (f) $14\frac{3}{7} - 9\frac{4}{5} =$
   (g) $8\frac{1}{3} - 4\frac{1}{2} =$
   (h) $17\frac{3}{7} - 10\frac{9}{10} =$
   (i) $15\frac{2}{5} - 11\frac{11}{12} =$
   (j) $16\frac{5}{12} - 9\frac{7}{10} =$
   (k) $29\frac{17}{24} - 15\frac{3}{4} =$
   (l) $28\frac{23}{40} - 15\frac{4}{5} =$

5.6 Multiplication of Fractions

When we multiply together two numbers greater than 1, the result is bigger than either of the original numbers. $2 \times 9 = 18$: 18 is bigger than either 2 or 9. $3 \times 5 = 15$: 15 is bigger than 3 or 5. This is because we have *two of* the nines and *three of* the fives. So we can replace the multiplication sign with the word 'of'.

What happens when we multiply fractions? Consider the multiplication $\frac{1}{2} \times \frac{1}{2}$, or $\frac{1}{2}$ of $\frac{1}{2}$ (Fig. 5.1).

A whole apple   Two halves

A half of
a half is
a quarter

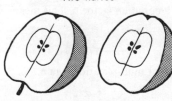

Fig. 5.1 A half of a half = a quarter

We see that

$$\frac{1}{2} \times \frac{1}{2} = \frac{1}{4}$$

Similarly, Fig. 5.2 makes it clear that

$$\frac{1}{2} \times \frac{1}{3} = \frac{1}{6}$$

and

$$\frac{1}{2} \times \frac{1}{4} = \frac{1}{8}$$

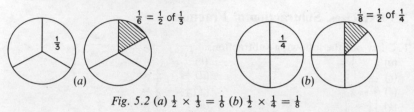

Fig. 5.2 (a) $\frac{1}{2} \times \frac{1}{3} = \frac{1}{6}$ (b) $\frac{1}{2} \times \frac{1}{4} = \frac{1}{8}$

In fact, to multiply fractions we simply *multiply the numerators and multiply the denominators.*

Examples

Multiply $\frac{1}{3}$ by $\frac{1}{6}$: $\frac{1}{3} \times \frac{1}{6} = \frac{1}{18}$

Multiply $\frac{1}{5}$ by $\frac{1}{4}$: $\frac{1}{5} \times \frac{1}{4} = \frac{1}{20}$

Multiply $\frac{1}{3}$ by $\frac{2}{5}$: $\frac{1}{3} \times \frac{2}{5} = \frac{2}{15}$

Some multiplications can be simplified before the final calculation.

Example

Multiply $\frac{2}{3} \times \frac{3}{8}$

$$\frac{2}{3} \times \frac{3}{8} = \frac{6}{24}$$

But $\frac{6}{24}$ is a fraction which is not in its lowest terms: both the numerator and the denominator have a common factor 6. This means we can cancel down by 6:

$$\frac{6}{24} = \frac{1}{4}$$

Let us look at our original multiplication again:

$$\frac{2}{3} \times \frac{3}{8}$$

We can see that the numerator 2 will cancel with the denominator 8, and the numerator 3 will cancel with the denominator 3:

$$\frac{2}{3}\frac{1}{1} \times \frac{3}{8}\frac{1}{4}$$

If we cancel these common factors we end up with

$$\frac{1}{1} \times \frac{1}{4} = \frac{1}{4}$$

So the rule for multiplying fractions is

Cancel if you can: then multiply the numerators and multiply the denominators.

Examples

Multiply $\frac{5}{8}$ by $\frac{2}{3}$

$$\frac{5}{\cancel{8}4} \times \frac{\cancel{2}1}{3}$$

$$= \frac{5}{12}$$

Multiply $\frac{7}{8}$ by $\frac{2}{3}$ and multiply the result by $\frac{3}{7}$
We can write this down as a single calculation:

$$\frac{\cancel{7}1}{\cancel{8}4} \times \frac{\cancel{2}1}{\cancel{3}1} \times \frac{\cancel{3}1}{\cancel{7}1}$$

$$= \frac{1}{4}$$

5.7 Exercises: Multiplication of Fractions

1. Multiply these fractions:

(a) $\frac{2}{3} \times \frac{3}{4} =$ (b) $\frac{3}{8} \times \frac{4}{9} =$

(c) $\frac{3}{8} \times \frac{4}{7} =$ (d) $\frac{5}{6} \times \frac{9}{10} =$

(e) $\frac{5}{9} \times \frac{3}{10} =$ (f) $\frac{7}{12} \times \frac{33}{42} =$

(g) $\frac{4}{7} \times \frac{14}{15} =$ (h) $\frac{14}{15} \times \frac{10}{21} =$

(i) $\frac{2}{3} \times \frac{9}{10} =$ (j) $\frac{19}{20} \times \frac{5}{19} =$

2. Multiply these fractions:

(a) $\frac{7}{12} \times \frac{2}{3} \times \frac{5}{7} =$ (b) $\frac{3}{10} \times \frac{3}{4} \times \frac{5}{9} =$

(c) $\frac{5}{8} \times \frac{3}{10} \times \frac{4}{9} =$ (d) $\frac{11}{12} \times \frac{3}{5} \times \frac{25}{33} =$

(e) $\frac{6}{7} \times \frac{14}{15} \times \frac{5}{8} =$ (f) $\frac{3}{7} \times \frac{5}{8} \times \frac{14}{15} =$

(g) $\frac{2}{3} \times \frac{9}{10} \times \frac{5}{8} =$ (h) $\frac{4}{9} \times \frac{3}{4} \times \frac{3}{5} =$

(i) $\frac{3}{5} \times \frac{4}{15} \times \frac{5}{8} =$ (j) $\frac{8}{9} \times \frac{3}{4} \times \frac{7}{15} =$

(k) $\frac{7}{10} \times \frac{15}{16} \times \frac{4}{7} =$ (l) $\frac{3}{4} \times \frac{20}{21} \times \frac{7}{10} =$

5.8 Multiplying Mixed Numbers

When we multiply mixed numbers we have to overcome a new difficulty: we know that $2 \times 2 = 4$, but just what $2\frac{1}{2} \times 2\frac{1}{2}$ comes to is not so easy to tell. We can discover the answer by common sense in simple cases—for example, $2\frac{1}{2} \times 2\frac{1}{2}$ is the same as $2 \times 2\frac{1}{2}$ plus another $\frac{1}{2} \times 2\frac{1}{2}$ Now $2 \times 2\frac{1}{2} = 5$ and $\frac{1}{2} \times 2\frac{1}{2} = 1\frac{1}{4}$, so adding these together we get $2\frac{1}{2} \times 2\frac{1}{2} = 6\frac{1}{4}$ This sort of solution is not always possible, and as a rule we must eliminate the mixed numbers first by changing them into 'top-heavy' fractions. We then multiply the numerators and denominators in the usual way, cancelling down if possible. If the result is itself a top-heavy fraction, we finally convert it into a mixed number.

Example

Multiply $1\frac{3}{8} \times 1\frac{1}{3}$

$$1\frac{3}{8} \times 1\frac{1}{3}$$

$$= \frac{11}{\underset{2}{8}} \times \frac{\overset{1}{4}}{3}$$

$$= \frac{11}{6}$$

$$= 1\frac{5}{6}$$

First, we change the mixed numbers to 'top-heavy' fractions. There are 8 eighths in the whole unit, and 3 more make 11 eighths. There are 3 thirds in one whole unit and 1 more makes 4 thirds. That gives us $\frac{11}{8} \times \frac{4}{3}$. Cancelling, and multiplying the numerators and the denominators gives us $\frac{11}{6}$. We finally change this 'top-heavy' fraction back into a mixed number by dividing the denominator into the numerator: 6 goes once into 11, with 5 sixths left over.

Now work through the following example, making sure you understand each step of the reasoning.

Example

$$1\frac{3}{4} \times 3\frac{1}{3} \times 3\frac{1}{7}$$

$$= \frac{\overset{1}{7}}{\underset{1}{\underset{1}{4}}} \times \frac{\overset{5}{10}}{3} \times \frac{\overset{11}{22}}{\underset{1}{7}}$$

$$= \frac{55}{3}$$

$$= 18\frac{1}{3}$$

5.9 Exercises: Multiplying Mixed Numbers

1. Multiply these mixed numbers:
   (a) $1\frac{1}{2} \times 1\frac{1}{3} =$ (b) $2\frac{3}{4} \times 1\frac{1}{11} =$
   (c) $2\frac{1}{4} \times 2\frac{2}{3} =$ (d) $4\frac{1}{2} \times 1\frac{5}{9} =$
   (e) $3\frac{1}{2} \times 1\frac{1}{7} =$ (f) $3\frac{1}{3} \times 1\frac{1}{5} =$
   (g) $4\frac{1}{5} \times 1\frac{1}{14} =$ (h) $9\frac{1}{3} \times 1\frac{2}{7} =$
   (i) $7\frac{1}{2} \times 3\frac{1}{5} =$ (j) $5\frac{1}{4} \times 3\frac{1}{7} =$

2. Multiply these mixed numbers:
   (a) $2\frac{1}{3} \times 4\frac{1}{2} \times 1\frac{1}{5} =$ (b) $3\frac{1}{2} \times 1\frac{1}{2} \times 2\frac{1}{7} =$
   (c) $5\frac{1}{2} \times 3\frac{1}{3} \times 1\frac{3}{11} =$ (d) $4\frac{1}{4} \times 2\frac{1}{4} \times 1\frac{1}{17} =$
   (e) $5\frac{2}{3} \times 2\frac{1}{3} \times 1\frac{4}{5} =$ (f) $7\frac{1}{3} \times 1\frac{1}{4} \times 2\frac{5}{11} =$
   (g) $3\frac{3}{4} \times 2\frac{1}{2} \times 1\frac{7}{15} =$ (h) $1\frac{7}{8} \times 1\frac{1}{3} \times 3\frac{1}{5} =$
   (i) $3\frac{1}{4} \times 2\frac{3}{4} \times 1\frac{3}{13} =$ (j) $2\frac{7}{10} \times 2\frac{3}{5} \times 1\frac{1}{9} =$
   (k) $3\frac{3}{5} \times 2\frac{1}{4} \times 2\frac{2}{9} =$ (l) $3\frac{7}{8} \times 2\frac{1}{4} \times 1\frac{1}{31} =$

5.10 Division of Fractions

The division process is one in which we see how many times one number will go into another. Thus $125 \div 5$ means 'how many times will 5 go into 125?' The answer is of course 25. Suppose the question had been $125 \div \frac{1}{5}$, the answer would have been 625, because $\frac{1}{5}$ goes 5 times into one whole unit, and 625 times into 125 whole units. Thus when we divide by a whole number the answer is smaller than the number we started with ($125 \div 5 = 25$) but when we divide by a proper fraction the answer is bigger ($125 \div \frac{1}{5} = 625$). Another example: $\frac{1}{2} \div \frac{1}{2} = 1$, because $\frac{1}{2}$ goes once into $\frac{1}{2}$.

Notice that $125 \div \frac{1}{5}$ is the same as $125 \times \frac{5}{1}$: common sense tells us that the answer to both is 625. We have not changed the answer by changing the $\div$ into $\times$, because at the same time we changed the divisor upside down.

$$\text{Thus } 40 \div \tfrac{1}{4} = 40 \times \tfrac{4}{1} = 160$$
$$\text{and } \tfrac{1}{2} \div \tfrac{1}{2} = \tfrac{1}{2} \times \tfrac{2}{1} = 1$$

Stated in its simplest way, the rule for dividing fractions says *turn the divisor upside down and multiply*. On no account turn the other number, the dividend, upside down; remember, the divisor is the number with the $\div$ sign in front of it.

Example

Divide $\frac{3}{4}$ by $\frac{5}{8}$

$$\tfrac{3}{4} \div \tfrac{5}{8}$$
$$= \tfrac{3}{4}_1 \times \tfrac{8^2}{5}$$
$$= \tfrac{6}{5}$$
$$= 1\tfrac{1}{5}$$

If mixed numbers are involved in the division, we must begin by changing them into 'top-heavy' fractions. Then we change the divisor upside down and multiply, as before.

Example

Divide $2\frac{1}{2}$ by $1\frac{3}{4}$

$$2\tfrac{1}{2} \div 1\tfrac{3}{4}$$
$$= \tfrac{5}{2} \div \tfrac{7}{4}$$
$$= \tfrac{5}{2}_1 \times \tfrac{4^2}{7}$$
$$= \tfrac{10}{7}$$
$$= 1\tfrac{3}{7}$$

5.11 Exercises: Division of Fractions

1. Carry out the following divisions:
   (a) $\frac{1}{2} \div \frac{1}{4} =$ (b) $\frac{7}{8} \div \frac{1}{4} =$
   (c) $\frac{3}{4} \div \frac{1}{8} =$ (d) $\frac{4}{5} \div \frac{4}{9} =$
   (e) $\frac{3}{5} \div \frac{7}{10} =$ (f) $\frac{3}{4} \div \frac{9}{10} =$
   (g) $\frac{7}{10} \div \frac{3}{8} =$ (h) $\frac{2}{3} \div \frac{5}{9} =$
   (i) $\frac{9}{10} \div \frac{2}{5} =$ (j) $\frac{11}{12} \div \frac{5}{8} =$

2. Carry out the following divisions involving mixed numbers:
   (a) $3\frac{3}{4} \div 1\frac{7}{8} =$ (b) $4\frac{1}{2} \div \frac{3}{4} =$
   (c) $2\frac{7}{10} \div 1\frac{1}{8} =$ (d) $5\frac{1}{3} \div \frac{8}{9} =$
   (e) $2\frac{1}{4} \div 3\frac{1}{2} =$ (f) $14\frac{1}{2} \div 2\frac{9}{10} =$
   (g) $3\frac{1}{8} \div 1\frac{3}{4} =$ (h) $6\frac{1}{4} \div 1\frac{2}{3} =$
   (i) $3\frac{1}{5} \div 1\frac{1}{5} =$ (j) $4\frac{1}{5} \div 2\frac{1}{3} =$

5.12 Mental Arithmetic Exercises

1. $38 + 97 + 329 =$
2. $468 - 379 =$
3. $2\,365 \times 8 =$
4. $4\,224 \div 6 =$
5. $1.6 + 2.75 + 0.35 =$
6. $3.8 \div 1.9 =$
7. $4.75 \times 0.5 =$
8. $2\,700 \div 300 =$
9. $\frac{1}{2} + \frac{1}{3} =$
10. $1\frac{3}{8} + 2\frac{1}{4} =$
11. $3\frac{7}{10} - 1\frac{3}{5} =$
12. What shall I pay altogether for 5 items at £48.00 each and 2 items at £24.00 each?
13. Change 275 minutes to hours and minutes.
14. $\frac{3}{5} \div \frac{7}{10} =$
15. $225 \div 15 =$

Unit Six

More Work with Fractions

6.1 Some Definitions

Mathematics, like all other subjects, has its own vocabulary of technical terms with which every student should become familiar. Some of the commoner words are defined here, and you should learn their meanings by heart.

A *digit* is any whole number from 0 (*zero*) to 9.

A *prime number* is a number which can be divided only by itself and 1. Thus 19 is a prime number, but 18 is not, since it can be divided exactly not only by 18 and 1 but also by 9, 2, 3 and 6.

A number is a *factor* of another number if it divides into that number an exact number of times. For example, 8 is a factor of 24, and so is 3.

A *common factor* of two or more numbers is a factor which will divide exactly into each of them. For example, 12 is a common factor of 36 and 48.

The *highest common factor* (HCF) of two or more numbers is the highest number that will divide exactly into each of them. Thus the HCF of 48 and 72 is 24, for 24 is the highest number that will divide exactly into 48 (twice) and 72 (three times).

A *multiple* of a number is one which contains it an exact number of times. For example, 72 contains 6 twelve times, so 72 is a multiple of 6.

A *common multiple* of two or more numbers is one which contains the other numbers an exact number of times. Thus 24 is a common multiple of 8 and 3, since it contains 8 three times and 3 eight times. 16 is not a common multiple of 8 and 3, since it contains 8 twice but does not contain 3 an exact number of times. Whenever we wish to find a common denominator in working out a fraction sum, we simply have to find a common multiple of the other denominators. For example, suppose we wish to add $\frac{1}{2}$ and $\frac{1}{3}$: the common denominator is 6 and we turn the $\frac{1}{2}$ to $\frac{3}{6}$ and the $\frac{1}{3}$ to $\frac{2}{6}$. So $\frac{1}{2} + \frac{1}{3} = \frac{5}{6}$.

A *lowest common multiple* (LCM) of two or more numbers is the smallest number that will contain them exactly. Thus 12 is the LCM of 4 and 3, since it is the lowest number both will divide into exactly.

6.2 Tests of Divisibility

Sometimes it is helpful to know whether a number will divide exactly into another number. In cancelling, for instance, it is useful to know some quick rules, or *tests of divisibility*.

Rules for 2, 4 and 8

A number will divide by 2 if it is an even number, that is, if it ends in 2, 4, 6, 8 or 0.

Examples.

26, 34, 58, 120 are all even numbers and therefore divisible by 2.

A number divides by 4 if the last two digits divide by 4.

Examples

524 divides by 4 because 24 (the last two digits) divide by 4. 1 732 divides by 4 because 32 (the last two digits) divides by 4.

A number divides by 8 if the last three digits divide by 8.

Examples

12 728 divides by 8 because 728 (the last three digits) divides by 8.

Rules for 3, 6 and 9

A number divides by 3 if the sum of the digits divides by 3.

Examples

1 028: the sum of $1 + 0 + 2 + 8 = 11$. 11 does not divide by 3 so 1 028 is not divisible by 3. 2 742: the sum of these digits is 15. 15 divides by 3 so 2 742 divides by 3.

A number divides by 6 if it is divisible by 3 and if it is also an even number.

Examples

306 is an even number. Is it divisible by 3? $3 + 0 + 6 = 9$: 9 divides by 3, so 306 divides by 3. As it is even it also divides by 6. 316: this is an even number. The sum of the digits is 10. 3 does not divide exactly into 10, so 316 is not divisible by 3. This means that 6 does not divide into it either.

A number divides by 9 if the sum of the digits divides by 9.

Examples

1 708: the sum of the digits is 16—this does not divide by 9 and hence 1 708 does not divide by 9. 2 304: the sum of the digits is 9, and 9 divides by 9, so 2 304 divides by 9.

Rules for 5, 25 and 125

A number divides by 5 if it ends in a 0 or a 5.

Examples

235; 710

A number divides by 25 if the last two digits divide by 25 or are 00.

Examples

175; 83 450

A number divides by 125 if the last three digits divide by 125 or are 000.

Examples

1 875; 17 000; 2 250

Rules for 10, 100, 1 000

A number divides by 10 if it ends in a 0, by 100 if it ends in 00, by 1 000 if it ends in 000, and so on.

There is no simple rule to test for divisibility by 7—you must try dividing it.

Rule for 11

This is a strange rule. *If the alternate digits are added up, and the two results taken away one from another, the number divides by 11 if the answer itself divides by 11 or is 0.*

Examples

Does 18 756 divide by 11?
Add alternate digits: $1 + 7 + 6 = 14$ and $8 + 5 = 13$.
Subtracting:
$$14 - 13 = 1$$

But 1 does not divide by 11; therefore 18 756 does not divide by 11.

Does 2 794 divide by 11?
$$2 + 9 = 11 \text{ and } 7 + 4 = 11$$
$$11 - 11 = 0$$
Therefore 2 794 does divide by 11.
$$2\ 794 \div 11 = \underline{\underline{254}}$$

6.3 Exercises: Prime Numbers, Factors and Multiples

1. Which of the numbers in each of the following sets are prime numbers?

   (a) 1, 2, 4   (b) 4, 7, 16
   (c) 3, 8, 11   (d) 5, 9, 12
   (e) 8, 13, 27   (f) 9, 18, 23
   (g) 7, 17, 29   (h) 6, 11, 19
   (i) 4, 13, 33   (j) 7, 27, 57

2. List the prime numbers between 1 and 30.

3. List the prime numbers between 40 and 60.

4. Write down the factors of the following numbers:

   (a) 12   (b) 15
   (c) 18   (d) 24
   (e) 27   (f) 36
   (g) 54   (h) 72
   (i) 80   (j) 84

5. Find any common factors for the numbers in each of the following sets (do not count 1 as a common factor):

   (a) 9, 12   (b) 14, 21
   (c) 8, 12   (d) 24, 40
   (e) 15, 25   (f) 36, 60
   (g) 18, 24   (h) 72, 80
   (i) 17, 34   (j) 16, 64

6. Find any common factors for the numbers in each of the following sets (do not count 1 as a common factor):

   (a) 16, 20   (b) 15, 35
   (c) 42, 70   (d) 36, 48
   (e) 60, 70   (f) 15, 45
   (g) 36, 54   (h) 12, 28
   (i) 19, 57   (j) 64, 80

7. Find the lowest common multiple of the numbers in each of the following sets:

   (a) 3, 4   (b) 5, 12
   (c) 4, 5   (d) 6, 4, 3
   (e) 2, 7   (f) 7, 3, 28
   (g) 3, 7   (h) 4, 6, 5
   (i) 4, 9   (j) 2, 3, 4

8. Find the lowest common multiple of the numbers in each of the following sets:

   (a) 5, 7   (b) 2, 5
   (c) 3, 5   (d) 2, 4, 9
   (e) 3, 5, 25   (f) 2, 3, 5
   (g) 4, 5, 25   (h) 2, 3, 7
   (i) 2, 5, 15   (j) 3, 4, 6

6.4 More Complex Fractions

Unit 5 explained how to carry out the four basic processes in fractions: addition, subtraction, multiplication and division. In business life complex problems arise which involve all these processes, and the results of the calculations may differ depending on which part was performed first. The question then is 'which shall we do first?'

Example

Calculate $\frac{1}{2} + \frac{2}{3} \times \frac{3}{4}$

Case 1. Addition first
If we do the addition first we get

$$\frac{1}{2} + \frac{2}{3} \times \frac{3}{4}$$

$$= \frac{3+4}{6} \times \frac{3}{4}$$

$$= \frac{7}{\cancel{6}2} \times \frac{\cancel{3}^1}{4}$$

$$= \frac{7}{8}$$

Case 2. Multiplication first
If we do the multiplication first we get

$$\frac{1}{2} + \frac{\cancel{2}^1}{\cancel{3}_1} \times \frac{\cancel{3}^1}{\cancel{4}_2}$$

$$= \frac{1}{2} + \frac{1}{2}$$

$$= 1$$

Clearly we must have a rule which tells us which to do first. The best rule, attributed to Mr E. J. Hopkins, is the 'BODMAS' rule, which says that complex fraction calculations should be worked out in the following order:

(a) **B**rackets first;
(b) **O**f next ('of' is like a bracket containing a multiplication sign). For example, in finding $1\frac{1}{2} \div \frac{2}{3}$ of 15, we must calculate $\frac{2}{3}$ of 15 as the first step;
(c) **D**ivision comes next;
(d) **M**ultiplication comes before addition and subtraction;
(e) **A**ddition is done before subtraction;
(f) **S**ubtraction is done last.

So in the present example we should follow the order in Case 2, carrying out the multiplication first. If we wanted to do the other part first we should have to make this clear by enclosing it in a bracket, thus:

$$\left(\frac{1}{2} + \frac{2}{3}\right) \times \frac{3}{4}$$

$$= \left(\frac{3 + 4}{6}\right) \times \frac{3}{4}$$

$$= \frac{7}{\cancel{6}2} \times \frac{\cancel{3}1}{4}$$

$$= \frac{7}{8}$$

Note that any part of a calculation which is not being dealt with at the moment is simply carried down to the next line and ignored until it is time to consider it. Never break up a sum and write it out in little pieces. *Write out the whole sum on every line as the calculation proceeds.*

Work through the following examples, making sure you understand the working in each.

Example

$$\frac{1}{2} + \frac{1}{3} \times \frac{1}{4} \left(\text{do the multiplication first; } \frac{1}{3} \times \frac{1}{4} = \frac{1}{12}\right)$$

$$= \frac{1}{2} + \frac{1}{12}$$

$$= \frac{6 + 1}{12} \qquad \text{(12 is the common denominator)}$$

$$= \frac{7}{12}$$

Example

$$\frac{3}{4} \div \frac{5}{8} - \frac{1}{3} \qquad \text{(do the division part first; change the divisor upside down and multiply)}$$

$$= \frac{3}{\cancel{4}1} \times \frac{\cancel{8}2}{5} - \frac{1}{3}$$

$$= \frac{6}{5} - \frac{1}{3}$$

$$= 1\frac{1}{5} - \frac{1}{3} \qquad \text{(now do the subtraction; 15 is the common denominator)}$$

$$= 1\frac{3 - 5}{15}$$

$$= \frac{13}{15}$$

Example

$$\frac{2}{3} \times \frac{3}{4} + \frac{5}{8} \div \frac{3}{4}$$

$$= \frac{2^1}{3_1} \times \frac{3^1}{4_2} + \frac{5}{8_2} \times \frac{4^1}{3}$$

$$= \frac{1}{2} + \frac{5}{6}$$

$$= \frac{3 + 5}{6}$$

$$= 1\frac{2^1}{6_3}$$

$$= 1\frac{1}{3}$$

Example

$$\left(3\frac{1}{5} - 2\frac{7}{8}\right) \div \left(4\frac{2}{3} - 3\frac{11}{30}\right)$$

$$= \left(1\frac{8 - 35}{40}\right) \div \left(1\frac{20 - 11}{30}\right)$$

$$= \frac{13}{40} \div 1\frac{9}{30}\frac{3}{10}$$

$$= \frac{13^1}{40_4} \times \frac{10^1}{13_1}$$

$$= \frac{1}{4}$$

6.5 Exercises: More Complex Fractions

Work out the following fraction calculations, remembering the BODMAS rule.

1. (a) $\frac{1}{2} \times \frac{2}{3} + \frac{1}{4} =$

   (c) $\frac{2}{5} + \frac{1}{3} \times \frac{6}{7} =$

   (e) $\frac{2}{6} + \frac{2}{3} \times \frac{3}{4} =$

   (g) $\frac{2}{3} \times \frac{9}{10} + \frac{3}{4} - \frac{1}{2} =$

   (i) $\frac{3}{4} \times \frac{2}{3} + \frac{4}{5} \times \frac{7}{8} =$

   (b) $\frac{3}{4} + \frac{3}{8} \times \frac{4}{5} =$

   (d) $\frac{3}{8} \times \frac{4}{9} + \frac{2}{3} =$

   (f) $\frac{1}{2} + \frac{1}{3} \times \frac{2}{5} - \frac{1}{4} =$

   (h) $\frac{7}{8} + \frac{2}{3} \times \frac{7}{12} \div \frac{7}{9} =$

   (j) $\frac{3}{5} \div \frac{7}{10} - \frac{5}{8} \div \frac{5}{6} =$

2. (a) $\frac{1}{2} + \frac{2}{3} \times \frac{3}{4} =$

   (c) $2\frac{3}{4} - \frac{1}{2} \div \frac{1}{3} =$

   (e) $\frac{2}{3} \times \frac{1}{2} + \frac{1}{4} \times \frac{2}{5} =$

   (g) $1\frac{2}{3} \div \frac{8}{9} - \frac{4}{5} \times \frac{7}{8} =$

   (i) $4\frac{1}{4} \times 1\frac{1}{2} - 3\frac{3}{4} \div 2\frac{1}{3} =$

   (b) $\frac{1}{3} + \frac{5}{6} \times \frac{3}{4} =$

   (d) $\frac{2}{3} - \frac{1}{2} \times \frac{2}{3} =$

   (f) $\frac{3}{10} \div \frac{1}{2} - \frac{2}{3} \times \frac{1}{4} =$

   (h) $2\frac{3}{4} \div 1\frac{1}{2} + 4\frac{2}{3} \div 1\frac{1}{9} =$

   (j) $5\frac{1}{3} \div 2\frac{2}{9} \times 3\frac{3}{4} + 1\frac{1}{2} =$

3. (a) $\frac{3}{4} \times (\frac{1}{2} + \frac{1}{3}) =$

   (c) $(4\frac{1}{2} + 3\frac{3}{4}) \div 3\frac{2}{3} =$

   (e) $(1\frac{3}{8} + 2\frac{1}{2}) \div 4\frac{3}{7} =$

   (g) $(1\frac{1}{2} \times 2\frac{1}{3} + \frac{2}{3}) \div 1\frac{7}{8} =$

   (i) $24\frac{1}{3} - (3\frac{3}{8} \times 7\frac{1}{9}) =$

   (b) $1\frac{3}{8} \div (\frac{2}{3} + \frac{5}{8}) =$

   (d) $(2\frac{2}{3} + 3\frac{3}{4}) \div 2\frac{1}{5} =$

   (f) $5\frac{1}{3} \div (2\frac{1}{2} + 3\frac{3}{4}) \times 7\frac{1}{2} =$

   (h) $2\frac{3}{4} + 1\frac{1}{2} \div (3\frac{3}{4} \times 2\frac{2}{5}) =$

   (j) $1\frac{1}{3} \div 1\frac{1}{5} \times (4\frac{1}{2} + 1\frac{4}{5}) =$

6.6 Mental Arithmetic Exercises

1. $47.5 + 32.6 + 84.75 =$
2. £320.85 − £217.65 =
3. £4 000 × 500 =
4. £7 265 ÷ 5 =
5. How many $2\frac{1}{2}$-litre bottles can be filled from a barrel holding 60 000 litres?
6. $1\frac{1}{2} + 2\frac{1}{3} + 3\frac{1}{6} =$
7. Change 2 450 centimetres to metres.
8. $\frac{2}{3} \times \frac{3}{5} \times \frac{7}{8} =$
9. How many minutes are there in 24 hours?
10. How many times will $1\frac{1}{4}$ divide into $7\frac{1}{2}$?
11. Three boxes contain respectively 5, 9 and 10 articles. If the articles are rearranged to give the same number in each box, how many will there be in each?
12. A housewife pays £5 deposit and 12 quarterly payments of £4.85 for a spin dryer. What was its total cost?
13. John runs $1\frac{1}{2}$ kilometres. Mary runs half as far as John. Peter runs half as far as Mary. How far does Peter run? (Give your answer as a fraction of a kilometre.)
14. What is the cost of 10 000 articles at £3.50 each?
15. Give the lowest common multiple of 24 and 36.

Unit Seven
The Metric System of Weights and Measures

7.1 The Metric System

In 1790, shortly after the Revolution, France invited Britain to join her in establishing an international system of weights and measures. No action was taken by Britain at this time, and France proceeded alone to adopt the system which became known as the *metric system*, a name derived from the basic unit of length, the metre. The metric system was soon adopted for scientific measurements. Its use for everyday measurements gradually became more widespread and by 1960 the general world trend was towards the use of the metric system. At the time of writing 143 countries have either already adopted the metric system or are in the process of changing over to its use. Only five countries have not made up their minds. Before many years have passed the entire world will be using the decimal system, which has much to recommend it. Metric calculations are simple and there are no complicated tables to learn as in the old imperial system. Most people only need to learn five measures of which three are metric; they are as follows:

the *metre* (m) for length;
the *litre* (l) for volume or capacity;
the *kilogram* (kg) for weight;
the *degree Celsius* (°C) for temperature (formerly Centigrade);
the *second* (s) for time.

These units are part of the International System of Units, or SI units, which covers all types of measurement. 'SI units' is short for the French name for the system, *Système International d'Unités*.

7.2 The Metric Units

The metric units were based on the most accurate scientific data available at the time of their introduction. The *metre* was based on the distance from the poles of the Earth to the equator, and was defined as one ten-millionth part of this distance. The *litre* was defined as the volume of a cube with a side one-tenth of a metre long. The *gram* was the weight of one-thousandth of a litre of water, measured under specified conditions of temperature and pressure. Since this is a very tiny measure, the *kilogram* (1 000 grams) has been chosen as the practical unit of weight for everyday use.

Metric units operate on a decimal system and calculations using them are very simple, since all three metric tables are similar and very easy to learn.

Table 7.1 Table of length (based on the metre)

10 millimetres (mm)	= 1 centimetre (cm)
10 centimetres	= 1 decimetre (dm)
10 decimetres	= 1 metre (m)
10 metres	= 1 decametre (dam)
10 decametres	= 1 hectametre (hm)
10 hectametres	= 1 kilometre (km)

Table 7.2 Table of weight (based on the gram)

10 milligrams (mg)	= 1 centigram (cg)
10 centigrams	= 1 decigram (dg)
10 decigrams	= 1 gram (g)
10 grams	= 1 decagram (dag)
10 decagrams	= 1 hectogram (hg)
10 hectograms	= 1 kilogram (kg)
1 000 kilograms	= 1 tonne (or metric ton)

Table 7.3 Table of capacity (based on the litre)

10 millilitres (ml)	= 1 centilitre (cl)
10 centilitres	= 1 decilitre (dl)
10 decilitres	= 1 litre (l)
10 litres	= 1 decalitre (dal)
10 decalitres	= 1 hectolitre (hl)
10 hectolitres	= 1 kilolitre (kl)

(*Note:* Wherever there is a risk of confusion with the figure one (1) the word litre should be written in full.)

Table 7.4 Table of time

60 seconds	= 1 minute
60 minutes	= 1 hour
24 hours	= 1 day
365 days	= 1 year

(There are 366 days in a leap year)

The first three tables may be written in a way that brings out the similarity between them, as follows:

1 000	100	10	1	$\frac{1}{10}$	$\frac{1}{100}$	$\frac{1}{1\,000}$
km	hm	dam	metre	dm	cm	mm
kg	hg	dag	gram	dg	cg	mg
kl	hl	dal	litre	dl	cl	ml

Only a few of these units are used commonly in everyday life. These important units are:

the kilometre, metre, centimetre and millimetre: the smallest of these is chiefly used in engineering;

the litre, half-litre and millilitre; the cubic centimetre (cm^3) is also often used to measure volumes in scientific work;

The tonne or metric ton, kilogram, half-kilogram, gram and milligram: the last two of these are very small, and are only important in scientific work.

7.3 Familiarization with Metric Units

It is very important, and very easy, for the student to become familiar with the metric system, and to be able to convert easily from one unit (say kilograms) to another unit in the same set (say grams). Since the relationship is a decimal one there is no real difficulty.

Example

Here is a weight in grams:

$$1\ 765.525\ g$$

change it from grams to kilograms.
Since 1 000 grams = 1 kilogram the number of grams can be changed to kilograms by dividing it by 1 000, that is, by pushing the number three places towards the right through the decimal point. There is only one kilogram, the rest is fractions of a kilogram.

$$1.765\,525\ kg$$

Now change this to hectograms. Every kilogram = 10 hectograms, so we need to multiply by 10, by pushing the whole number to the left one place. We then have

$$17.655\,25\ hg$$

Similarly we can change our original weight in grams to milligrams by multiplying by 1 000, pushing the number three places to the left, and we get

> 1 765 525. mg (the decimal point can be omitted here)

Clearly milligrams are very small. There are 1 000 of them in a gram, and 1 000 000 of them in a kilogram.

Example

Here is a distance in metres:

> 27 550.5 m

Change it to kilometres (1 000 m = 1 km):

> 27.550 5 km

Change it to centimetres (1m = 100 cm):

> 2 755 050. cm (the decimal point can be omitted here)

7.4 Exercises: Simple Metric Activities

1. Change each of the following lengths in metres to (i) kilometres (km), (ii) centimetres (cm), (iii) millimetres (mm):

   (a) 2 756 metres
   (b) 3 818 metres
   (c) 4 265.5 metres
   (d) 5 872.75 metres
   (e) 175 650 metres
   (f) 189 265 metres
   (g) 38 565.725 metres
   (h) 72 469.585 metres
   (i) 27.956 metres
   (j) 138.721 metres

2. Change each of the following weights in grams to (i) kilograms (kg), (ii) milligrams (mg):

   (a) 2 756.5 grams
   (b) 3 812.5 grams
   (c) 7 256.425 grams
   (d) 8 497.256 grams
   (e) 27 284.3 grams
   (f) 385 625.712 grams
   (g) 45.856 grams
   (h) 38.721 grams
   (i) 145.979 grams
   (j) 156.958 grams

3. Change each of the following capacities in litres to (i) millilitres (ml), (ii) centilitres (cl), (iii) decilitres (dl):

   (a) 2.5 litres
   (b) 3.8 litres
   (c) 47.5 litres
   (d) 27.9 litres
   (e) 8.765 litres
   (f) 9.214 litres
   (g) 385.725 litres
   (h) 396.321 litres
   (i) 726.942 litres
   (j) 459.725 litres

7.5 Problems Involving Metric Units

Most metric calculations which occur in business life are simple.

Example

A garage fuel tank contains 55 000 litres of petrol. 400 motorists demand 20 litres each, 850 demand 10 litres each and 1 250 demand 5 litres. What reserves are left in the tank?

We must first calculate the quantity of fuel sold.

$$
\begin{aligned}
400 \times 20 \text{ litres} &= \quad 8\,000 \text{ litres} \\
850 \times 10 \text{ litres} &= \quad 8\,500 \text{ litres} \\
1\,250 \times 5 \ \text{ litres} &= \quad 6\,250 \text{ litres} \\
\hline
&\quad 22\,750 \text{ litres sold}
\end{aligned}
$$

Now we deduct this quantity from the opening stock to find the closing stock.

$$
\begin{aligned}
\text{Total at start} \quad &= \quad 55\,000 \text{ litres} \\
\text{Subtract sales} \quad &\quad -22\,750 \text{ litres} \\
\hline
\text{Reserves in stock} &= \quad 32\,250 \text{ litres}
\end{aligned}
$$

Example

A tea blender is mixing a blend from three varieties of tea.

Type A is in two sacks each of 100 kg
Type B is in two sacks each of 75 kg
Type C is in one sack of 55 kg

The mixture will be marketed in packets each weighing 125 g. How many packets will be made up from this quantity of tea?

$$
\begin{aligned}
\text{Total weight} &= (2 \times 100) \text{ kg} + (2 \times 75) \text{ kg} + 55 \text{ kg} \\
&= 200 \text{ kg} + 150 \text{ kg} + 55 \text{ kg} \\
&= 405 \text{ kg} \\
405 \text{ kg} &= 405\,000 \text{ g} \\
\text{Number of packets} &= \frac{405\,000}{125} \\
&= 3\,240 \text{ packets}
\end{aligned}
$$

7.6 Exercises: Problems Involving Metric Units

1. A metric ton of sugar (1 000 kg) was made up into packets containing 500 g and 250 g. There were 480 of the larger packets and the rest were small. How many small packets were there?

2. How many cartons of raisins can be filled from a container holding 25 metric tons, if each carton has 500 g of fruit in it?

3. 125 g of tea costs 25p. What shall I pay for the canteen supplies for the month of December—45 kg?

4. A supermarket retails potatoes in bags containing 5 kg and $2\frac{1}{2}$ kg. A farmer supplies a lorry load weighing 15 tonnes. 1 500 of the 5-kg bags are made up and the rest of the potatoes are put into $2\frac{1}{2}$-kg bags. How many of these are there?

5. From a stock of 6 000 litres of wine the following bulk quantities are sold: 500 litres, 280 litres, 850 litres, 1 200 litres and 60 litres. What stock is still available?

6. From a granary holding 25 000 kg of wheat, supplies are dispatched to four towns, as follows: Town A, 5 800 kg; Town B, 6 500 kg; Town C, 3 150 kg; Town D, 580 kg. What quantity is left at the granary?

7. Dried fruit is retailed in packets of 125 g and 250 g. A warehouseman makes up 20 000 packets of the larger size and 36 000 packets of the smaller size. What quantity of fruit will he need?

8. Cheese is sold in packets labelled with their weight in grams. A supermarket packaging department cuts and wraps cheeses as follows: 200 packets labelled 125 g, 240 packets labelled 100 g, 480 packets labelled 200 g and 150 packets labelled 500 g. How much cheese altogether did the department cut and wrap? Give your answer in kilograms.

9. Milk lorries bringing milk in from farms carry 25 000 litres. The milk from six such lorries is made up into cartons holding 1 litre and 1 half-litre. If there are 80 000 litre cartons how many half-litre cartons are made up?

10. If the price of sugar is £42 per 100 kg, calculate the cost of 5 deliveries which weigh respectively 3 tonnes, 3.5 tonnes, 8 tonnes, 11 tonnes and 13.5 tonnes (1 tonne = 1 000 kg).

11. A traveller charges his firm for the following distances travelled in a week:

Monday 85 km	Thursday 224 km
Tuesday 132 km	Friday 18 km
Wednesday 48 km	Saturday 43 km

He is allowed to claim 15p for each kilometre travelled. What will be the value of his travel claim for the week?

12. An aircraft flies the following distances at fuel costs of 37.5p per kilometre. Calculate the total fuel bill.

Monday 2 850 km	Thursday 4 325 km
Tuesday 4 750 km	Friday 5 165 km
Wednesday 2 875 km	Saturday 8 235 km

7.7 Imperial Weights and Measures

The changeover from imperial weights and measures to metric units is gathering pace in Britain and should soon be complete. There is therefore little point in including in this book exercises and activities to give you practice in the use of the old imperial units. The only sensible thing to do is to *think metric* and *act metric*, using metric measurements. For a variety of reasons, however, we shall probably continue to meet references to the old measures for some time to come. In literature, and in historical and contemporary records, for example, students may come across references to the old measurements, while statistics for past years record many facts that were collected in the old units. This section therefore gives the tables of the principal imperial weights and measures, together with ways of converting imperial units to metric units.

Table 7.5 Table of length

12 inches = 1 foot
3 feet = 1 yard
22 yards = 1 chain
10 chains = 1 furlong
8 furlongs = 1 mile

Useful links with the metric system (correct to the number of decimal places shown):

1 metre = 39.37 inches
8 kilometres = 5 miles

Table 7.6 Table of weight

16 ounces = 1 pound (lb)
14 lb = 1 stone
2 stones = 1 quarter
4 quarters = 1 hundredweight (cwt)
20 cwt = 1 ton

Useful link with the metric system:

1 kilogram = 2.2 lb

Table 7.7 Table of capacity

4 gills = 1 pint
2 pints = 1 quart
4 quarts = 1 gallon
2 gallons = 1 peck
4 pecks = 1 bushel
8 bushels = 1 quarter

Useful link with the metric system:

1 litre = 1.76 pints

Unit Eight
Simple Ratios and Proportions

8.1 What is a Ratio?

A ratio is a relationship between two quantities expressed in numbers of units (of weight or speed, for instance) which enables us to compare them with one another. It is often very convenient to compare things in this way. For example, two motor vehicles may be travelling at different speeds, 60 km per hour and 30 km per hour. The ratio of their speeds to one another is said to be

$$60 : 30$$

(which is read 'as sixty is to thirty').

Ratios, like fractions, are usually given in their simplest forms (or *lowest terms*). We can cancel down by dividing both parts of the ratio by the same number. Thus

$$60 : 30$$
$$= \quad 6 : 3 \text{ (dividing both sides by 10)}$$
$$= \quad 2 : 1 \text{ (dividing both sides by 3)}$$

and the speeds may be said to be in the ratio 'as 2 is to 1'.

Two weights, such as 5 kg and 1 tonne, may be compared only if we *change them to the same units*. At present the weights are expressed in different units of measurement. If we turn the 1 tonne to 1 000 kg, so that both are in the same units, we can say that the weights are in the ratio

$$5 \text{ kg} : 1 \text{ 000 kg}$$

We can leave out the names of the units, so that we just have a relationship between two numbers:

$$5 : 1 \text{ 000}$$
$$= 1 : 200$$

Sometimes the ratio comes down to small whole numbers but cannot be simplified any further. For example, the ratio of the daily outputs of two factories may be 35 units to 40 units:

$$35 : 40$$
$$= \quad 7 : 8$$

This may be sufficient to give a clear picture to the managers of the two factories. If not we can go one stage further, dividing each side by 7:

$$7 : 8$$
$$= 1 : 1\tfrac{1}{7}$$
$$\text{or } 1 : 1.1428 \text{ etc.}$$

When a ratio is reduced to the point where one side is 1, we have gone as far as we can in simplifying it. This form is useful for comparing one ratio with another. Suppose, for example, that 18 applicants out of 54 failed to gain admission to a medical college, while 22 candidates out of 68 failed to gain admission to a veterinary college. The ratios of failures to total candidates are as follows:

Medical college	Veterinary college
18 : 54	22 : 68
9 : 27	11 : 34
1 : 3	1 : 3.09

The second of these ratios is a little awkward, because 11 will not divide exactly into 34 and we must state the ratio to a certain number of decimal places, depending on the degree of accuracy required.

Example

Express the ratio between 25 m and 1 km as a ratio in its lowest terms.

First we must turn the two distances to the same units; then we cancel both parts of the ratio as far as possible.

$$25 \text{ m} : 1 \text{ km}$$
$$= 25 \text{ m} : 1\,000 \text{ m}$$
$$= 25 : 1\,000$$
$$= 5 : 200$$
$$= 1 : 40$$

The first length is to the second length as 1 is to 40, that is, 25 m is contained in 1 km 40 times.

8.2 Exercises: Simple Ratios

1. Express the following ratios as simply as possible in the form $a : b$.
   - (a) £5 to £100
   - (b) £50 to £100
   - (c) £75 to £100
   - (d) £14 to £56
   - (e) 60 m to 300 m
   - (f) 50 km to 125 km
   - (g) 48 cm to 120 cm
   - (h) 16 cm to 80 cm

2. Express the following ratios as simply as possible in the form $a : b$, remembering that both parts of the ratio must be in the same units:
   - (a) 10 m to 1 km
   - (b) 50p to £10
   - (c) 12 cm to 1.68 m
   - (d) 30 seconds to 1 minute 45 seconds
   - (e) 5 millilitres to 2 litres
   - (f) 240 m to 12 km
   - (g) 5 minutes to $2\frac{1}{2}$ hours
   - (h) 30 minutes to 1 day

3. Express the following ratios in the form $1 : x$. (Write down the ratio; then reduce one side of the ratio to 1 and divide the other out *correct to 2 places of decimals*.)

(a) 24 tonnes to 64 tonnes

(b) 12 cm to 45 cm

(c) 5p to 18.5p

(d) 7 square metres to 24 square metres

(e) 18 kg to 57 kg

(f) 4 km to 27.7 km

(g) 7 people per thousand people

(h) 9 days to 3 weeks 3 days

4. (a) A hotel charges £15 per night in the winter and £25.50 per night in the summer. What is the ratio of winter to summer prices?

(b) A man earns £6 000 per year (after deductions) and spends £4 500 per year. What is the ratio of his savings to his earnings?

(c) The tax on an income of £8 700 is £1 450. What is the ratio of tax to income?

(d) Two cars cost £4 500 and £5 500. After one year they are worth £3 250 and £4 000 respectively. What are the ratios of their prices (i) when new and (ii) secondhand? (Answers correct to 2 decimal places.)

(e) An electronic printing calculator costs £95. A mini-computer with printer costs £1 425. What is the ratio of their prices?

(f) What is the ratio of the commissions of two business representatives, one of whom receives £7 950 and the other £6 916.50?

(g) A batch of coins is made of 32 kg of copper and 256 kg of nickel. What is the ratio of copper to nickel in the coinage alloy?

(h) A bankrupt owes £28 900 and his goods when sold fetch £3 400. What is the ratio of cash available to debts payable?

8.3 Proportional Parts

Sometimes in business or professional life we have to share things proportionately. For instance, an inheritance might be shared in the proportions of $2 : 1 : 1$ between a son and two daughters. We can see that there are four portions, of which the son will have two and the daughters one each. The son will therefore get $\frac{2}{4} = \frac{1}{2}$ of the inheritance and the daughters $\frac{1}{4}$ each. Similarly, suppose that three children are to share an inheritance in the proportions $3 : 2 : 1$. This time there will be six shares, of which one child will have three shares, the next two, and the last one share only. We therefore have:

$$\text{First child receives} \quad \tfrac{3}{6} = \tfrac{1}{2}$$
$$\text{Second child receives} \quad \tfrac{2}{6} = \tfrac{1}{3}$$
$$\text{Third child receives} \quad \tfrac{1}{6}$$

Example

Profits are shared between three partners A, B and C in the proportions $3 : 2 : 2$. If the total profits are £27 580 how much does each partner get?

$$3 + 2 + 2 = 7 \text{ shares in all}$$

Partner A gets $\frac{3}{7} \times £27\,580 = 3 \times £3\,940$ (dividing by 7)
$$= £11\,820$$

Partner B gets $\frac{2}{7} \times £27\,580 = 2 \times £3\,940$
$$= £7\,880$$

Partner C also receives   £7 880

Example

Profits are shared between three partners X, Y and Z so that X has twice as much as Y who has three times as much as Z. If the total profits are £2 760, what will each receive?

Start with the partner getting the lowest share:

Z gets 1 share
Y gets three times Z's share = 3 shares
X gets twice as much as Y = 6 shares
Therefore there are $1 + 3 + 6 = 10$ shares in all.

$$1 \text{ share} = £\frac{2\,760}{10} = £276$$

Thus Z gets £276

Y gets £276 $\times$ 3 = £828

Z gets £276 $\times$ 6 = £1 656

Check: Total of £276 + £828 + £1 656 = £2 760

8.4 Exercises: Proportional Parts

1. Share the following sums of money in the proportions shown:
   (a) £285 in the proportions $3:2$
   (b) £330 in the proportions $2:1$
   (c) £480 in the proportions $5:1$
   (d) £560 in the proportions $4:3$
   (e) £720 in the proportions $5:4$
   (f) £1 785 in the proportions $8:7$
   (g) £7 236 in the proportions $5:4$
   (h) £2 421 in the proportions $4:3:2$
   (i) £5 533 in the proportions $4:4:3$
   (j) £19 875 in the proportions $8:4:3$

2. Share the following weights in the proportions shown:
   (a) 350 kg in the proportions 3 : 2
   (b) 472 kg in the proportions 3 : 1
   (c) 582 kg in the proportions 3 : 2 : 1
   (d) 4 734 kg in the proportions 5 : 2 : 2
   (e) 2 850 kg in the proportions 12 : 12 : 1
   (f) 5 000 tonnes in the proportions 5 : 3 : 2
   (g) 4 802 tonnes in the proportions 3 : 2 : 2
   (h) 3 250 tonnes in the proportions 2 : 2 : 1
   (i) 1 760 tonnes in the proportions 4 : 4 : 3
   (j) 1 582 tonnes in the proportions 3 : 3 : 1

3. Profits are shared among three partners X, Y and Z in such a way that X has twice as much as Y who has three times as much as Z. What will each receive if the profits are £8 750?

4. Profits are shared among four partners A, B, C and D so that A and B each get three times what D gets, while C gets twice D's share. What will each receive if the total profits are £4 950?

5. Food is shared among three famine-stricken villages in a relief campaign, the available food being shared according to the number of families. In village A there are 28 families, in village B 17 families and in village C 9 families. The relief column brings in 10 800 kilograms of food. How much should each village receive?

6. The marks in an examination paper total 120. They are distributed between three questions in the ratio 6 : 5 : 4. How many marks can be gained for each question?

7. Divide £198 between X, Y and Z so that X has twice as much as Y who has half as much again as Z. How much does each receive?

8.5 Changing Things in Direct Proportion

Many business calculations are based on simple proportion. For example: 2 tonnes of sulphur cost £360.50. What shall I pay for 5 tonnes? If the price is to be at the same rate per tonne I shall pay more for 5 tonnes than for 2 tonnes, *in direct proportion*: we must find the cost of 1 tonne, and then multiply this by 5. This procedure is called the *unitary method*, that is, the method of finding what 1 unit will cost.

Unitary method calculations always take three lines of working. Line 1 states what you know already. Line 2 tells you how to find what 1 unit will be. Line 3 tells you what you need to know. The actual calculations are not done until you get to the third line.

Example

In our earlier example we have:

Line 1   2 tonnes of sulphur cost £360.50

Line 2   1 tonne costs $\dfrac{£360.50}{2}$ (dividing by 2)

Line 3   5 tonnes cost $\dfrac{£360.50}{2} \times 5 = £180.25 \times 5$

$$= £901.25$$

Example

A stay at the George Hotel costs £198.80 for 7 days. How much will it cost for a stay of 15 days at the same rate?

Line 1   7 days cost £198.80

Line 2   1 day costs $\dfrac{£198.80}{7}$ (dividing by 7)

Line 3   15 days cost $\dfrac{£198.80}{7} \times 15$

$$= £28.40 \times 15$$
$$= £426.00$$

$$\begin{array}{r} 28.40 \\ 15 \\ \hline 284\ 00 \\ 142\ 00 \\ \hline £426.00 \end{array}$$

Example

A manufacturer pays £2 800 for 35 machines; how much will 60 cost?

35 machines cost £2 800

1 machine costs $\dfrac{£2\ 800}{35}$

60 machines cost $\dfrac{£2\ \cancel{800}^{400}}{\cancel{35}\ 7\ 1} \times \cancel{60}^{12}$

$$= £4\ 800$$

8.6 Exercises: Unitary Method Calculations

1. Do these simple proportion calculations in your head and write down the answers. In each case find the cost of 1 unit first.
   (*a*) 3 cost 6p. How much for 5?
   (*b*) 2 cost 7p. How much for 3?
   (*c*) 4 cost 12p. How much for 7?
   (*d*) 7 cost 21p. How much for 10?

(e) 18 cost 36p. How much for 25?

(f) 15 cost 45p. How much for 18?

(g) 5 cost £40. How much for 7?

(h) 6 cost £96. How much for 5?

(i) 12 cost £240. How much for 20?

(j) 15 cost £60. How much for 25?

2. Do these direct proportion sums by the unitary method, each time setting out three lines of working and then doing the calculation.

(a) 12 similar motor vehicles cost altogether £58 800. What will 7 cost?

(b) 3 colour television sets cost £594. What will 8 cost at the same rate?

(c) 4 typewriters cost £244.80. What will 7 cost at the same rate?

(d) 5 sewing machines cost £365.50. What will 9 cost at the same rate?

(e) 4 washing machines cost £875. What will it cost to install 15 of these machines in a launderette? (No charge is made for installation.)

(f) 72 vacuum cleaners cost £2 304. What will 120 cost at the same rate?

(g) A hotel charges £133.00 per week. What will be the charge for 4 days at the same rate?

(h) Renting a television set costs £78 per year. What will be the rent for three weeks at the same rate?

(i) A railway ticket for a journey of 70 kilometres costs £4.55. What will it cost at the same rate for a journey of 120 kilometres?

(j) An airline flight of 2 400 kilometres costs £124.80. What will it cost at the same rate for a flight of 3 200 kilometres?

8.7 Mental Arithmetic Exercises

1. £47.50 + £38.70 + £25.65 =

2. £273.00 − £145.85 =

3. 7 236 × 7 =

4. £43.850 ÷ 5 =

5. How many 25-gram packets can be made up from 1 kilogram?

6. How many centimetres are there in 1.5 metres?

7. How many litres are there in 2.75 kilolitres?

8. How many days are there from 4 July to 18 August inclusive?

9. $4\frac{1}{2} + 3\frac{7}{8} + 1\frac{1}{4} =$

10. $\frac{3}{4} \div \frac{7}{8} =$

11. What is the profit on 24 items bought at £1.55 each and sold at £2.25 each?

12. Share £3 800 between Mr A and Mr B in the ratio of 10 : 9.

13. If 5 similar items cost £12.50 what will 7 of them cost?

14. If partners share profits in a ratio of $\frac{3}{5}$ to $\frac{2}{5}$, what will each receive on a transaction where a vehicle costing £600 is sold for £720?

15. What will it cost to build a fence on a garden frontage 24 metres long if the 2-metre panels cost £6 each and the posts £1.50 each? Labour costs £15, and other materials £2. (Ignore the widths of the posts.)

Unit Nine

Percentages

9.1 What are Percentages?

The word *percentage* comes from the Latin word for 100, *centum*, and the word *per*, translated here as 'out of'. Percentage thus means 'out of 100'. For example, the question 'what percentage of troops were taken ill with malaria?' means 'how many troops *out of each hundred* were struck down by malaria?'

It seems that people can imagine 100 fairly easily, and can therefore readily visualize '30 out of 100' or '75 out of 100'. To pick a smaller number like 5 gives less divisions for use in describing situations, while a very large number like 1 000 or 1 000 000 would give more divisions than we usually need. The statement that '4 792 articles were exported out of a total production of 9 584' is not very easy to grasp. To say that '50 out of every 100'—50 per cent—went to exports gives a much clearer idea.

The sign % is used for 'per cent', so that 17 per cent is often written 17%, and 50 per cent, 50%.

9.2 The Common Percentage Groups

It is useful to be familiar with the values of the commoner fractions when they are expressed as percentages. Those most often met with are as follows, and you should learn them by heart:

$$\frac{3}{4} = \frac{75}{100} = 75\% \qquad\qquad \frac{1}{3} = \frac{33\frac{1}{3}}{100} = 33\frac{1}{3}\%$$

$$\frac{1}{2} = \frac{50}{100} = 50\% \qquad\qquad \frac{2}{3} = \frac{66\frac{2}{3}}{100} = 66\frac{2}{3}\%$$

$$\frac{1}{4} = \frac{25}{100} = 25\%$$

$$\frac{1}{10} = \frac{10}{100} = 10\% \qquad\qquad \frac{1}{5} = \frac{20}{100} = 20\%$$

$$\frac{3}{10} = \frac{30}{100} = 30\% \qquad\qquad \frac{2}{5} = \frac{40}{100} = 40\%$$

$$\frac{7}{10} = \frac{70}{100} = 70\% \qquad\qquad \frac{3}{5} = \frac{60}{100} = 60\%$$

$$\frac{9}{10} = \frac{90}{100} = 90\% \qquad\qquad \frac{4}{5} = \frac{80}{100} = 80\%$$

$$\frac{1}{20} = \frac{5}{100} = 5\%$$

$$\frac{1}{40} = \frac{2\frac{1}{2}}{100} = 2\frac{1}{2}\%$$

$$\frac{1}{80} = \frac{1\frac{1}{4}}{100} = 1\frac{1}{4}\%$$

$$\frac{1}{6} = \frac{16\frac{2}{3}}{100} = 16\frac{2}{3}\%$$

$$\frac{5}{6} = \frac{83\frac{1}{3}}{100} = 83\frac{1}{3}\%$$

$$\frac{1}{8} = \frac{12\frac{1}{2}}{100} = 12\frac{1}{2}\%$$

$$\frac{3}{8} = \frac{37\frac{1}{2}}{100} = 37\frac{1}{2}\%$$

$$\frac{5}{8} = \frac{62\frac{1}{2}}{100} = 62\frac{1}{2}\%$$

$$\frac{7}{8} = \frac{87\frac{1}{2}}{100} = 87\frac{1}{2}\%$$

9.3 Changing Fractions and Decimals to Percentages

Fractions, decimals and percentages are all linked together, and in business life often have to be converted from one to another. We must be familiar with these conversions: the rules for them are very simple.

Rule 1: *To change a fraction to a percentage write down the fraction and multiply it by* $\dfrac{100}{1}$

Example

Change the following fractions to percentages:

$$\tfrac{1}{2}; \tfrac{5}{12}; \tfrac{7}{20}; 1\tfrac{1}{2}$$

$$\frac{1}{2}_1 \times \frac{100}{1}^{50} = 50\%$$

$$\frac{5}{12}_3 \times \frac{100}{1}^{25} = \frac{125}{3} = 41\frac{2}{3}\%$$

$$\frac{7}{20}_1 \times \frac{100}{1}^{5} = 35\%$$

$$1\frac{1}{2} \times \frac{100}{1} = \frac{3}{2} \times \frac{100}{1}^{50} = 150\%$$

Rule 2: *To change a decimal to a percentage multiply the decimal by 100 and put the % sign.*

Example

Change the following decimals to percentages:

$$0.55; \ 0.725; \ 0.8125; \ 1.50$$

Remember that we multiply a decimal fraction by 100 by moving the number two decimal places to the left. Then:

$$0.55 \times 100 = \underline{55\%}$$

$$0.725 \times 100 = \underline{72.5\%}$$

$$0.8125 \times 100 = \underline{81.25\%}$$

$$1.50 \times 100 = \underline{150\%}$$

9.4 Exercises: Changing Fractions and Decimals to Percentages

1. Change the following fractions to percentages:
   (a) $\frac{1}{2}$ (b) $\frac{1}{4}$ (c) $\frac{1}{5}$ (d) $\frac{3}{10}$
   (e) $\frac{7}{10}$ (f) $\frac{3}{20}$ (g) $\frac{1}{8}$ (h) $\frac{3}{8}$
   (i) $\frac{9}{20}$ (j) $\frac{7}{8}$ (k) $\frac{5}{12}$ (l) $\frac{3}{4}$

2. Change the following mixed numbers to percentages:
   (a) $1\frac{1}{2}$ (b) $1\frac{3}{4}$ (c) $1\frac{5}{8}$ (d) $1\frac{7}{10}$
   (e) $2\frac{3}{20}$ (f) $3\frac{4}{5}$ (g) $4\frac{3}{8}$ (h) $5\frac{3}{5}$
   (i) $6\frac{13}{20}$ (j) $2\frac{1}{3}$ (k) $3\frac{2}{3}$ (l) $4\frac{5}{8}$

3. Change the following decimals to percentages:
   (a) 0.55   (b) 0.75   (c) 0.36   (d) 0.28
   (e) 0.41   (f) 0.58   (g) 0.65   (h) 0.73
   (i) 0.855   (j) 0.725   (k) 0.964   (l) 0.785

9.5 Changing Percentages to Fractions and Decimals

Rule 3: *To change a percentage to a fraction write down the whole number of the percentage as the numerator, and write down 100 as the denominator. Then cancel if you can.*

Example

Change the following percentages to fractions:
$$64\%; \ 75\%; \ 58\%; \ 62.5\%; \ 150\%$$

$$64\% = \frac{\overset{16}{\cancel{64}}}{\underset{25}{\cancel{100}}} = \frac{16}{25} \text{ (cancelling by 4)}$$

$$75\% = \frac{\overset{3}{\cancel{75}}}{\underset{4}{\cancel{100}}} = \frac{3}{4} \text{ (cancelling by 25)}$$

$$58\% = \frac{\overset{29}{\cancel{58}}}{\underset{50}{\cancel{100}}} = \frac{29}{50} \text{ (cancelling by 2)}$$

$$62.5\% = \frac{62\frac{1}{2}}{100} = \frac{125}{200} = \frac{5}{8}$$

$$150\% = \frac{150}{100} = \frac{3}{2} = 1\frac{1}{2}$$

The fourth of these examples involves a decimal fraction as a percentage. We deal with this by writing 62.5 as $62\frac{1}{2}$, getting rid of the fraction in the usual way by multiplying both the numerator and the denominator by the necessary figure—in this case, 2.

Rule 4: *To change a percentage to a decimal write down the percentage and divide it by 100.*

Example

Change the following percentages to decimals:

$$72\%; 85\%; 61.25\%; 150\%$$

Remember that we divide a decimal fraction by 100 by moving the number through two decimal places to the right.

$$72\% = 72.00 \div 100 = 0.72$$
$$85\% = 85.00 \div 100 = 0.85$$
$$61.25\% = 61.25 \div 100 = 0.6125$$
$$150\% = 150.00 \div 100 = 1.50$$

9.6 Exercises: Changing Percentages to Decimals and Fractions

1. Change the following percentages to fractions in their lowest terms:
   (a) 30%   (b) 40%   (c) 80%   (d) 96%
   (e) 28%   (f) 36%   (g) $83\frac{1}{3}\%$ (h) $12\frac{1}{2}\%$
   (i) $16\frac{2}{3}\%$ (j) $37\frac{1}{2}\%$ (k) $87\frac{1}{2}\%$ (l) $41\frac{2}{3}\%$

2. Change the following percentages to fractions in their lowest terms:
   (a) 90%   (b) 60%   (c) 12%   (d) 78%
   (e) 56%   (f) 48%   (g) $27\frac{1}{2}\%$ (h) $68\frac{3}{4}\%$
   (i) $33\frac{1}{3}\%$ (j) 85%   (k) 88%   (l) 55%

3. Change the following percentages to decimal fractions:
   (a) 31%   (b) 36%   (c) 72%   (d) 65%
   (e) 45.5%   (f) 62.5%   (g) 73.5%   (h) 85.8%
   (i) 41.35%   (j) 65.35%   (k) 87.60%   (l) 92.59%

9.7 Finding a Percentage of a Quantity

In business we often have to calculate a certain percentage of a given quantity, for example 10 per cent of a sum of money, or 30 per cent of a quantity of raw material of some sort, and we frequently calculate discounts to customers, or profit margins on goods for sale, in percentage terms. Always the process is very simple, but we have to use our basic arithmetical processes accurately so that we do not make errors.

Rule 5: *Write down the percentage required and multiply it by the original quantity.*

Example

Our firm adds on $33\frac{1}{3}$ per cent to cost prices to find its selling prices. Calculate how much we should add to items costing (*a*) 84 pence; (*b*) £5.25; (*c*) £180.

Note that $33\frac{1}{3}$ per cent is one of the common percentages (see Section 9.2) which we know is $\frac{1}{3}$. All we need to do, therefore, is to write down $\frac{1}{3}$ and multiply.

(*a*) $33\frac{1}{3}\% \times 84$ pence $= \frac{1}{\cancel{3}_1} \times \cancel{84}^{28}$ pence $= \underline{\underline{28 \text{ pence}}}$

(*b*) $33\frac{1}{3}\%$ of £5.25 $= \frac{1}{\cancel{3}_1} \times \cancel{£5.25}^{1.75} = \underline{\underline{£1.75}}$

(*c*) $33\frac{1}{3}\%$ of £180 $= \frac{1}{\cancel{3}_1} \times \cancel{£180}^{60} = \underline{\underline{£60}}$

If the percentage is not a well-known fraction, we may need to multiply out the calculation, but the work is still essentially simple.

Example

What is 17% of (*a*) £5 200, (*b*) £755?

(*a*) 17% of £5 200 $= \frac{17}{\cancel{100}_1} \times \cancel{5\,200}^{52}$

$= 17 \times 52$

$$
\begin{array}{r}
17 \\
\times\ 52 \\
\hline
34 \\
850 \\
\hline
884
\end{array}
$$

$= \underline{\underline{£884}}$

(*b*) 17% of £755 $= \frac{17}{100} \times £755$

$= 17 \times £7.55$

$$
\begin{array}{r}
7.55 \\
\times\ \ 17 \\
\hline
52\ 85 \\
75\ 50 \\
\hline
128.35
\end{array}
$$

$= \underline{\underline{£128.35}}$

9.8 Exercises: Finding a Percentage of a Quantity

1. Calculate the following percentage parts:
   (*a*) 50% of £120
   (*b*) 25% of £600
   (*c*) 75% of £240
   (*d*) 20% of £1 200
   (*e*) 10% of £4 800
   (*f*) $33\frac{1}{3}\%$ of £450
   (*g*) $66\frac{2}{3}\%$ of £720
   (*h*) 40% of £800

2. Calculate the following percentage parts:
   (a) $12\frac{1}{2}\%$ of £800
   (c) $16\frac{2}{3}\%$ of £660
   (e) $2\frac{1}{2}\%$ of £50
   (g) 5% of £250

   (b) $37\frac{1}{2}\%$ of £400
   (d) 15% of £780
   (f) 35% of £150
   (h) $62\frac{1}{2}\%$ of £480

3. Calculate the following percentage parts:
   (a) 12% of £1 400
   (c) 16% of £1 800
   (e) 22% of £550
   (g) 34% of £720

   (b) 72% of £1 000
   (d) 32% of £500
   (f) 56% of £480
   (h) 84% of £420

4. Calculate the following percentage parts:
   (a) 24% of 300 tonnes
   (c) 42% of 480 kg
   (e) 38% of 25 km
   (g) 88% of 2 000 litres

   (b) 66% of 5 000 tonnes
   (d) 44% of 720 kg
   (f) 28% of 250 km
   (h) 17% of 400 litres

9.9 Discounts

It is a common business practice to deduct a certain percentage from the price of an article. This reduction in price is called a *discount* and there are three chief types: cash discounts, settlement discounts and trade discounts.

Cash discounts are given to people who pay cash for goods. They are commonly about 5 per cent, but on more profitable items, or when trade is bad and extra inducements are necessary to coax customers into buying, as much as 10 or even 20 per cent may be offered.

Settlement discounts are given to customers who normally buy on monthly terms, and settle their debts on receiving a monthly statement. The discount given is not great, perhaps $2\frac{1}{2}$ or 5 per cent, but it is still welcome to the debtor and represents a useful reduction in costs.

Trade discounts are much larger, and are given to traders who buy wholesale and sell retail. They are rarely less than 20 per cent and often as high as 55 per cent, depending on the rate of turnover. The articles purchased are usually offered at a 'recommended retail price', and it is convenient to invoice them at this price. Such an invoice might read as follows:

20 Slumbersweet divan beds at £80 = £1 600

The £80 is the recommended retail price. Clearly the retailer will not buy at £80 and sell at £80. The wholesaler therefore deducts trade discount at an agreed rate, thus giving the retailer a reasonable profit margin. The invoice might therefore read:

20 Slumbersweet divan beds at £80 = £1 600
Less 40% trade discount   =   640
                                     ————
                                     £960
                                     ════

Example

A tailor allows his customer 5 per cent cash discount. What will the customer pay for a suit priced at £78.50?

$$\text{Discount} = \frac{\cancel{5}^{1}}{\cancel{100}_{20}} \times £78.50$$

$$= \frac{£7.850}{2}$$

$$= £3.92\tfrac{1}{2}$$

Customer pays £78.50 − £3.92½ = £74.57½

Care is needed in the first line of this calculation: the zero in the decimal fraction cannot be cancelled as it might be in a whole number. The best way to complete the working is to divide both the numerator and the denominator by 10, by moving both numbers one place through the decimal point to the right. The numerator thus changes from £78.50 to £7.850, and the denominator, 20, changes to 2.

Example

A firm receives a statement on October 31 which reads 'To account rendered £295. Settlement discount 2½% cash 30 days'. It decides to pay at once after deducting the permitted discount. What will be the value of the cheque sent in payment?

$$\text{Value of account} = £295$$

$$\text{Discount} = 2\tfrac{1}{2}\% \text{ of } £295$$

$$= \frac{1}{\cancel{40}_{8}} \times £\cancel{295}^{59}$$

$$= £7.37\tfrac{1}{2}$$

But cheques cannot be made out for odd halfpennies.

$$\text{Therefore value of cheque} = £295 - £7.38$$

$$= £287.62$$

Example

A wholesaler gives his customers 45 per cent trade discount on all orders. What will a retailer pay for goods whose catalogue price is £380?

$$\text{Catalogue price} = £380$$

$$\text{Less } 45\% \text{ trade discount} = \frac{\cancel{45}^{9}}{\cancel{100}_{20_1}} \times £\cancel{380}^{19}$$

$$= £171$$

Retailer pays £380 − £171 = £209

9.10 Exercises: Discounts

1. Work out the following cash discounts:
   (a) 5% of £50   (b) $2\frac{1}{2}$% of £80
   (c) 10% of £240   (d) 5% of £25
   (e) $2\frac{1}{2}$% of £420   (f) 5% of £40
   (g) 10% of £55   (h) 15% of £65

2. Work out the following settlement discounts, if necessary to the nearest penny.
   (a) $2\frac{1}{2}$% of £48   (b) $2\frac{1}{2}$% of £36
   (c) $2\frac{1}{2}$% of £72.00   (d) $2\frac{1}{2}$% of £50.50
   (e) $2\frac{1}{2}$% of £95.60   (f) 5% of £27.50
   (g) 5% of £42.40   (h) 5% of £86.30

3. Work out the following trade discounts, if necessary to the nearest penny.
   (a) $33\frac{1}{3}$% of £125   (b) $33\frac{1}{3}$% of £175
   (c) 40% of 65   (d) 40% of £88
   (e) 45% of £72.50   (f) 45% of £195.50
   (g) 30% of £640   (h) 55% of £85.65

4. A trader orders goods at a catalogue price of £350. He is given a 25 per cent trade discount on the invoice and is then allowed to deduct 5 per cent from the final (i.e. net) invoice price if he pays cash. He does pay cash, so what does he pay?

5. A trader orders goods at a catalogue price of £165. He is given a trade discount of 20 per cent on the invoice and a settlement discount of $7\frac{1}{2}$ per cent off the final invoice price if he pays within 7 days. What will he finally pay for these goods if he pays promptly?

6. A trader orders goods at a catalogue price of £285. He is given a trade discount of 45 per cent, and then a cash discount of $2\frac{1}{2}$ per cent on the final invoice price. What does he pay in the end for these goods?

9.11 Mental Arithmetic Exercises

1. $127 + 242 + 563 =$
2. $327 - 209 =$
3. $259 \times 50 =$
4. $7\,368 \div 8 =$
5. $1\frac{1}{2} + 2\frac{2}{3} =$
6. $0.5 \times 0.42 =$
7. What shall I pay for 30 items at £1.15 each?
8. What is the value of £275 × 20?
9. Divide £16 in the ratio 5 : 3.

10. VAT is payable at a rate of 15 per cent on certain items. What will be the tax on a spin dryer costing £84 before tax?
11. Change 35 per cent to a common fraction.
12. Discount of $12\frac{1}{2}$ per cent is given off all marked prices in a sale. What shall I pay for an item marked £36.00?
13. How many days are there from 11 June to 20 September inclusive?
14. If items cost £54 a dozen what will 7 cost?
15. If a train travels at 84 kilometres per hour for $3\frac{1}{2}$ hours, how far will it go?

Unit Ten

Simple Averages

10.1 What are Averages?

The word *average* comes from an Arabic word meaning 'damaged goods'. From the earliest times Arab traders had a custom about goods that were deliberately thrown overboard at sea in an attempt to save a vessel in difficulties. This custom ruled that those who were the losers should be compensated by those whose goods were saved. The loss was shared equally among all parties. So if £10 000 of Mr A's goods were sacrificed to save £90 000 of goods altogether, Mr A would be given £9 000 compensation, leaving £81 000 for those whose goods were saved. The English word 'average' is thus linked with its Arab associations, and today the law of General Average is still an important part of insurance law.

Averages are part of the branch of mathematics called *statistics*, which is more fully described in Units 30–33. There are several different types of average (see Unit 33) but in this Unit we are concerned with the simple average, more correctly called the *arithmetic mean*, which is found by sharing the sum of the quantities concerned equally between the number of quantities.

Thus, suppose we need to know the average age of five young people attending an adventure playground on a particular morning, who are aged 6, 8, 11, 12 and 13 respectively. We begin by adding up the ages of the children: $6 + 8 + 11 + 12 + 13 = 50$ years; when we divide by 5 this shares out equally (*averages*) at 10 years each. If the ages of the young people had been 7, 7, 8, 11 and 17 the average would still have been 10 years: $7 + 7 + 8 + 11 + 17 = 50$, and $\frac{50}{5} = 10$.

Whenever we wish to calculate averages we must start with a collection of figures from which to draw our conclusions. In a textbook these figures are given by the author in various examples and questions, but in real life the figures must be collected. We might collect sales figures from the various departments of a store and find the average departmental sales, for example. These collections of figures are called *data*.

10.2 Finding a Simple Average

The rule for finding simple number averages is: *add up the data provided and divide by the number of quantities.*

Example

Find the average age of five students aged 17, 19, 23, 24 and 27.

Sum of the ages = 17 + 19 + 23 + 24 + 27 = 110
Average   = 110 ÷ 5 (because there are 5 students)
             = 22

Example

Find the average age of 6 students who ages are listed below:

(a)   17 years   3 months
(b)   17 years   5 months
(c)   17 years 11 months
(d)   18 years   4 months
(e)   18 years   6 months
(f)   18 years   7 months

Total = 108 years   0 months

Note that the number of months added together comes to 36. There are 12 months in a year, so 36 months make 3 years; we write a zero in the months column and carry 3 into the years column.

Average age = 108 years ÷ 6
              = 18 years

If the answer to an average sum does not work out exactly, we must use our common sense on the degree of accuracy required. Often an answer correct to one place of decimals will be quite good enough.

Example

A theatrical performance is given 5 times, and the audiences numbered 721, 854, 1 027, 1 063, 1 170. What was the average attendance?

First find the total attendance:

$$
\begin{array}{r}
721 \\
854 \\
1\ 027 \\
1\ 063 \\
1\ 170 \\
\hline
4\ 835
\end{array}
$$

Average attendance =   4 835 ÷ 5
           =   967

10.3 Exercises: Simple Averages

1. Find the average of each of the following sets of data:
   (*a*) 3, 7, 8   (*b*) 4, 9, 11
   (*c*) 3, 5, 7, 9   (*d*) 7, 11, 13, 17
   (*e*) 3, 5, 9, 12, 16   (*f*) 4, 6, 7, 10, 13
   (*g*) 1, 2, 3, 5, 8, 11   (*h*) 4, 5, 7, 9, 12, 17
   (*i*) 259, 412, 736   (*j*) 425, 387, 296, 512

2. Find the average of each of the following sets of data:
   (*a*) 14 kg, 13 kg, 70 kg, 51 kg
   (*b*) 29 kg, 37 kg, 55 kg, 24 kg, 30 kg
   (*c*) 17 hr 30 min, 16 hr 40 min, 15 hr 20 min, 22 hr 10 min
   (*d*) 5 hr 50 min, 8 hr 40 min, 7 hr 25 min, 6 hr 30 min, 5 hr 10 min
   (*e*) 27.5 tonnes, 32.3 tonnes, 18.7 tonnes, 19.1 tonnes

10.4 Averages of Large Numbers

Sometimes we can take a short cut in finding the average of large numbers or large quantities, especially if the numbers are not very different from each other.

Example

Find the average of the following numbers:

$$17\,250;\ 17\,350;\ 17\,450$$

Clearly all the numbers contain at least 17 000, so we can ignore that part of the sum.

Thus
$$17\,250 = 17\,000 + 250$$
$$17\,350 = 17\,000 + 350$$
$$17\,450 = 17\,000 + 450$$

Now find the average of 250, 350 and 450:

$$250 + 350 + 450 = 1\,050$$
$$\text{Average} = \frac{1\,050}{3}$$
$$= 350$$

Then the average we want is $17\,000 + 350$
$$= 17\,350$$

We could have used the fact that all the numbers have at least 17 250 in them, and regarded them as:

$$17\,250 + 0$$
$$17\,250 + 100$$
$$17\,250 + 200$$

The average of 0, 100 and 200 $= \dfrac{300}{3} = 100$.

Then the average we want is 17 250 + 100

$$= \underline{\underline{17\ 350}}$$

This type of short cut makes the calculation of averages of big numbers much easier.

10.5 Exercises: Averages of Large Numbers

1. Find the average of the following sets of numbers, using the method of the example in Section 10.4:
   (a) 1 567, 1 595, 1 995, 1 607
   (b) 3 028, 3 054, 3 087, 3 094, 3 092
   (c) 425, 395, 414, 397, 436, 501
   (d) 550, 565, 575, 585, 540, 580, 546
   (e) 41 727, 48 725, 49 324

2. Find the average of the following sets of numbers:
   (a) 3.4, 3.6, 3.5, 3.7, 3.8
   (b) 4.75, 3.25, 3.75, 4.55, 5.45
   (c) 14.5, 15.3, 15.8, 15.7, 15.6, 15.5
   (d) 21.5, 23.7, 25.6, 20.5, 20.9, 20.6, 21.9
   (e) 18.75, 18.77, 18.79, 19.15, 19.79

3. At a series of concerts the attendances were 1 473, 1 568, 1 572 and 1 495. What was the average attendance?

4. At a series of theatrical performances the attendances were successively 2 859, 2 759, 2 638, 3 124 and 3 250. What was the average attendance?

5. Outputs of cars from six manufacturing plants in the month of December were as follows: 27 280, 29 756, 30 150, 33 721, 25 011, 27 902. What was the average output?

10.6 Weighted Averages

The word *weight* here means 'emphasis'. Sometimes in calculating averages one of the numbers involved may have greater emphasis than the other.

Example

2 candidates receive 70 marks in an examination and the third 49 marks. What was the average mark?

Clearly the 70 has greater weight than the 49, and should be counted twice. We must multiply 70 × 2 = 140 and then add 49, because the total mark obtained by the candidates was 70 + 70 + 49.

$$140 + 49 = 189$$
$$\text{Average} = \dfrac{189}{3} = 63$$

Example

3 children are 11 years old, 4 are 13 years old, 2 are 14 years old and 5 are aged 15 years. What is the average age?

Here we must multiply each age by the appropriate weighting and add them together, to obtain the total age of all the children. Then we divide by the number of weights, that is, by the total number of children.

$$
\begin{array}{ccc}
Weighting & & Age \\
3 & \times & 11 = 33 \\
4 & \times & 13 = 52 \\
2 & \times & 14 = 28 \\
5 & \times & 15 = 75 \\
\overline{14} & & \overline{188}
\end{array}
$$

$$188 \div 14$$

$$
\begin{array}{r}
13.4 \\
14\,)\overline{188} \\
14 \\
\overline{48} \\
42 \\
\overline{60} \\
56 \\
\overline{4}
\end{array}
$$

$$= \underline{\underline{13.4 \text{ years}}}$$

10.7 Exercises: Weighted Averages

1. Find the average weight of the following sets of parcels:
   (a) 2 parcels weighing 400 g each and 3 parcels weighing 100 g each
   (b) 4 parcels weighing $\frac{1}{2}$ kg each, 2 parcels weighing 300 g each and one parcel of 200 g
   (c) 3 packets weighing 120 g each and 2 packets weighing 70 g each
   (d) 2 crates weighing 62.5 kg and 4 crates weighing 55.25 kg (answer to the nearest kilogram)
   (e) 4 crates weighing 5.2 kg and 6 crates weighing 3.6 kg

2. Find the average weight in kilograms of the members of each of the following families, correct to one decimal place:
   (a) Family A: two weigh 75 kg each, one weighs 62 kg and three weigh 48.5 kg each
   (b) Family B: one weighs 82 kg, two weigh 68 kg each and the fourth weighs 64 kg
   (c) Family C: one weighs 51.5 kg, three weigh 54 kg each and two weigh 57.8 kg each
   (d) Family D: one weighs 55 kg, two weigh 72 kg each and two weigh 74.5 kg each

(e) Family E: three weigh 48 kg each, two weigh 57 kg each, one weighs 64 kg and the last member of the family weighs 67.5 kg.

3. A firm makes up wage packets as follows: 7 men get £85.50 each, 3 men get £82.50, 14 men get £76.80 and 6 get £65.00. Work out the average wage correct to the nearest penny.

4. In an examination taken by 20 students 3 score 72%, 2 score 69%, 1 scores 68%, 5 score 62%, 4 score 58%, 2 score 48% and the others get 46%, 41% and 33% respectively. What is the average mark?

5. A racing driver does 12 practice laps. 3 are timed at 9 min 14 s, 2 at 9 min 17 s, 2 at 9 min 12.5 s and the rest as follows: 9 min 22 s, 9 min 21.4 s, 9 min 14.8 s, 9 min 12.8 and 9 min 33 s. What was his average time? Answer correst to the nearest tenth of a second.

6. 15 bob sleigh runs are timed as follows: 4 took 1 min 58 s, 3 took 1 min 56.5 s, 2 took 1 min 50.5 s. The others took as follows: 2 min 3.4 s, 2 min 1.8 s, 1 min 59 s, 1 min 57 s, 1 min 55.5 s and 1 min 53 s. Find the average time for a run. Answer correct to the nearest tenth of a second.

7. A cargo of merchandise for export moved to the docks required the following loads:
2 containers each weighing 28 tonnes
3 containers each weighing 17.5 tonnes
12 containers each weighing 5.8 tonnes
2 containers each weighing 27.5 tonnes
What was the average weight of a container? Answer correct to 0.1 tonne.

8. A cargo of goods imported from Hong Kong is cleared to a warehouse in eleven containers. Of these, 3 weigh 24.5 tonnes, 3 weigh 22.8 tonnes, 2 weigh 21.65 tonnes and the other three weigh 18.7 tonnes, 16.5 tonnes and 14.25 tonnes respectively. What is the average weight of a container correct to the nearest 0.1 tonne?

10.8 Mental Arithmetic Exercises

1. 2.5 m + 3.7 m + 11.6 m =
2. £27.50 − £13.85 =
3. £4 270 ÷ 20 =
4. £8 165 + £7 248 + £3 868 =
5. 14.72 × 0.5 =
6. $1\frac{5}{8} + 2\frac{2}{5} =$
7. What is the average of 7, 11 and 12?
8. How many metres are there in 24.78 kilometres?
9. Divide up 85 pence in the ratio 9 : 8.
10. Write down $\frac{5}{8}$ as a decimal fraction.
11. What is the average of £500, £650 and £950?

12. A farmer is paid 20 per cent by a Farm Prices Support Fund on top of the prices he gets in the market. If his wheat crop fetched £24 850 in the market what payment did he receive?

13. In the following, what number is missing? 2 : 3 as ? : 24

14. What is the total weight in kilograms of three parcels weighing 65 g, 365 g and 4.25 kg respectively?

15. If 7 items cost £280 what will 4 cost?

Unit Eleven

The Use of Electronic Calculators

11.1 The Electronic Calculator

At this stage it is appropriate to mention electronic calculators again. We have covered the basic processes of arithmetic and from now on we shall be applying them to many business situations, sometimes using very large numbers. If you want to use a calculator you may do so, providing you thoroughly understand the procedures studied in earlier Units. You must know what you are doing and *why you are doing it*. Owning a calculator does not mean you can relax and leave it all to the machine. Far from it. You cannot use the machine properly if your knowledge of basic calculations is weak.

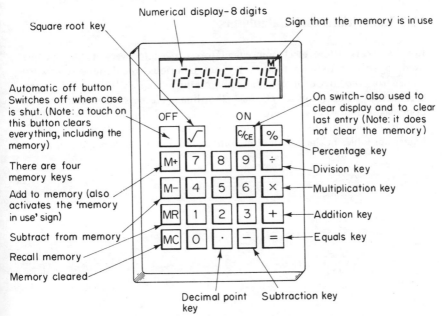

Fig. 11.1   A typical layout for a pocket calculator

A relatively inexpensive pocket calculator will perform all the calculations needed in an ordinary business and can effect great savings in time by cutting out hours spent on the routine arithmetical processes.

Before you decide to buy a particular model of calculator, you should consider carefully what you will want to do with it. All calculators will add subtract, multiply and divide. If you are going to use it frequently to calculate VAT, for instance, or to carry out a great many foreign currency conversions, you may find that a *constant factor* facility will be useful. This allows you to multiply or divide a series of numbers by the same number without having to enter each calculation separately. Some models calculate *percentages, mark-ups* and *discounts* directly. A *memory* facility is convenient if you often have to do rather complicated calculations, and a *clear last entry* facility allows you to correct a mistake in an entry without having to go all the way back to the beginning of your calculation. If you are going to study statistics beyond the elementary level, you will need a *square root* facility.

There are many layouts for calculators. Remember that even though two calculators may look very much alike, they do not necessarily work in the same way and they may be operated quite differently. Study the instruction booklet which comes with your calculator and learn how to use it properly. Practise with it until you can use it easily and speedily.

Some larger desk calculators print out the calculations and their results on rolls of paper. In these larger machines omissions or wrong entries can readily be detected by comparing the printed list with the original documents.

11.2 Logarithms and Calculators

For 250 years before electronic calculators came into everyday use, people used logarithms to help them carry out laborious calculations (the word comes from the Greek for 'calculating with numbers'). Few businessmen, however, use logarithms nowadays, since all ordinary business calculations can be done easily and accurately with an electronic calculator. If you wish to learn how to use logarithms, you will find full details of the method and a set of logarithm tables in the companion volume, *Success in Mathematics*.

Unit Twelve

Foreign Money and Exchange Calculations

12.1 Foreign Money Systems

Every country around the world has its own money system imposed by the State, which lays down the name of the currency and its sub-division into smaller coins. Practically all currencies now work on a *centesimal* system, that is, a system with a unit of currency which is equivalent to 100 smaller coins. A few use a *millesimal* system with 1 000 small coins equal to the unit of currency. One or two, where the main unit of currency has a very small value, have abandoned any coin smaller than this unit. Thus the Italian lira (at the time of writing the exchange rate is 2 291 lire = £1) and the yen (about 410 yen = £1) have no subdivisions.

Table 12.1 Some important currencies

Country	Unit of currency	Smaller denomination
Australia	dollar	100 cents
Austria	schilling	100 groschen
Bahrain	dinar	1 000 fils
Belgium	franc	100 centimes
Brazil	cruzeiro	100 centavos
Canada	dollar	100 cents
Cyprus	pound	1 000 mils
Denmark	krone	100 oere
Finland	markka	100 pennis
France	franc	100 centimes
Germany (West)	Deutschemark	100 pfennigs
Greece	drachma	100 lepta
India	rupee	100 paise
Italy	lira	—
Japan	yen	—
Libya	dinar	1 000 dirhams
Netherlands	guilder	100 cents
Nigeria	naira	100 kobos
Norway	krone	100 oere
Portugal	escudo	100 centavos
South Africa	rand	100 cents
Spain	peseta	100 centimos

Country	Unit of currency	Smaller denomination
Sweden	krona	100 oere
Switzerland	franc	100 centimes
Tanzania	shilling	100 cents
Turkey	Turkish lira	100 kurus
United Kingdom	pound	100 pence
United States	dollar	100 cents
USSR	rouble	100 roubles
Yugoslavia	dinar	100 paras

12.2 Rates of Exchange

At one time an international agreement called the Bretton Woods Agreement fixed the rates of exchange of currencies with one another, and their values were not allowed to change more than 1 per cent. Today all currencies are *floating*, that is, changing from day to day according to the laws of supply and demand. A currency that is in strong demand floats upward to higher prices. A currency in poor demand floats downwards until it is cheap enough for foreigners to want it.

Everyone buying goods or services must pay for them in the currency of the country that sells them. Thus an Englishman wishing to buy Nigerian timber must pay in naire, and one wishing to buy motor cars from Detroit must pay in American dollars. A Spaniard wishing to buy British machinery must buy pounds on the foreign exchange market, through his local bank. All imports to the United Kingdom must be financed by buying the currency required on the foreign exchange market through a dealer, usually a major bank.

Exchange rates are quoted daily in the newspapers, on the financial page. Usually they give the highest and lowest prices of the day, so that businessmen know the range of prices the previous day and can work out roughly how much they will get for the orders received from overseas, or how much they will need for imports they intend to buy from foreigners.

12.3 Changing British Currency to Foreign Currency

Currency exchange rates are usually quoted in the newspapers like this: £1 = 2.03$ or £1 = 8.9 French francs. When rates are quoted in this way with the £s as 1 (unit) we change sterling to foreign money by *multiplying* the sterling by the rate of exchange. We change foreign money to sterling by *dividing* by the rate of exchange.

Very rarely exchange rates are quoted the other way round, for example, £0.49 = 1$. Such a rate would be changed to a rate per £1 before calculations.

Example

A British businessman sells machinery valued at £10 000 to an American customer at a time when the rate of exchange is £1 = 1.71 $. What will he receive?

$$£10\,000 = 10\,000 \times 1.71\,\$$$
$$= 17\,100\,\$$$

Example

A British secretary decides to take £150 on her Spanish holiday. The rate of exchange at the time is £1 = 184.50 pesetas. How many pesetas does she receive?

$$£150 = 150 \times 184.50$$

$$
\begin{array}{r}
184.50 \\
150 \\
\hline
18\,450\,00 \\
9\,225\,00 \\
\hline
27\,675.00 \\
\end{array}
$$

$$= 27\,675 \text{ pesetas}$$

In calculations like these a *rough estimate* is always a useful check. In this example

$$
\begin{array}{r}
100 \times 184 = 18\,400 \\
50 \times 184 = 9\,200 \\
\hline
27\,600 \\
\end{array}
$$

So the British citizen will get about 27 600 pesetas to spend in Spain. Clearly our answer to this calculation is of the correct order.

12.4 Exercises: Changing Pounds into Foreign Currency

Change the following numbers of pounds into foreign currency at the exchange rates indicated:

1. £100 to US dollars at £1 = 1.92 $
2. £100 to French francs at £1 = 10.52 fr
3. £100 to German D-marks at £1 = 4.30 Dm
4. £1 000 to Swiss francs at £1 = 3.37 fr
5. £1 000 to Canadian dollars at £1 = 2.28 $
6. £1 000 to Japanese yen at £1 = 413 yen
7. £10 000 to Italian lire at £1 = 2 221 lire
8. £10 000 to Bahrain dinars at £1 = 0.55 dinars
9. £10 000 to Finnish markka at £1 = 8.51 markka
10. £10 000 to Brazilian cruzeiros at £1 = 275.0 cruz

11. £500 to US dollars at £1 = 1.98 $
12. £600 to French francs at £1 = 10.52 fr
13. £300 to Dutch guilders at £1 = 4.68 guilders
14. £800 to Norwegian krone at £1 = 11.1 k
15. £12 200 to Swiss francs at £1 = 3.42 Swiss francs

12.5 Changing Foreign Currency to British Currency

Where a British firm earns currency from foreigners by exporting goods or services, the currency earned is changed into British money through the foreign exchange market. We must now *divide* the foreign money we have earned by the exchange rate, to find out how much sterling we are entitled to.

Thus when the £1 is valued at 1.70 dollars the British businessman who earns 5 000 dollars will receive £1 for every 1.70 dollars and his total receipts will be

$$5\,000 \div 1.7$$
$$= 50\,000 \div 17$$
$$= £2\,941.18$$

Example

Change 45 000 Deutschemarks to pounds sterling when £1 = 4.5 Dm.

$$\text{Number of pounds} = 45\,000 \div 4.5$$
$$= 450\,000 \div 45$$
$$= £10\,000$$

Example

Change 24 000 Bahrain dinars to pounds sterling when £1 = 0.45 Bahrain dinars.

$$\text{Number of pounds} = 24\,000 \div 0.45$$
$$= 2\,400\,000 \div 45$$

```
          53 333.33
45 ) 2 400 000
       2 25
        150
        135
        150
```

$$= £53\,333.33 \qquad \text{etc.}$$

12.6 Exercises: Changing Foreign Currency to Pounds Sterling

1. (a) Change 30 000 Austrian schillings to pounds when £1 = 30 sch.
   (b) Change 34 000 Swiss francs to pounds when £1 = 3.4 Swiss francs.
   (c) Change 1 860 pesetas to pounds when £1 = 186 pesetas.
   (d) Change 27 800 Danish krone to pounds when £1 = 13.9 krone.
   (e) Change 2 460 Portuguese escudos to pounds when £1 = 123 escudos.

2. (a) Change 36 000 Belgian francs to pounds when £1 = 72 francs.
   (b) Change 44 800 Canadian dollars to pounds when £1 = 2.24 dollars.
   (c) Change 54 000 French francs to pounds when £1 = 10.8 francs.
   (d) Change 140 700 Dutch guilders to pounds when £1 = 4.69 guilders.
   (e) Change 69 000 000 lire to pounds when £1 = 2 300 lire.

3. In the following calculations, give your answers correct to the nearest penny.
   (a) Change 400 US dollars to pounds when £1 = 1.88 dollars.
   (b) Change 500 Swiss francs to pounds when £1 = 3.42 francs.
   (c) Change 800 Spanish pesetas to pounds when £1 = 185 pesetas.
   (d) Change 500 Norwegian krone to pounds when £1 = 10.98 krone.
   (e) Change 3 000 Japanese yen to pounds when £1 = 412 yen.

12.7 Mental Arithmetic Exercises

1. 327 + 249 + 253 =
2. How many pence are there in £2.37?
3. Multiply 3 295 × 5.
4. 2 764 − 1 237 =
5. Divide 4 325 by 12.
6. $4\frac{1}{2} + 2\frac{1}{3} =$
7. What is 25 per cent of 164 metres?
8. What is 5 per cent of £180?
9. Multiply 3.5 by 0.7.
10. Change £50 to francs when 8.50 fr = £1.
11. 2 000 × 750 =
12. How many grams are there in $2\frac{1}{2}$ kilograms?
13. How many minutes are there in 3 hours and 37 minutes?
14. A debt is payable on the 60th day after March 31. What day is that?
15. How many pounds sterling will I get for 36 800 pesetas when 184 pesetas = £1?

Unit Thirteen

Simple Interest

13.1 Introduction

Interest is money paid for the use of borrowed money. It is paid by the borrower for the facility of being able to borrow it. The sum of money which is borrowed is called the *principal*, and the period of time for which it is borrowed is called the *duration* of the loan. Interest is calculated as a percentage of the principal; the percentage agreed between the borrower and the lender is called the *interest rate*. Usually the rate is fixed on an annual basis; it is then expressed as 'so much per cent *per annum*'.

For instance, suppose I borrow a principal sum of £1 000 for one year at 14 per cent interest per annum, that is, I pay £14 interest for every £100 borrowed. As I am borrowing £1 000 – that is, 10 × £100 – I shall have to pay 10 × £14 = £140 for the use of the money for one year.

Generally speaking, interest is paid to the lender at an agreed date in the year; as the years go by the sum borrowed remains unchanged. Interest paid like this is called *simple interest*. Sometimes, however, the interest is not paid to the lender, but is added to the amount of the loan. The borrower then has to pay interest on the interest—as well as the interest on the original loan—and this is called *compound interest* (see Unit 26).

13.2 The 'Interest for One Year' Method

We can use simple arithmetic to find the interest payable for a single year. If the loan under consideration is for more than one year we can then find the total interest for the whole period of the loan by multiplying the interest payable for one year by the number of years the loan is to run.

Example

Calculate the simple interest on £600 for 4 years at 6 per cent per annum.

First calculate the interest for 1 year on a principal of £600:
Interest at 1 per cent = £6
Interest at 6 per cent = £36 (6 × 6)
Interest for 4 years   = £144 (4 × 36)

Example

Calculate the simple interest on £525 for 3 years at 8 per cent per annum.

First calculate the interest for 1 year on a principal of £525:
Interest at 1 per cent = £5.25
Interest at 8 per cent = £42.00 (5.25 × 8)
Interest for 3 years   = £126.00 (42 × 3)

Example

Calculate the simple interest on £470.40 for $3\frac{1}{2}$ years at $12\frac{1}{2}$ per cent per annum.

Note that $12\frac{1}{2}$ per cent is a percentage which is a simple fraction of 100 per cent (see Section 9.2)—it is one-eighth. It is therefore easy to work the interest out on a single line by calculating one-eighth of the principal.

Interest for 1 year on a principal of £470.40:
Interest at $12\frac{1}{2}$ per cent ($\frac{1}{8}$)   =   £58.80
Interest for 3 years   = £176.40 (58.80 × 3)
Add interest for $\frac{1}{2}$ year   =   £29.40 (58.80 ÷ 2)

Interest for $3\frac{1}{2}$ years   = £205.80

13.3 Exercises: Simple Interest by the 'Interest for One Year' Method

1. Find the simple interest payable on each of the following loans:
   (a) £300 at 4 per cent per annum for 3 years
   (b) £500 at 6 per cent per annum for 4 years.
   (c) £700 at 8 per cent per annum for 3 years
   (d) £1 000 at 7 per cent per annum for 5 years
   (e) £400 at 10 per cent per annum for 4 years
   (f) £800 at 6 per cent per annum for 6 years
   (g) £1 200 at 9 per cent per annum for 4 years
   (h) £2 000 at 5 per cent per annum for 5 years
   (i) £8 000 at 6 per cent per annum for 3 years
   (j) £12 000 at 7 per cent per annum for 7 years

2. Find the simple interest payable on each of the following loans:
   (a) £250 at 5 per cent per annum for 8 years
   (b) £350 at 6 per cent per annum for 4 years
   (c) £550 at 10 per cent per annum for 5 years
   (d) £850 at 8 per cent per annum for 3 years
   (e) £325 at 8 per cent per annum for 3 years
   (f) £575 at 10 per cent per annum for 8 years

(g) £626 at 6 per cent per annum for 4 years
(h) £925 at 12 per cent per annum for 7 years
(i) £1 175 at 15 per cent per annum for 10 years
(j) £1 225 at 10 per cent per annum for 8 years.

3. Find the simple interest payable on each of the following loans (give the answers correct to the nearest penny):

(a) £625 at 15 per cent per annum for $4\frac{1}{2}$ years
(b) £440 at 14 per cent per annum for $6\frac{1}{2}$ years
(c) £740 at 16 per cent per annum for $2\frac{1}{2}$ years
(d) £480 at 17 per cent per annum for $3\frac{3}{4}$ years
(e) £1 850 at 15 per cent per annum for $2\frac{1}{2}$ years
(f) £1 720 at 18 per cent per annum for $1\frac{3}{4}$ years
(g) £2 525 at 14 per cent per annum for $7\frac{1}{2}$ years
(h) £3 725 at 15 per cent per annum for $6\frac{1}{2}$ years
(i) £10 500 at 10 per cent per annum for $2\frac{3}{4}$ years
(j) £12 500 at 12 per cent per annum for $3\frac{1}{4}$ years

13.4 The Formula Method

Any simple interest problem can be solved by applying the formula:

$$Interest\ payable = \frac{Principal \times Rate\ of\ interest \times Time\ in\ years}{100}$$

This is abbreviated to

$$I = \frac{P \times R \times T}{100}$$

which we can write simply as

$$I = \frac{PRT}{100}$$

The 100 appears in the formula because the rate of interest is always given as a rate *per cent*, so that 6 per cent, for instance, appears in the formula as $\frac{6}{100}$.

To calculate the interest on a loan we simply write down the formula and then substitute into it the figures for that particular loan.

Example

Find the simple interest payable on a loan of £500 at 6 per cent per annum for five years.

$$Formula:\quad I = \frac{PRT}{100}$$

Substituting the figures into the formula:

$$I = \frac{500 \times 6 \times 5}{100}$$

$$= \frac{5 \times 6 \times 5}{1} \text{ (cancelling by 100)}$$

$$= \underline{\underline{£150}}$$

Example

Find the simple interest on £625 for 8 years at $7\frac{1}{2}$ per cent per annum.

$$\text{Formula:} \quad I = \frac{PRT}{100}$$

Substituting the figures into the formula:

$$I = \frac{625 \times 7\frac{1}{2} \times 8}{100}$$

The $7\frac{1}{2}$ must be changed to $\frac{15}{2}$, so that

$$I = \frac{625 \times 15 \times 8}{100 \times 2}$$

$$= \frac{25 \times 15}{1} \text{ (cancelling by 25, 2 and 4)}$$

$$= \underline{\underline{£375}}$$

Example

Find the simple interest on £420 for $3\frac{1}{2}$ years at $12\frac{1}{2}$ per cent per annum.

$$\text{Formula:} \quad I = \frac{PRT}{100}$$

Substituting the figures into the formula, and writing the $3\frac{1}{2}$ as $\frac{7}{2}$ and the $12\frac{1}{2}$ as $\frac{25}{2}$:

$$I = \frac{420 \times 7 \times 25}{100 \times 2 \times 2}$$

$$= \frac{21 \times 7 \times 5}{2 \times 2} \text{ (cancelling by 10, 2 and 5)}$$

$$= \frac{735}{4}$$

$$= \underline{\underline{£183.75}}$$

13.5 Exercises: Simple Interest by the Formula Method

1. Find the simple interest payable on each of the following loans:
   (a) £625 at 5 per cent per annum for 4 years
   (b) £750 at 6 per cent per annum for 3 years.
   (c) £850 at $2\frac{1}{2}$ per cent per annum for 4 years
   (d) £275 at $7\frac{1}{2}$ per cent per annum for 8 years
   (e) £875 at 8 per cent per annum for $3\frac{1}{2}$ years
   (f) £925 at $6\frac{1}{2}$ per cent per annum for 4 years
   (g) £350 at $8\frac{1}{2}$ per cent per annum for 6 years
   (h) £720 at 10 per cent per annum for $2\frac{1}{2}$ years
   (i) £360 at $7\frac{1}{2}$ per cent per annum for 6 years
   (j) £420 at $11\frac{1}{2}$ per cent per annum for 4 years

2. Find the simple interest payable on each of the loans summarized in the following table:

	Principal £	Rate per cent per annum	Duration in years
(a)	1 275	8	3
(b)	800	$6\frac{1}{2}$	$2\frac{1}{2}$
(c)	1 640	$7\frac{1}{2}$	$4\frac{1}{2}$
(d)	625	10	5
(e)	1 880	$5\frac{1}{2}$	$6\frac{1}{2}$
(f)	7 720	$5\frac{1}{2}$	7
(g)	440	$6\frac{1}{2}$	$3\frac{1}{2}$
(h)	375	8	$5\frac{1}{2}$
(i)	1 600	$10\frac{1}{2}$	$2\frac{1}{4}$
(j)	4 000	$11\frac{1}{4}$	$3\frac{1}{4}$
(k)	1 640	$11\frac{1}{2}$	$2\frac{1}{2}$
(l)	2 000	$12\frac{1}{2}$	$4\frac{1}{2}$
(m)	3 200	9	$3\frac{3}{4}$
(n)	6 400	$10\frac{1}{2}$	$7\frac{1}{2}$
(o)	2 400	$7\frac{1}{2}$	$2\frac{1}{4}$
(p)	12 000	16	$3\frac{1}{2}$
(q)	8 500	$17\frac{1}{2}$	$4\frac{1}{4}$
(r)	15 000	21	$2\frac{1}{2}$
(s)	25 000	$22\frac{1}{2}$	$6\frac{1}{2}$
(t)	30 000	$17\frac{1}{2}$	$5\frac{1}{2}$

13.6 Rearranging Formulae

Sometimes we are not asked to find the simple interest on a sum of money, but to find some other item, such as the rate of interest, or the number of years that an investment must continue to earn a certain sum of money. This can be done quite easily by rearranging the formula.

Consider the formula in the form we have already learned:

$$I = \frac{PRT}{100}$$

This type of formula is called an equation, because one quantity is said to be equal to another. If we wish to rearrange a formula we can do so by using the rule for equations. This says: *an equation will still be true if the same operation is carried out on both sides of it.* Therefore:

1. An equation will still be true if you add the same quantity to both sides. Take the equation $1 = 1$. If we added 2 to both sides we get $1 + 2 = 1 + 2$ or $3 = 3$. The equation is still true.
2. An equation will still be true if you subtract the same quantity from both sides. Take the equation $9 = 5 + 4$. If we take 3 from both sides we get $9 - 3 = 5 + 4 - 3$ or $6 = 6$. The equation is still true.
3. An equation will still be true if you multiply both sides by the same quantity. Take the equation $7 = 7$. If we multiply both sides by 3 we have $7 \times 3 = 7 \times 3$ or $21 = 21$. The equation is still true.
4. Similarly an equation will still be true if we divide both sides by the same quantity. For example, take the equation $8 = 8$. Dividing both sides by 4 we have $\frac{8}{4} = \frac{8}{4}$ or $2 = 2$.

So the general rule for rearranging an equation is to ensure that you always do the same thing to both sides of it.

Returning to the simple interest formula

$$I = \frac{PRT}{100}$$

this formula can be used to calculate the simple interest on a sum of money at a certain rate of interest over a certain period of time. Supposing I know the interest earned, but not the rate of interest? How shall I rearrange the formula to find out the rate of interest? It is quite simple if we keep to the rules of equations. We wish to rearrange the formula to give us the rate:

$$R = ?$$

To do this we remove everything else from the side that has R in it.
Take the original formula:

$$I = \frac{PRT}{100}$$

Remove the 100 by multiplying both sides by 100:

$$100I = \frac{PRT}{100} \times 100$$

The hundreds on the right-hand side cancel out, leaving

$$100I = PRT$$

Remove the P by dividing both sides by P:

$$\frac{100I}{P} = \frac{PRT}{P}$$

The Ps on the right-hand side cancel out leaving

$$\frac{100I}{P} = RT$$

Remove the T by dividing both sides by T:

$$\frac{100I}{PT} = \frac{RT}{T}$$

The Ts on the right-hand side cancel out, leaving the final formula:

$$\frac{100I}{PT} = R$$

This can be turned round for convenience, to read

$$R = \frac{100I}{PT}$$

and the formula has been rearranged.

Conclusion. We can rearrange the original formula to tell us three things: (a) the rate, (b) the principal invested (c) the number of years for which the principal was invested. The four formulae are:

$$\text{Simple interest formula} \qquad I = \frac{PRT}{100}$$

$$\text{`Rate' formula} \qquad R = \frac{100I}{PT}$$

$$\text{`Principal' formula} \qquad P = \frac{100I}{RT}$$

$$\text{`Number of years' formula} \qquad T = \frac{100I}{PR}$$

Example

Find the rate of simple interest earned when a principal of £750 earns interest of £210 in 4 years.

Using the 'rate' formula we have:

$$R = \frac{100I}{PT}$$

$$= \frac{100 \times 210}{750 \times 4} \text{ (this cancels easily)}$$

$$= 7\%$$

(A rate will always be an answer 'per cent'.)

Example

Find the sum of money invested when £600 simple interest is earned in 3 years at 8 per cent.

Using the 'principal' formula we have:

$$P = \frac{100I}{RT}$$

$$= \frac{100 \times 600}{3 \times 8} \text{ (this cancels easily)}$$

$$= £2\,500$$

(The principal will always be a sum of money in £s.)

Example

Find how many years it will take for an investment of £1 200 invested at 5 per cent to earn simple interest of £210. Using the 'number of years' formula we have:

$$T = \frac{100I}{PR}$$

$$= \frac{100 \times 210}{1\,200 \times 5} \text{ (this cancels easily)}$$

$$= \frac{7}{2}$$

$$= 3\tfrac{1}{2} \text{ years}$$

(The time will always be an answer in years.)

13.7 Exercises: More Difficult Simple Interest Calculations

1. Find the rate of interest earned on each of the following loans.

	Principal	Interest earned	Number of years
(a)	£500	£100	4
(b)	£800	£224	$3\frac{1}{2}$
(c)	£1 200	£240	$2\frac{1}{2}$
(d)	£1 550	£372	4
(e)	£2 350	£1 269	$4\frac{1}{2}$

2. Find the principal invested in each of the following loans.

	Interest earned	Rate per cent	Number of years
(a)	£252	6	3
(b)	£200	10	4
(c)	£240	12	$2\frac{1}{2}$
(d)	£260	8	5
(e)	£348.75	$7\frac{1}{2}$	3

3. How long were the following sums of money invested if they earned the interest shown in the table, calculated at the rates given?

	Principal	Interest earned	Rate per cent
(a)	£800	£120	6
(b)	£700	£196	8
(c)	£640	£384	12
(d)	£1 400	£661.50	$10\frac{1}{2}$
(e)	£3 500	£831.25	$9\frac{1}{2}$

13.8 Mental Arithmetic Exercises

1. 833 + 247 + 348 =
2. How many pence are there in £13.25?
3. Multiply 3 784 × 4.
4. 1 835 − 1 327 =
5. Divide 5 760 by 6.

6. $4\frac{1}{3} + 2\frac{1}{2} + 1\frac{3}{8} =$
7. What is 20 per cent of £750?
8. What is the average of 7, 9, 10, 13, 16 and 17?
9. Multiply 7.5 by 0.6.
10. What is the simple interest on a loan of £400 for 2 years at 8 per cent per annum?
11. $400 \times 500 =$
12. How many millilitres are there in 1.5 litres?
13. How many minutes are there in 6 hours 47 minutes?
14. How many days are there from August 4 to September 5 inclusive?
15. How many pounds sterling shall I get for 25 000 000 lire when 2 000 lire = £1?

Unit Fourteen

Hire Purchase

14.1 Introduction

When a family or a businessman requires a relatively expensive article such as a motor car, a refrigerator, a television set or a vacuum cleaner it may be impossible for the purchaser to pay the full price of the article at once. To overcome this difficulty the system of hire purchase was developed. The idea is that the purchaser pays only a small part of the purchase price at the beginning. This part is called the *deposit*. The rest of the money is often provided by an organization called a *finance company*, which lends the money to the purchaser by paying the shopkeeper. This part of the purchase price is called the *balance due*. The finance company now adds on interest at a fixed rate—say 15 per cent—for every year the loan is outstanding. If the purchaser is to repay in one year, 15 per cent will be added to the balance due. If he is to repay in two years 30 per cent will be added; if three years are needed 45 per cent will be added.

The balance due, with the interest, will be paid in weekly or monthly sums called *instalments*. Thus there will be 12 equal monthly instalments or 52 equal weekly instalments if repayment is to be in one year. Until the last payment is made the purchaser does not own the goods; they are only on hire to him from the finance company. As soon as the last instalment is paid the goods become the property of the buyer, who has now purchased them in full. In the United Kingdom, the Consumer Credit Act 1974 attempts to prevent unfair treatment of hire purchasers by laying down strict rules about consumer credit agreements, and by setting up the Office of Fair Trading to supervise them.

14.2 Calculations about Hire Purchase

Whenever calculations have to be made about hire purchase the following questions must be asked:

What was the selling price of the goods?
What was the deposit to be?
What rate of interest is to be added, and for how many years?
How many instalments are to be paid?

If we have this information we can solve most hire purchase problems.

Example

Mrs Jones buys a television set for £250 on hire purchase. She pays a deposit of 20 per cent, and interest is charged on the balance due at 15 per cent per annum for two years. She will pay the instalments monthly over this period. How much is each instalment?

Selling price = £250
Deposit = 20% = $\frac{20}{100}$ = $\frac{1}{5}$ of the selling price = £50
Balance due = £250 − £50 = £200
Interest added = 15% for 2 years = 30% = $\frac{30}{100}$ = $\frac{3}{10}$

$$\frac{3}{10} \text{ of } £200 = £60$$

Total to pay = £200 + £60 = £260
Number of instalments = 12 monthly instalments for 2 years
$$= 24 \text{ instalments}$$
So each instalment = $£\frac{260}{24}$ = $£\frac{130}{12}$ = $£\frac{65}{6}$

$$= £10.83 \text{ to nearest penny}$$

14.3 Exercises: Easy Problems in Hire Purchase

1. Find the amount of each instalment in the hire purchase agreements summarized in the following table. (Answer correct to the nearest penny.)

	Selling price of goods	Deposit payable	Rate of interest per annum	No. of years	Instalments payable
(a)	£120	£20	10%	1	monthly
(b)	£180	£30	10%	2	monthly
(c)	£165	£45	10%	2	monthly
(d)	£270	£70	10%	2	monthly
(e)	£340	£40	10%	2	monthly
(f)	£225	£25	15%	2	monthly
(g)	£375	£75	15%	2	monthly
(h)	£125	£25	15%	2	monthly
(i)	£56.50	£6.50	15%	1	monthly
(j)	£92.40	£12.40	15%	1	monthly

2. Find the amount of each instalment in the hire purchase agreements summarized in the table on page 108. (Answer correct to the nearest penny.)

	Selling price (£)	Deposit payable (£)	Rate of interest (% per annum)	No. of years	Instalments payable
(a)	215	35	10	2	monthly
(b)	385	35	10	2	monthly
(c)	420	40	15	2	monthly
(d)	16	4	15	1	monthly
(e)	168	18	20	2	monthly
(f)	420	50	15	2	monthly
(g)	380	30	$12\frac{1}{2}$	2	monthly
(h)	760	120	$12\frac{1}{2}$	2	monthly
(i)	540	140	15	2	weekly
(j)	250	50	15	2	weekly

3. Find the amount of each instalment in the hire purchase agreements summarized below. Answer correct to the nearest penny. (In each question, decide carefully how many weeks—52, 104, 130 or 156—the total cost must be divided by, in order to find the weekly instalments.)

	Selling price (£)	Deposit payable (£)	Rate of interest (% per annum)	No. of years	Instalments payable
(a)	120	12	25	1	weekly
(b)	150	30	20	1	weekly
(c)	180	30	15	1	weekly
(d)	160	40	15	1	weekly
(e)	250	40	$33\frac{1}{3}$	1	weekly
(f)	300	50	15	2	weekly
(g)	450	90	$12\frac{1}{2}$	2	weekly
(h)	950	150	10	$2\frac{1}{2}$	weekly
(i)	1 250	125	10	$2\frac{1}{2}$	weekly
(j)	1 500	150	15	3	weekly

Unit Fifteen

Receipts and Payments

15.1 The Ledger

Whenever money is received and paid the record of receipts and payments is kept on a page called an *account*, in a book called the *ledger*. The word 'ledger' means 'the one that lies' and it refers to the book in constant use in the early 'counting houses', and for that reason kept lying open on the desk ready to record any receipt or payment.

Nowadays, ledgers need not be books at all. Card-index systems are commonly used, and some ledgers are computerized. All such systems, however, obey the same general rules.

A simple cash account is recorded as shown in Figs. 15.1 and 15.2.

You will see that the ledger page is divided down the centre, and the two sides are ruled in exactly the same way.

The left-hand side is called the *debit side*, and is used to record all money received. Money may be received as original capital from the owners of the business (or in the case of a club, from its members). It may also be received in payment for goods supplied or for services rendered.

The right-hand side is called the *credit side*, and is used to record all payments made. Payments are made for goods or services supplied by other firms.

The number on the page in the top right-hand corner is called the *folio number*. It tells us the page in the ledger on which the cash account appears.

The two columns marked F are *folio columns*, where page numbers of other accounts may be recorded. Whenever any transaction takes place two accounts are affected, and the entry in the folio column indicates in which account, and upon what page of that account, the other half of the *double entry* appears. (These double entries give the system its name—Double Entry Bookkeeping.) For example, if the sales on April 2 are also recorded in the Sales Account (to show that the goods have gone out, in return for the cash that came in) the folio number of the Sales Account would be written in the folio column to show where this other half of the record could be found.

15.2 Cash Receipts and Payments: A Simple Cash Account

Fig. 15.2 shows a simple Cash Account, with some typical receipts and payments.

Let us examine the entries one by one.

Cash Account L 1

19 . . Month	Day	Details	F	£	p	19 . . Month	Day	Details	F	£	p
		Debit side: On this side we record any cash received. Debit cash account whenever cash is received						*Credit side:* On this side we record any cash paid. Credit cash account whenever cash is paid out			

Fig. 15.1 The layout of a simple Cash Account

Cash Account

L 1

19.. April				£	p		19.. April				£	p
1	Opening balance	B/d		100	00		1	Office equipment	L 15		35	00
2	Fees received	L 27		6	00		1	Purchases	L 17		23	00
2	Sales	L 31		4	50		3	Purchases	L 17		6	40
5	Fees received	L 27		3	50		6	Equipment hire	L 29		3	00
6	Sales	L 31		4	40		7	Stationery	L 18		1	25
							7	Balance	C/d		49	75
				£118	40						£118	40
April 8	Balance	B/d		49	75							

Fig. 15.2 A simple Cash Account

April 1   Opening balance. Clearly cash cannot be paid out unless there is some money in the till or cash box. The first debit entry will therefore record the balance available at the start of the day or week: here it is £100.

April 1   Office equipment £35.00. This sum was paid out for the purchase of some item of office equipment. Such items are bought to be used in the business, and are called *assets.*

April 1   Purchases £23.00. Purchases are items bought to sell again, that is, they are the ordinary stock-in-trade of the businessman. The item on April 3 is similar. On both occasions cash has been paid out.

April 2   Fees received £6.00. This item shows that cash was received for some service rendered to a client. The item on April 5 is similar.

April 2   Sales £4.50. This shows that cash was received for goods supplied to a customer. The entry on April 6 is similar.

April 6   Equipment hire and *April 7   Stationery* are two more items paid out.

The abbreviation 'B/d' beside the balance means *brought down* from the previous day, week or month, and 'C/d' means *carried down* to the following day, week or month.

The cash account is *balanced off* at the end of the day in a busy office, or at the end of the week in a smaller organization. To do this, the two sides are added up thus:

Debit side	*Credit side*
£	£
100.00	35.00
6.00	23.00
4.50	6.40
3.50	3.00
4.40	1.25
118.40	68.65

The credit side (the total of money paid out) is then subtracted from the debit side (the total of money received):

$$
\begin{array}{r}
£ \\
118.40 \\
-\ 68.65 \\
\hline
49.75 \\
\end{array}
$$

This balance of cash in hand should agree with the actual cash in the cash box. If this is so then the account can be regarded as correct, and is then balanced off. This means that the balance of £49.75 is inserted on the credit side, and the two sides are totalled as shown in Fig. 15.2. The balance is then carried down to the debit side.

15.3 Exercises: Simple Cash Receipts and Payments

For these exercises you must either rule up suitable paper, or obtain a small supply of ledger paper from a stationer's shop.

1. Enter the following items in a simple Cash Account. Its folio number is L27.

June 19 . .

   1 Balance of cash in hand £100.00; paid wages £45.50; paid postage £1.15, telegrams £2.50.

   2 Bought coffee £1.80; bought stationery £2.10; cash sales brought in £25.50.

   3 R. Johnson sent £2.40 to us in cash; P. Laker sent cash £8.80 to us; we sent £2.15 to R. Lewisham in cash.

   4 Paid office expenses £2.25 and window cleaner £2.30; cash sales from till £35.50.

Balance off the account and bring down the cash balance.

2. Enter the following items in a Cash Account, balance off at the end, and bring down the balance:

April 19 . .

   1 Balance of cash in hand £42.50

   2 Paid for insurance £8.50

   3 Paid garage expenses £14.53

   4 Cash sales from till records £42.80

   5 Paid wages £46.10

   6 Paid to M. Richardson £14.25

   7 Paid to Betta Sauces Ltd. £5.80

   8 Paid office expenses £1.50; cash sales from till £48.50

   10 Paid to M. Light £37.50; paid to P. Rogers £4.10

   15 R. Jones paid us the sum of £41.54

   23 Received from D. Hammond £4.25

   25 Paid to K. Baker £16.63

   27 Paid for office expenses £2.55

   29 Cash sales from till records £37.85

3. Enter the following items in a Cash Account:

July 19 . .

   1 Balance of cash in hand £46.50

   2 Paid for postage £3.00

   2 Paid office expenses £2.75

   2 M. Warner paid us £45.50; paid P. Wright £7.30

   3 Paid wages £46.60

   3 Paid to D. Cartier £4.75

   3 Paid to H. Higgins £3.25

   3 Paid repairs £4.60

   4 Cash sales from till records £88.50

   4 R. Green paid us the sum of £27.50

    4 Received from M. Parsons £2.25
    5 Paid to C. Wescombe £3.25
    5 Paid for office expenses £1.35
    5 Cash sales from till records £42.45

Balance the account and bring down the balance at the end of the week ready for next day.

4. Enter the following items in a Cash Account, balance off at the end, and bring down the balance:

May 19 . .
    1 Balance of cash in hand £17.20
    2 Paid for repairs to front door £3.25
    2 Paid motor vehicle expenses £5.72
    2 Cash sales as recorded in till £149.50
    3 Paid wages to office cleaner £39.80
    3 Paid to M. Rossiter £4.75
    3 Paid to K. Lacey £2.75
    4 Paid office expenses £2.50
    4 Cash sales as recorded in till £42.75
    4 R. Jones paid us the sum of £13.75
    5 Received from T. Lester £27.25
    5 Paid to Anne Agent £34.50
    5 Paid for office expenses £1.55
    5 Cash sales as per till roll £74.52

15.4 Receipts and Payments by Cheque: A Simple Bank Account

Although money is received in cash and paid in cash every day, there are great disadvantages in cash transactions. From the point of view of security alone it is unwise to pay large amounts in cash; payment by cheque is much safer. It is also much more convenient; for example, to pay £350 in cash means counting out notes to that value, and this can be a tiresome business. A cheque is written easily, whatever the value.

When cheques are received or paid out they are dealt with in exactly the same way as cash, but of course the account is not called a Cash Account, but a Bank Account. A typical Bank Account is shown in Fig. 15.3.

Look at these entries one by one.

On April 1 the opening balance carried down from the previous month was £275.00.

On April 2 cheques were paid out to the Cambridgeshire County Council, to the Eastern Electricity Board and to the Post Office. All cheques paid out are entered on the credit side.

Bank Account   L 4

19.. April			£	p		19.. April			£	p
1	Opening Balance	B/d	275	00		2	Cambridgeshire CC	L 49	15	00
3	M. Byron	L 181	35	00		2	Eastern Electricity	L 62	5	50
						2	Post Office	L 73	3	50
						5	T. Bold and Sons	L 48	125	00
						6	Balance	C/d	161	00
			£310	00					£310	00
April 7	Balance	B/d	161	00						

Fig. 15.3 A simple Bank Account

On April 3 a cheque was received from M. Byron. All cheques received are debited.

On April 5 a cheque was paid out to T. Bold and Sons.

At the end of the period—in this case, one week—the two sides are totalled as follows:

Debit side:	Credit side
£	£
275.00	15.00
35.00	5.50
310.00	3.50
	125.00
	149.00

The difference between the two sides is found:

$$
\begin{array}{r}
£ \\
310.00 \\
-\ 149.00 \\
\hline
161.00 \\
\hline
\end{array}
$$

This balance is entered on the credit side, and the two sides are then totalled. The balance is then brought down to the debit side.

15.5 Exercises: Receipts and Payments by Cheque

1. Enter the following items in a simple Bank Account.

April 19..
    1 Opening balance of £500.00 in the bank; paid £20.00 to R. Johnson
    1 Y. Smith paid us £15.10 by cheque
    2 J. Rogers paid us £48.50 by cheque
    2 Paid R. Morecambe £165.50 for goods supplied
    3 Paid by cheque rent £35.00
    4 Paid by cheque repairs £42.50
    4 R. Laws paid us £4.20
    5 Paid by cheque for electric stove £46.50
Balance off the Bank Account and bring down the balance.

2. Enter the following items in a Bank Account, balance off at the end and bring down the balance.

February 19..
    1 Balance of cash at bank £375.20
    1 Paid for insurance £5.50
    2 Paid garage expenses £2.75 by cheque

2 M. Taylor paid by cheque for goods supplied £48.50

3 Paid wages £57.50

3 Paid to M. Harper £4.75 by cheque

3 Paid R. Palmer £16.65 by cheque

4 Paid office expenses £7.85 by cheque

4 R. Thomas paid us £24.16 by cheque

4 R. Jones paid us the sum of £36.50 by cheque

5 Paid to M. Soames £13.75 by cheque

6 Paid for office expenses £16.20

6 N. Thomas paid us £10.75 by cheque

3. Enter the following items in a Bank Account, and balance off the account at the end of the week.

May 19..

14 Balance in bank £785.50; paid £14.22 rent by cheque; paid M. Brown £5.00 by cheque

17 D. Spires gave a cheque for £42.50 for goods to be delivered that day

18 Paid rates by cheque £17.50

18 R. Milton paid by cheque £10.50 for account rendered on May 1

18 M. Tyce paid his account, value £64.70 by cheque

19 Paid wages by cheque £67.50

20 Received cheque from Customs and Excise, VAT refunded £36.50

15.6 Bank Overdrafts

With a Cash Account you can never spend more than you have in the cash box, for you cannot take more money out of the till than is already in it. With a Bank Account, provided the bank manager agrees, it is possible to pay out a cheque for which there are really no funds. This is called a *bank overdraft* and amounts to a temporary loan from the bank. An example of such a situation is illustrated in Fig. 15.4.

Here the payments out are greater than the funds available. Consequently, when balanced off, the account has the credit side greater than the debit side. The balance inserted on the debit side is carried down to the credit side as a bank overdraft.

19..			£ p	19..			£ p
July 1	Balance	B/d	127 50	July 2	M. Ruback	L 47	65 80
4	T. Smith	L 39	5 50	5	Tree Products Ltd.	L 59	138 50
6	Balance	C/d	86 80	6	M. Large	L 49	15 50
			£219 80				£219 80
				July 7	Balance	B/d	86 80

Bank Account   L 4

Fig. 15.4 *A Bank Account ending with an overdraft*

15.7 Exercises: Bank Accounts with Overdrafts

1. Enter the following items in a Bank Account, balance off at the end and bring down the balance, which is an overdraft.

March 19 . .
   1 Balance of cash at bank £42.00
   2 Paid for repairs to window £7.55 by cheque
   3 Paid M. Roberts £130.00 by cheque
   4 B. Brown paid us by cheque £27.50
   5 Paid wages £75.10 by cheque
   6 Paid to M. Hobart £15.75 by cheque
   7 Paid to R. Sidney £24.85 by cheque
   8 Paid office expenses £16.25 by cheque
   9 M. Lyons paid us by cheque £42.50

2. Enter the following items in a simple Bank Account.

June 19 . .
   1 Balance of cash in bank £37.50; paid wages by cheque £56.65; drew money from bank for office use £20.00; paid R. Johns by cheque £73.15
   2 Bought goods for canteen by cheque £6.85; bought stationery £3.10 by cheque; bought typewriter by cheque £185.00
   3 R. Masters sent us £12.15 cheque; B. Brown sent us a cheque for £13.85; sent £26.15 to R. Jones by cheque
   4 R. Howell paid us by cheque £34.20

Balance off the Bank Account and bring down the balance, which is an overdraft.

15.8 Book-keeping for the Small Business

In this Unit we have taken a brief look at the ledger, and in particular the Cash Account and the Bank Account. If you wish to study book-keeping further, either to take employment in an accounts department or for the purpose of running your own business, you will find two other Success Study-books useful: *Success in Principles of Accounting* and its associated *Answer Book*. *Success in Principles of Accounting* covers all the elementary book-keeping required for any business, while in the *Answer Book* every question in the main text has an answer fully worked out in correct style. Another useful book is *Simplified Book-keeping for Small Businesses* (available from George Vyner Ltd), which describes the Simplex Book-keeping System.

15.9 Mental Arithmetic Exercises

1. $4\frac{1}{4} + 2\frac{2}{3} =$
2. $2\frac{2}{5} - 1\frac{3}{4} =$
3. $\frac{3}{8} \times \frac{3}{4} \times \frac{2}{9} =$
4. $\frac{5}{8} \div \frac{7}{12} =$
5. $0.56 + 0.24 + 3.75 =$
6. $31.5 - 17.6 =$
7. £850 × 7 =
8. Share £48 between two partners in the ratio 7 : 5.
9. An article costing £250 including interest charges is bought for £25 deposit and ten monthly instalments. How much is each instalment?
10. What is the average of 16, 22, 30 and 36?
11. Change £24.50 to Deutschemarks at 4 Dm = £1.
12. Three items cost £50 each and five others cost £30 each. What is the average cost?
13. What is the simple interest on £550 for 3 years at 7 per cent per annum?
14. If a will orders that £42 000 is to be shared between three brothers in the ratio 3 : 2 : 1, what will each get?
15. What is the total cost of an article bought on hire purchase for £150 deposit and 24 monthly payments of £25?

Unit Sixteen

The Petty-cash Book

16.1 The Imprest System

One of the commonest ways of recording receipts and payments is to use a *petty-cash book* kept on the *imprest system*. The word *petty* means 'small' or 'unimportant'. This system is commonly used by firms who settle their main debts by cheque, leaving minor items to be paid for from the petty cash.

In the imprest system, a certain sum of money is advanced to the person keeping the record—in this case the petty-cashier. From this sum of money any minor expenses can be paid out. Any small sums received are added to the imprest, and included in the reckoning at the end of a fixed period, usually a week.

The imprest system has the following advantages:

(*a*) It saves the time of the chief cashier, who is a busy person with many responsibilities.

(*b*) It trains young staff to be responsible about money and accurate in accounting for it.

(*c*) The sum impressed is small, and unlikely to prove a temptation either to the person in charge of it or to others in the office.

(*d*) It enables a great saving of time to be effected in the posting of small items to the ledger accounts, since it uses an analysis system which collects these items—for example, small payments—together into weekly or monthly totals, which are then posted to the ledger accounts.

16.2 The Layout of the Petty-cash Book

This is best understood by studying the example given in Fig. 16.1. Petty-cash rulings vary; some books have as many as 40 analysis columns. In examination questions a student is usually advised to use only four or five analysis columns.

Notice that the page, shown in Fig. 16.1, is divided from top to bottom by a triple line, placed to the left to allow plenty of room for the analysis columns.

The imprest of money advanced by the chief cashier to the petty-cashier is entered on the debit side as money received. We also have on this side a sum received from a debtor named Jones, and a sum received (from a member of staff) for a private telephone call.

On the payments side each entry is made twice: first in the total column, then again in whichever analysis column is appropriate. These analysis

'Middle' of the book

Dr.

Month Day	Details	F	£	p
19.. Dec. 1	Imprest	CB1	50	00
3	R. Jones	L62	14	56
5	Telephone Exp.	L29	3	27
		£	67	83
19.. Dec. 9	Balance	B/d	6	60
7	Restored imprest	CB5	43	40

Month Day	Details	PCV	Total £ p	Postage £ p	Travelling £ p	Stationery £ p	Sundry Expenses £ p	Sales Returns £ p	F	Ledger Accounts £ p
19.. Dec. 1	Stamps	1	12 50	12 50						
1	Bus fares	2	0 63		0 63					
2	Postage	3	1 55	1 55						
2	Envelopes	4	4 25			4 25				
2	Refreshments	5	2 65				2 65			
3	R. Smith	6	13 25						L14	13 25
3	T. Peters	7	4 72						L27	4 72
4	Sales Returns	8	8 00					8 00		
5	Postage	9	2 55	2 55						
5	Train fares	10	6 38		6 38					
6	Notepaper	11	4 75			4 75				
			61 23	16 60	7 01	9 00	2 65	8 00		17 97
6	Balance	C/d	6 60	(L7)	(L9)	(L15)	(L17)	(L18)		
		£	67 83							

Fig. 16.1 A simple petty-cash book

columns enable us to discover how much is spent each week on each analysed item—postage, travelling and so forth.

The ledger column on the right is used for items which cannot be collected together; for instance, Mr Smith's and Mr Peters' cheques are kept separate. The folio column enables these items to be posted separately to the accounts of these suppliers.

At the end of the week the imprest is nearly used up, and it is necessary to claim some more. The credit side of the book is added and cross-totted to see if the total of £61.23 spent agrees with the totals of the other columns when they are added together. If not, a mistake has been made somewhere.

The debit side is now totalled and the balance in hand is worked out: it comes to £6.60. Does this agree with what is in the till? If it does the book is balanced off and the balance brought down.

When the book is presented to the chief cashier and checked, the imprest will be restored to £50 by giving the petty cashier the £43.40 required.

Petty-cash vouchers (PCVs) are documents which are obtained when money is spent, to prove that payments have been made. For example, when buying stationery the receipt given by the shopkeeper becomes the petty-cash voucher

	2 March	
Envelopes	003.25	+
Paste	001.20	+
Pens	000.62	+
Eraser	000.60	+
Wrapping paper	003.75	+
	009.42	TL
	009.45	AT
	000.03	CH

AT — Amount Tendered
TL — Total
CH — Change   PCV 8

Fig. 16.2 A petty-cash voucher from outside the business

(Fig. 16.2). Sometimes we cannot obtain these (for example, for train fares) and the person claiming the fares fills up an 'internal' petty-cash voucher (Fig. 16.3). These vouchers are filed and numbered and the numbers are entered in the PCV column.

petty-cash claim			
name: R. Cox		date: 1 May 19..	
required for Travelling expenses		amount	
Fares to London Airport		5	40
Fares to Wimbledon		1	60
	total:	7	00
signed: R.Cox	passed: CWR	folio PCV 4	

Fig. 16.3 An internal petty-cash voucher, authorized by the manager

The folio numbers of the ledger accounts are shown either at the foot of the analysis columns (for example, L7 for postage account) or in the special folio columns provided for individual items (such as L14 and L27 for Mr Smith's and Mr Peters' cheques).

16.3 Exercises: Petty-cash

A suitable supply of petty-cash paper is needed for these exercises. Any stationers' shop will supply a ruled paper, which you can adapt, if necessary. Alternatively you can rule your own, similar to the one in Fig. 16.1, and photocopy a few sheets.

1. Using petty-cash paper open D. Benson's petty-cash book on April 7, 19 . ., with an initial balance of £4.35. Then enter the cash given to the petty-cashier by the proprietor to restore the imprest to £25.00, and the following transactions:

April 19 . .

7 Pays postage £0.66 and bus fares £0.60; pays R. Collins's account £5.32
8 Receives from a member of staff £1.57 for a private telephone call; pays postage £0.86, stationery £2.50
9 Pays postage £0.64, train fares £3.65; parking meter charge £0.60
10 Purchases, for office use: sticky-tape dispenser £3.27; office cleaning materials £4.51; M. Brown, a debtor, pays Benson in cash £3.45
11 Pays postage £1.29; buys cakes for typist's tea-break £2.38

The petty-cash book has analysis columns for postage, travelling expenses, office-cleaning expenses, stationery and sundry expenses, and a ledger accounts column for recording payments to creditors or for the purchase of assets. Balance the book at the end of the week, ready to present to the proprietor for checking. Invent suitable folio and petty-cash voucher numbers.

2. Enter the following items in R. Norris's petty-cash book which has five columns, for postage, fares, office sundries, repairs and ledger accounts. Invent sensible folio numbers and petty-cash voucher numbers.

July 19 . .

15 Draws petty-cash imprest £25.00; pays postage £3.50
16 Pays fare £1.28; buys ball of string £0.75; pays plumber to clear drain £8.75, and a creditor, T. Bright, £4.75. R. Brown, a debtor, pays Norris in cash £17.25
17 Pays postage £1.55; buys stationery £3.50; buys cleaning materials £2.35
18 Pays R. Jones £1.45; member of staff pays £1.35 for private telephone call; pays fares £0.86
19 Pays fares £2.35; pays for repairs to door £5.85; pays M. Knight £3.25; pays postage £1.50

Balance the book and restore the imprest to £25.00.

3. A petty-cash book is kept on the imprest system, the amount of the imprest being £25.00. It has five analysis columns: postage and stationery, travelling expenses, carriage, office expenses and ledger accounts. Give the ruling for the book and enter the following transactions of the petty-cashier.

January 19 . .

14 Petty cash in hand £2.25; receives cash to make up the imprest; buys stamps £6.00
15 Pays railway fares £4.25; bus fares £0.65; telegrams £2.35
16 Pays carriage on small parcels £1.33; pays railway fares £2.36; buys stationery £2.68
17 Pays for repairs to window £7.65; pays T. Smith's account for December £8.55. R. Morgan pays in cash £15.50 which he owes us
18 Pays for tea for visitor £1.86

Balance the petty-cash book as on January 18 and bring down the balance. Invent suitable folio numbers and petty-cash voucher numbers.

4. R. Duncan keeps a petty-cash book with three analysis columns: postages, cleaning and sundries. On June 29, 19 . ., the petty-cashier reaches the bottom of a page, and carries forward the following totals:

	£
Imprest	25.00
Total expenditure	11.30
Postage	6.14
Cleaning	3.22
Sundries	1.94

The following payments were made on the last two days of the month:

	£
29 Postages	2.13
30 Cleaning materials	2.22
Bus fare	0.65
Postages	0.96

Write up the petty-cash book as it would appear for the last two days of the month, balance the book and restore the imprest. Invent sensible petty-cash voucher numbers, and ledger folio numbers.

Unit Seventeen

Prices, Practice and Simple Costing

17.1 Calculating Prices

One of the commonest business activities is the calculation of prices. Everything bought and sold, every job and every contract has its price. It is not easy to fix prices so as to content both parties to a bargain, and there is usually a special department in firms to estimate prices.

Many simple price calculations can be performed mentally, but others require the use of pencil and paper, or perhaps of an electronic calculator (see Unit 11) or a ready-reckoner (see Section 25.3).

The following examples illustrate some simple price calculations which can easily be done mentally.

Example

What is the cost of 3 electric hair-dryers at £5.95 each?

We can say: £5.95 is almost £6
$$3 \times £6 = £18$$
Now deduct 3×5 pence $= 15$p
Price of 3 hair-dryers is £17.85

Example

What is the cost of 6 paperback thrillers at £1.50 each?

We can say: £1.50 $= £1\frac{1}{2}$
$6 \times 1 = 6$ and $6 \times \frac{1}{2} = 3$
Total cost $= £6 + 3 = £9$

17.2 Exercises: Simple Price Calculations

1. Calculate each of the following prices:
   (a) 3 loaves at 43p each
   (b) 2 packets of detergent at $67\frac{1}{2}$p each
   (c) 4 tyres at £16.99 each
   (d) 4 books at £4.65 each
   (e) 8 chops at 77p each
   (f) 5 box files at £1.85 each
   (g) 5 magazines at 85p each
   (h) 8 m² of carpet at £8.95 per m²
   (i) 6 blankets at £9.55 each
   (j) 10 rose bushes at £2.85 each

2. Calculate the following bills:
   (a) 4 rolls wallpaper at £4.55 per roll
      3 packets cellulose paste at 43½p each
      1 brush at £2.35½
   (b) 3 lamb chops at 37p each
      2 steaks at 65p each
      2 packets of sage and onion stuffing at 22½p each
   (c) 3 lunches at £2.35 each
      3 desserts at 45p each
      1 biscuits and cheese at 60p
      3 coffees at 25p each
   (d) 5 copies of *Astronomy for Amateurs* at £2.55 each
      4 copies of *The Sky at Night* at £3.60 each
      3 copies of *Worlds in Collision* at £4.85 each
   (e) 2 cabinets (grey) at £67.50 each
      1 desk at £85.00
      4 desk trays at £2.87½ each
      3 sets of desk tray risers at 43½p per set

3. Work out the prices of the following imports from European firms, in the currency given.
   (a) 500 Desktronic calculators at 235.50 D-marks each
   (b) 200 'Italia' radial tyres at 22 500 lire each
   (c) 400 bottles Gaulloise brandy at 22.50 francs per bottle
   (d) 300 cuckoo clocks at 52.50 Swiss francs each
   (e) 1 100 Dutch cheeses at 18.54 guilders each
   (f) 400 German typewriters at 925 D-marks each
   (g) 300 Dutch trucks at 10 450 guilders each
   (h) 500 French gowns at 425 francs each
   (i) 250 Danish sides of bacon at 96 krone each
   (j) 250 crates Norwegian frozen fish at 84 krone per crate

17.3 Finding Prices by the Practice Method

Many price calculations are easily performed by the *practice method*. This method is easiest to explain in terms of examples.

Example

Find the cost of 96 articles at £1.85 each.

The method starts with a very simple line, and the rest of the calculation is worked out in terms of this original line. In this example, we may regard the cost of one article, £1.85, as

$$£1.85 = £1 + 50p + 25p + 10p$$

Line 1 96 articles at £1	= £ 96	(an easy first line)
Line 2 96 articles at 50p	= £ 48	($\frac{1}{2}$ of line 1)
Line 3 96 articles at 25p	= £ 24	($\frac{1}{2}$ of line 2)
Line 4 96 articles at 10p	= £9.60	($\frac{1}{10}$ of line 1)

$$96 \text{ articles at } £1.85 = \underline{£177.60}$$

Example

Find the cost of 1 800 metres of cloth at £4.78 per metre.

$$£4.78 = £1 + £3 + 50p + 25p + 1p + 2p$$

Line 1 1 800 m at £1	= £1 800	(an easy first line)
Line 2 1 800 m at £3	= £5 400	(3 × line 1)
Line 3 1 800 m at 50p	= £ 900	($\frac{1}{2}$ of line 1)
Line 4 1 800 m at 25p	= £ 450	($\frac{1}{2}$ of line 3)
Line 5 1 800 m at 1p	= £ 18	($\frac{1}{100}$ of line 1)
Line 6 1 800 m at 2p	= £ 36	(2 × line 5)

$$1\ 800 \text{ m at } £4.78 = \underline{£8\ 604}$$

The best rule is: *always start with a £ line.*
Thus a calculation involving £2.55 is worked out with £1, £1, 50p and 5p lines. One involving £0.75 is worked out with a £1 line first (which is not added into the answer) and from this a 50p line and a 25p line are worked out: adding these gives the answer needed.

17.4 Exercises: Prices by the Practice Method

1. Find the cost of the following purchases using the practice method:
   (a) 45 articles at £1.75 each
   (b) 86 articles at £1.60 each
   (c) 48 articles at £1.85 each
   (d) 72 articles at £1.80 each
   (e) 65 articles at £1.35 each

2. Find the cost of the following rolls of cloth:
   (a) 48 m at £3.65 per metre
   (b) 38 m at £2.35 per metre
   (c) 27 m at £4.42 per metre
   (d) 60 m at £3.68 per metre
   (e) 28 m at £2.82 per metre

3. Find the cost of the following lorry loads at the quoted rates per tonne:
   (a) 32 tonnes at £2.55 per tonne
   (b) 18 tonnes at £2.85 per tonne
   (c) 22 tonnes at £3.68 per tonne
   (d) 25 tonnes at £2.15 per tonne
   (e) 11 tonnes at £0.78 per tonne

17.5 Simple Costing Activities

Many firms raise a *cost sheet* for every job that is started and record on it every item of expense that is incurred. The various costs can then be added together to give the total cost of the job. From this cost sheet a final charge for the job can then be calculated, so that a bill can be sent to the customer. Sometimes a contract price will already have been agreed, and the cost sheet will then be used for comparing the actual cost with the estimated cost quoted to the customer. If the true cost looks like being greater than the estimate it may be possible to come to some arrangement with the customer. If not, the firm will at least be better informed, and able to avoid making the same mistake again.

Often it is necessary to add on a percentage of the costs recorded, to allow for overhead expenses. For example, a component used in a repair job may be priced at £5 but the paperwork, correspondence, transport and so on involved in obtaining the component may add considerably to this cost. Experience might lead us to believe that a 100 per cent *oncost*—that is, a sum of money equal to 100 per cent of the price of the component—should be added to make sure that a fair share of these overheads is included in the costs charged to the customer. Other costs of the contract may be subject to higher or lower oncost rates.

Fig. 17.1 shows a typical cost sheet; many different kinds are in use.

17.6 Exercises: Simple Cost Sheets

Make a number of copies of the cost sheet in Fig. 17.1 and use them to record the costs for the following jobs performed by A. Builder for his customers:
1. Serial No. 1: Mr J. Smith, 22 Hill Street, Somerton.
   Garage erection and alterations to outhouses
   Materials used: 5 000 bricks £800.00; lime and sand £75.00; guttering £32.00; piping £45.00; roofing felt and tar £26.50; set of doors £96.50; locks and brackets £12.50
   Machine shop expenses: welding £14.15; fitting and repairing £28.85; milling £41.50
   Delivery of repaired parts: £10.35
   Transfers from other departments: insurance £4.50; labour £234.50; drawing office £32.50; Buying Department £3.55

Cost sheet serial number _____

Name of customer _____

Address _____

_____

Job description _____

Materials and components	F	£	Machine shop expenses	F	£	Transport and travel	F	£
Total			Total			Total		
Add oncost at 100%			Add oncost at 250%			Add oncost at 50%		
Section total			Section total			Section total		

Other charges	F	£	Summary	
				£
			Materials etc.	
			Machine shop expenses	
			Transport and travel	
			Other charges	
			Total costs	
			Add profit	
			Invoice total	
Total			Notes	
Add oncost at 50%				
Section total				

Fig. 17.1 A cost sheet

Record these costs in the appropriate columns, total them, add on the rate of oncost shown, and carry the final total to the summary. Profit is to be £365.

2. Serial No. 2: Mr E. Varley, 5 High Road, Cambridge.
   Alterations to windows and doors
   Materials used: 1 patio door £175.00; 2 windows at £35.75 each; plaster £12.50; paints etc. £18.50

Transport: lorry expenses £14.55; fares £8.15

Transfers from other departments: accounts £8.50; drawing office £32.50; security £12.28; labour £74.50

Record these costs, add on the appropriate rate of oncost, carry the totals to the summary and add the profit which is to be £103.

3. Serial No. 3: Mr J. Simmons, 24 Botney Drive, Willenham.
   Redecorations
   Materials used: 12 rolls paper at £5.80 per roll; paint £22.34; sundries £2.25
   Transport: £13.50
   Wages Department transfer £67.50; Interior Design Department transfer £20.00

Record these costs, add the various oncosts and carry the figures to the summary. The profit is to be £65.

4. Serial No. 4: Mr E. Morton, 25 Highcliff Road, Coton.
   Re-roofing and external repairs
   Materials used: timber £148.50; tiles £84.25; cement and sand £24.25
   Machine shop charges: wrought iron work £25.80; welding £15.75
   Transport and travelling: lorry charges £14.25; van charges £15.50; fares £8.25
   Other departments: drawing office £18.50; wages £266.50; general administration £15.00

Record these costs, add on the appropriate oncost figure, carry the totals to the summary section and add on the profit, which is £220.

17.7 Mental Arithmetic Exercises

1. £3.52$\frac{1}{2}$ × 6 =
2. £8.15 − £4.38$\frac{1}{2}$ =
3. 2$\frac{3}{4}$ × 1$\frac{1}{11}$ =
4. How many decimetres in 2$\frac{1}{2}$ metres?
5. Change 62$\frac{1}{2}$ per cent to a fraction.
6. What common factor is there of 14 and 49?
7. 0.65 × 5 =
8. 2 300 × 500 =
9. £74.60 is changed into 10-pence pieces. How many are there?
10. What is 22$\frac{1}{2}$ per cent as a fraction?
11. What is the sale price of items costing £185 and sold at 33$\frac{1}{3}$ per cent profit?
12. What is the simple interest on £500 for two years at 7 per cent per annum?
13. Two brothers share an inheritance, one taking $\frac{4}{7}$ and the other $\frac{3}{7}$. If it totalled £42 000 how much did each get?
14. Round off the number 42 756 to the nearest thousand.
15. A German visitor exchanges 87 Deutschemarks into pounds sterling. The rate of exchange is 4.35 Dm = £1. How many pounds sterling does he receive?

Unit Eighteen

Buying and Selling

18.1 Cost Price, Mark-up and Selling Price

The trader, or merchant, buys goods to sell again. It is a useful function in at least two ways. First, by buying the goods and so becoming their owner, the trader relieves the grower, or perhaps the manufacturer, of any worry that the goods will not be sold. Second, he distributes them, making them available to the people who want to buy them, perhaps shipping them halfway round the world, and often dividing large loads—in crates or barrels, for instance—into conveniently small packages.

In return he hopes to sell the goods for more money than he paid for them. He *marks up* the goods from the *cost price* to a higher price, which becomes his *selling price*. When he sells them to his customer he ceases to be the owner. His reward for carrying the risks and for performing other useful services such as transport, breaking bulk, packaging and so forth is the *profit* he has made on the transaction.

Mark-up is often worked out in percentage terms, using the formula

$$Cost\ price + mark\text{-}up = selling\ price$$

Example

A trader buys potatoes from a farmer at £2.25 per sack and adds $33\frac{1}{3}$ per cent mark-up. What is his selling price?

$$
\begin{aligned}
\text{Cost price} + \text{mark-up} &= \text{selling price} \\
\text{Selling price} &= £2.25 + (33\tfrac{1}{3}\% \text{ of } £2.25) \\
&= £2.25 + (\tfrac{1}{3} \text{ of } £2.25) \\
&= £2.25 + £0.75 \\
&= \underline{\underline{£3.00}}
\end{aligned}
$$

Example

A trader buys flour at £6.80 per sack and adds 50 per cent mark-up. What is his selling price?

$$
\begin{aligned}
\text{Cost price} + \text{mark-up} &= \text{selling price} \\
&= £6.80 + (50\% \text{ of } £6.80) \\
&= £6.80 + (\tfrac{1}{2} \text{ of } £6.80) \\
&= £6.80 + £3.40 \\
&= \underline{\underline{£10.20}}
\end{aligned}
$$

Example

A trader buys articles at £4.80 each. He adds a mark-up of 25 per cent. What will his selling price be?

$$\text{Cost price} + \text{mark-up} = \text{selling price}$$
$$\text{Selling price} = £4.80 + (25\% \text{ of } £4.80)$$
$$= £4.80 + (\tfrac{1}{4} \text{ of } £4.80)$$
$$= £4.80 + £1.20$$
$$= £6.00$$

18.2 Exercises: Cost Price and Selling Price

1. If mark-up is fixed at 25 per cent, work out the selling prices of goods of which the cost prices are as follows:

   (a) 40p   (b) 60p
   (c) £1.00   (d) £1.30
   (e) £1.50   (f) £4.50
   (g) £7.80   (h) £15.00
   (i) £32.00   (j) £38.50

2. If mark-up is fixed at 40 per cent, work out the selling prices of goods of which the cost prices are as follows:

   (a) £1.00   (b) £2.50
   (c) £4.80   (d) £12.00
   (e) £13.20   (f) £15.60
   (g) £18.00   (h) £24.50
   (i) £35.00   (j) £48.00

3. If mark-up is fixed at 150 per cent, work out the selling prices of goods of which the cost prices are as follows:

   (a) £0.50   (b) £0.80
   (c) £1.50   (d) £1.80
   (e) £5   (f) £15.50
   (g) £24.40   (h) £45.00
   (i) £75.00   (j) £124.00

18.3 Selling Prices, Margins and Mark-downs

In the retail trade many calculations are based upon selling prices rather than cost prices. One reason for this is that in large retail organizations, such as multiple shops and chain stores, the mark-up to the cost price is often added on *before* the goods are sent out to branches. The branch manager receives the goods already marked with their selling price, and he never knows the cost price to Head Office. This system makes it easy to control the branches, for a branch manager must have the full value of the goods supplied available in the shop. Either he has the goods in stock, or he must have sold them in which case he should have the money. If he has less than the full value this must be because he is dishonest or inefficient—perhaps some member of staff is stealing the money, or shop-lifters are stealing the goods.

So shop-keepers tend to talk in terms of selling prices rather than of cost prices, and in terms of margins of profit rather than of mark-ups.

The *margin of profit* is the percentage that has to be subtracted from the selling price to give the cost price. The formula is

$$Selling\ price\ -\ margin\ =\ cost\ price$$

Example

A retailer sells an article for £45. The margin of profit is $33\frac{1}{3}$ per cent. What was the cost price?

$$\begin{aligned}
\text{Cost price} &= \text{selling price} - \text{margin} \\
&= £45 - (33\tfrac{1}{3}\% \text{ of } £45) \\
&= £45 - (\tfrac{1}{3} \text{ of } £45) \\
&= £45 - £15 \\
&= £30
\end{aligned}$$

It often happens that an item of stock becomes shop-soiled or damaged, or becomes unfashionable. To clear the item the selling price may be reduced or *marked down*. A mark-down is always made *from the selling price*.

Example

An article for sale at £15 is damaged by sunlight and marked down by 10 per cent. What is the final sale price?

$$\begin{aligned}
\text{Mark-down} &= 10\% \text{ of } £15 \\
&= \tfrac{1}{10} \times £15 \\
&= £1.50 \\
\text{Final sale price} &= £15 - £1.50 \\
&= £13.50
\end{aligned}$$

18.4 Exercises: Margins and Mark-downs

1. Work out the cost prices of each of the items of which the selling prices and margins of profit are as follows:

(a) 60p; 50%   (b) £1.20; 25%
(c) £2.50; 20%   (d) £3.30; $33\frac{1}{3}$%
(e) £4.00; 25%   (f) £5.50; 50%
(g) £7.50; $33\frac{1}{3}$%   (h) £12.50; 20%
(i) £25.00; 50%   (j) £100; 40%

2. A retailer's shop is damaged by flooding from burst pipes, and he decides to mark down all his stock in order to clear it. Work out the marked-down prices of the items whose original selling prices and mark-downs are as follows:

(a) 80p; 10%   (b) 65p; 10%
(c) £1.30; 20%   (d) £1.50; 25%
(e) £2.40; 10%   (f) £2.75; 20%
(g) £3.60; $33\frac{1}{3}$%   (h) £4.20; 10%
(i) £15.00; 5%   (j) £27.00; 5%

18.5 The Relationship between Mark-up and Margin

Many business calculations involve mark-ups and margins and the connexions between them, which are often very simple. Consider a mark-up of 50 per cent or $\frac{1}{2}$.

Cost price + (50% of cost price) = selling price

Suppose the cost price is £100 (the particular figure we choose does not affect the result of the calculation):

$$\text{Selling price} = £100 + (50\% \text{ of } £100)$$
$$= £100 + £50$$
$$= £150$$

Now the mark-up of £50 is also the margin of profit. A margin, however, is always considered in terms of the selling price, and the £50, which is $\frac{1}{2}$ of the cost price, is $\frac{50}{150} = \frac{1}{3}$ of the selling price. So *a mark-up of $\frac{1}{2}$ on the cost price is equal to a margin of $\frac{1}{3}$ off the selling price.*

Now suppose that we mark up the same goods by $33\frac{1}{3}$ per cent:

Cost price + ($33\frac{1}{3}$% of cost price) = selling price
$$\text{Selling price} = £100 + (33\frac{1}{3} \text{ of } £100)$$
$$= £133\frac{1}{3}$$

But this mark-up of £$33\frac{1}{3}$, which is $\frac{1}{3}$ of the cost price, is $\dfrac{33\frac{1}{3}}{133\frac{1}{3}} = \frac{1}{4}$ of the selling price. So *a mark-up of $\frac{1}{3}$ of the cost price is equal to a margin of $\frac{1}{4}$ off the selling price.*

In fact we can build up a table like this:

Mark-up		*Margin*
$\frac{1}{2}$ on to the cost price	=	$\frac{1}{3}$ off the selling price
$\frac{1}{3}$ on to the cost price	=	$\frac{1}{4}$ off the selling price
$\frac{1}{4}$ on to the cost price	=	$\frac{1}{5}$ off the selling price
$\frac{1}{5}$ on to the cost price	=	$\frac{1}{6}$ off the selling price
etc.		etc.

This relationship holds good no matter how far we carry it. Consider a retailer who adds 5 per cent ($\frac{1}{20}$) to his cost price to find his selling price and, again, suppose the goods cost him £100.

$$\text{Cost price} + (5\% \text{ of cost price}) = \text{selling price}$$
$$\text{Selling price} = £100 + (5\% \text{ of } £100)$$
$$= £100 + £5$$
$$= £105$$

Now, what is the margin of profit? Clearly it is $\frac{5}{105}$ of the selling price. But $\frac{5}{105}$ = $\frac{1}{21}$. So $\frac{1}{20}$ on to the cost price = $\frac{1}{21}$ off the selling price, and our relationship still holds good.

Example

A shopkeeper marks up an article by 25 per cent on cost price, and sells it for £6. (*a*) What was the margin on selling price? (*b*) What did the item cost him originally?

$$\text{Mark-up on cost price} = 25\% = \frac{1}{4}$$
$$\frac{1}{4} \text{ on the cost price} = \frac{1}{5} \text{ off the selling price}$$
$$\text{Margin} = \frac{1}{5} = 20\%$$

$$\text{Original cost} = £6 - (\frac{1}{5} \text{ of } £6)$$
$$= £6 - £1.20$$
$$= £4.80$$

Check: cost price + mark-up = selling price

$$£4.80 + (25\% \text{ of } £4.80) = £4.80 + £1.20 = £6$$

When the mark-up is not an easy fraction like 25 per cent, the calculation is done in just the same way. Consider a 40 per cent mark-up of goods costing £100:

$$\text{Cost price} + \text{mark-up} = \text{selling price}$$
$$\text{Selling price} = £100 + (40\% \text{ of } £100)$$
$$= £100 + £40$$
$$= £140$$

The margin—£40—is $\frac{40}{140}$, that is, $\frac{2}{7}$ of the selling price.

Example

A retailer marks up an article by 60 per cent on the cost price, and sells it at £12. (*a*) What was the margin on his selling price? (*b*) What did it originally cost him?

First we calculate the margin corresponding to a mark-up of 60 per cent and again we can do this by considering a consignment of goods costing the retailer £100:

$$\text{Cost price} + \text{mark-up} = \text{selling price}$$
$$\text{Selling price of this consignment} = £100 + (60\% \text{ of } £100)$$
$$= £100 + £60$$
$$= £160$$
$$\text{Margin on selling price} = \frac{60}{160} \times 100\%$$
$$= \frac{3}{8} \times 100\%$$
$$= 37\frac{1}{2}\%$$

So original cost of article sold for £12 $= £12 - (\frac{3}{8} \times £12)$
$$= £12 - £\frac{9}{2}$$
$$= £12 - £4\frac{1}{2}$$
$$= £7.50$$

Check: Cost price + mark-up = selling price

$$£7.50 + (60\% \text{ of } £7.50)$$
$$= £7.50 + (\tfrac{3}{5} \text{ of } £7.50)$$
$$= £7.50 + £4.50$$
$$= £12$$

18.6 Exercises: The Relationship between Mark-up and Margin

1. The following selling prices were obtained by marking up the cost price of

each article by the percentage indicated. What was the cost price of each article to the retailer?

(a) £5.00; 25%   (b) £10.00; 25%
(c) £4.50; 50%   (d) £12.00; 20%
(e) £12.60; 50%   (f) £24.00; 20%
(g) £1.60; $33\frac{1}{3}$%   (h) £2.80; $33\frac{1}{3}$%
(i) £14.00; $16\frac{2}{3}$%   (j) £2.80; $16\frac{2}{3}$%

2. The following selling prices were obtained by marking up the cost price of each article by the percentage indicated. What was the cost price of each article to the retailer?

(a) £7; 40%   (b) £4.20; 40%
(c) £29; 45%   (d) £5.80; 45%
(e) £62; 55%   (f) £9.30; 55%
(g) £16; 60%   (h) £4.80; 60%
(i) £27; 80%   (j) £4.50; 80%

3. The following problems all concern mark-ups and margins.

(a) A dealer sells a diamond ring for £759, thus making a profit of 32 per cent on his cost price. Find the price that he paid for the ring.   (RSA)

(b) A dealer sells a gold watch for £551, thus making a profit of 45 per cent on his cost price. Find the price that he paid for the watch.   (RSA)

(c) The marked price of a watch is £75.50, which represents an increase of 25 per cent on the cost price. Find the cost price.   (RSA)

(d) The marked price of a watch is £76.80, which represents an increase of 20 per cent on the cost price. Find the cost price.   (RSA)

(e) A man sells a house for £25 800, gaining 72 per cent on his cost price. How much did he pay for the house? What was his profit?

(RSA adapted)

(f) A man sells a house for £43 240, gaining 84 per cent on his cost price. How much did he pay for the house? What was his profit?

(RSA adapted)

18.7 Mental Arithmetic Exercises

1. $387 + 429 + 516 =$
2. $0.45 \times 0.7 =$
3. $4\frac{1}{2} + 3\frac{7}{10} =$
4. £47.50 × 7 =
5. Change $\frac{2}{3}$ to a percentage.
6. What is the total cost of 7 articles at 65 pence each and 3 articles at 75 pence each?
7. What is the lowest common multiple of 2, 3 and 4?
8. How many days are there from 24 March to 18 May inclusive?
9. How many days were there altogether in the years 1981 and 1982?
10. £26.07 ÷ 11 =
11. Express $22\frac{1}{2}$ per cent as a fraction.

12. A man leaves his wife half his property, his son one-third and his two daughters the rest divided equally between them. How much does each daughter get if he leaves £18 000?
13. A car travels at 45 kilometres per hour for 3 hours, and at 75 kilometres per hour for 2 hours. What was the car's average speed for the whole journey?
14. What is the gross profit if a firm takes £20 000 in its tills and the margin on selling price is 25 per cent?
15. What will 12 Italian car tyres cost in pounds sterling if the Italian price is 50 000 lire each and the rate of exchange is £1 = 2 500 lire?

Note on Mental Arithmetic Questions

Although the term 'mental arithmetic' implies that the work is done in one's head, in examinations – and in real life – it is usual to jot down partial answers on a spare piece of paper. To assist the candidate most examination papers in mental arithmetic have a section of the paper where the answers are to be written, and another section alongside it headed 'You may make notes of working here if you wish'. An example of such a layout, with a typical question is given below. From now on, in this book, you may use a piece of scrap paper to jot down partial answers to the mental arithmetic questions. These are increasing in difficulty as we cover the syllabus requirements of the various examination bodies.

Example

	Question	Answer	You may use this space for notes if required
14.	What will 20 German cars cost in pounds sterling if the import price per car is 18 000 Dm and the rate of exchange is £1 = 4 Dm?	£90 000	£4 500 per car

Unit Nineteen

More About Cost Price and Selling Price

19.1 Profits, Mark-ups and Margins

Today, perhaps more than at any other time in history, people are conscious of the need to ensure fair profit margins in business. It does nothing to simplify the problems if misunderstandings exist about the true profit figure. For instance, a shopkeeper might say to a customer, 'I am charging you £4 for this item, of which 25 per cent—£1—is my gross profit.'

In fact the 25 per cent is the margin, but gross profit should be calculated on cost price, not on selling price. The selling price of this item is £1 more than the cost price of £3, and the shopkeeper's true gross profit is therefore $33\frac{1}{3}$ per cent, not 25 per cent.

A wide variety of problems arise over these matters of profits and prices. They usually hinge around this basic point about cost prices and selling prices. This is why the businessman must be quite clear in his own mind what he is talking about: is the profit he wishes to make related to cost price or selling price? Is the discount he is thinking of related to list price (the price the manufacturer or wholesaler recommends him to charge the customer) or to the selling price—which may be the same as the list price or may be some other price?

Example

A retailer can buy freezers at a list price of £80 less a trade discount of 25 per cent. If he buys at this price and sells at the list price what percentage profit will he make? At what price must he sell a freezer if he wishes to make only 20 per cent on his outlay?

$$\text{Cost price of a freezer} = \text{£80 less 25\% trade discount}$$
$$= \text{£80} - \text{£20}$$
$$= \text{£60}$$

If it is sold at the list price, £80, the profit $= \text{£20}$

$$\text{Percentage profit} = \frac{\text{profit}}{\text{cost price}} \times 100\%$$

$$= \tfrac{20}{60} \times 100\%$$
$$= 33\tfrac{1}{3}\%$$

Selling price if only 20% profit is made on outlay

$$= \text{outlay} + 20\%$$
$$= \text{£60} + (20\% \text{ of £60})$$
$$= \text{£60} + \text{£12}$$
$$= \text{£72}$$

Example

A manufacturer sells goods valued at £36 800, of which 35 per cent is profit. What was the cost of manufacture of these products?

$$\text{Sales} = £36\ 800$$
$$\text{Profit margin} = 35\% \text{ of this sales figure}$$
$$= \tfrac{35}{100} \times £36\ 800$$
$$= 35 \times £368$$

$$\begin{array}{r} 368 \\ \times\ 35 \\ \hline 1\ 840 \\ 11\ 040 \\ \hline 12\ 880 \end{array}$$

$$= £12\ 880$$
$$\text{Cost of sales} = £36\ 800 - £12\ 880$$
$$= £23\ 920$$

Example

A shopkeeper prices an article in his shop at 40 per cent above cost price. During a sale he reduces this price by 20 per cent. What percentage profit (calculated on the original cost price) does he now make on the article?

$$\text{Suppose the article costs } £100\text{:}$$
$$\text{Selling price} = £100 + (40\% \text{ of } £100)$$
$$= £100 + £40$$
$$= £140$$
$$\text{Reduction for sale} = 20\% \text{ of } £140$$
$$= \tfrac{1}{5} \text{ of } £140$$
$$= £28$$
$$\text{Sale price} = £112$$
$$\text{Profit} = £12$$
$$\text{Percentage profit on original cost price} = \tfrac{12}{100} \times 100\% = \underline{\underline{12\%}}$$

Example

A shopkeeper wishes to price his goods so that he will make a profit of 25 per cent on cost price after allowing a cash discount of 5 per cent. What will he charge for an article which cost him £152?

$$\text{Cost price} = £152$$
$$\text{Final price desired} = £152 + (25\% \text{ of } £152)$$
$$= £152 + £38$$
$$= £190$$

But this price allows for a deduction of 5 per cent for cash discount; that is, £190 = $\tfrac{95}{100}$ of the marked price. To obtain the marked price we divide by 95 —giving us $\tfrac{1}{100}$ of the marked price—and then multiply by 100.

$$\text{Marked price} = £190 \times \tfrac{100}{95} = \underline{\underline{£200}}$$

19.2 Exercises: Prices and Profits

1. A retailer can buy television sets at a list price of £78 each, less a trade discount of $33\frac{1}{3}$ per cent. (*a*) What profit will he make if he sells at the list price? (*b*) What price should he sell at if he wishes to make a profit of only 20 per cent on his outlay?

2. A retailer can buy typewriters at a list price of £108 each, less a trade discount of $33\frac{1}{3}$ per cent. (*a*) What profit will he make if he sells at the list price? (*b*) What price should he charge if he decides to make a profit of only $16\frac{2}{3}$ per cent on his outlay?

3. A retailer can buy radiators at a list price of £60 each, less a trade discount of 45 per cent. (*a*) What profit will he make if he decides to sell at the list price? (*b*) What price should he charge if he decides instead to make a profit of 60 per cent on his outlay?

4. A retailer can buy bicycles at a list price of £81 each, less a trade discount of $33\frac{1}{3}$ per cent. (*a*) What profit will he make if he sells at the list price? (*b*) What price should he charge if he decides to make a profit of 30 per cent on his outlay?

5. A retailer can buy cars at a list price of £4 500 each, less a trade discount of $16\frac{2}{3}$ per cent. (*a*) What profit will he make if he decides to sell at the list price? (*b*) What price should he charge if he decides instead to make a profit of $12\frac{1}{2}$ per cent on his outlay?

6. A businessman's total sales are £280 500. Of this he estimates 15 per cent is profit. (*a*) What was the cost of the goods to him originally? (*b*) What would his sales total have been if he had sold these goods at a profit of 20 per cent on cost?

7. A businessman's total sales for the year are £13 550. Of this he calculates 22 per cent is profit. (*a*) What was the total cost to him of the goods sold? (*b*) What would his sales figure have been if he had added 40 per cent to cost prices to get his selling prices?

8. A businessman's total sales for the year are £29 500. Of this he calculates 28 per cent is profit. (*a*) What was the total cost to him of the goods sold? (*b*) What would his sales figure have been if he had added 35 per cent to cost prices to get his selling prices?

9. A businessman's total sales are £92 740. Of this he estimates 40 per cent is profit. (*a*) What was the cost of this merchandise to him originally? (*b*) What would his sales total have been if he had sold the goods at a profit of 25 per cent on cost?

10. A builder buys a plot of land for £30 000 and builds 4 bungalows on it. His building costs (materials, wages, etc.) are £9 500 for each bungalow. To the total cost price of each bungalow he adds his profit of 48 per cent. Find (*a*) the selling price of each bungalow, (*b*) the total profit made by the builder.   (RSA adapted)

11. A builder buys a plot of land for £27 500 and builds 5 bungalows on it. His building costs (materials, wages, etc.) are £11 800 for each bungalow. To the total cost price of each bungalow he adds his profit of 35 per cent. Find (a) the selling price of each bungalow, and (b) the total profit made by the builder.

12. A motor car manufacturer exports cars to Canada. He estimates that for each car his total costs will be £6 350 and his profit is 38 per cent of the total cost. Find the selling price of the car (a) in pounds sterling, (b) in dollars and cents given that £1 = 1.78 Canadian dollars.

13. A manufacturer of light aeroplanes exports to Australia. He estimates that for each aircraft his total costs will be £37 800 and his profit is 45 per cent of the total cost. Find the selling price of the aircraft (a) in pounds sterling, (b) in dollars and cents given that £1 = 1.64 Australian dollars.

14. A manufacturer issues a price list of his goods. The retailer when buying from the manufacturer receives a discount of 25 per cent off the list price. A customer buying these goods for cash at the list price from the retailer is allowed a discount of 5p in the pound. Calculate the percentage gross profit that the retailer will make when he sells these goods for cash.

(RSA, COS)

19.3 Stock-taking

Stock-taking is the counting and valuation of the stock held by a business. It is done at the end of the financial year to assist profit calculations. In general, by law, stock-taking must be done in such a way that goods are valued at cost price, unless for some unusual reason they have deteriorated so that their net realizable value is below their cost.

The owner of a small business may find it difficult to take stock for the purposes of calculating profits, since the end of a financial year often falls on a week-day when he has customers to serve and perhaps staff to supervise as well. A sole trader often therefore decides to do his stock-taking on a Sunday, or on his early-closing day, even though this is not the last day of the financial year. He then calculates his true closing-stock figure by taking into account any changes in the stock position that may occur in the two or three days between the stock-taking date and the end of the financial year.

Example

Tom Smith decides to postpone his stock-taking until Sunday April 5, although his financial year ends on March 31. He values the stock held on April 5 at £6 700. In the first five days of April the following events have occurred:

(a) takings at the tills totalled £455;
(b) goods priced at £160 were also sold on credit;
(c) goods costing £480 were delivered by suppliers;
(d) a customer returned goods originally sold to him for £30.

Tom has always fixed his selling prices by adding 25 per cent to his cost prices. What was his true closing-stock figure on March 31?

We must think very clearly about these figures. Taking (a) and (b) together, we see that

Sales during the first five days of April = £455 + £160
= £615

Since these goods were unsold on March 31 they were still in stock at that date and must be added back; but this adding back must be in terms of their cost price, not their selling price. To find out what the cost price was we must deduct one-fifth from £615 (since Tom's 25 per cent (one-quarter) mark-up is equivalent to a 20 per cent (one-fifth) profit margin).

$$£615 - (\tfrac{1}{5} \text{ of } £615) = £615 - £123$$
$$= £492$$

Valued at cost price, these items were worth £492; the stock in hand must therefore be *increased* by £492 to give the true March 31 figure.

The goods delivered by the suppliers (c) in the first five days of April were clearly not in stock on March 31 and must be *deducted* from the stock figure.

The goods returned by the customer (d) in early April (£30 at selling price) must also be *deducted* from the stock figure since they were not in stock on March 31. This deduction must be made.at cost price; £30 − ($\tfrac{1}{5}$ of £30) = £24.

Closing stock on April 5		£6 700
Add sales made in early April (at cost price)		£ 492
		£7 192
Deduct (at cost price)		
Goods taken into stock in early April	£480	
Returns in the same period	£24	
		£ 504
Closing stock at March 31		£6 688

If Tom Smith had valued his stock on Sunday March 29, the adjustments would have had to be made the opposite way. Sales made in the last two days of March would have been *deducted* from the March 29 figure (since they were lost to stock before the end of the year). Stock received and returns by customers would have been *added in* to give the true end-of-the-year position.

19.4 Exercises: Stock-taking Problems

In each of the exercises on page 146, show your working clearly.

1. R. and T. Traders are retailers whose financial year ended on Thursday March 31. They took stock on the following Saturday after closing their premises for the day, and then presented the accountant with the following figures:

	£
Stock at cost on Saturday April 2	3 180
Cost price of goods taken into stock from suppliers delivering on April 1 and 2	340
Sales on April 1 and 2 (cash takings)	88
Credit sales on these days	108
Credit note to customer for goods returned on April 1	32

R. and T. Traders add 33⅓ per cent to cost prices to fix their selling prices. Calculate the correct stock figure for March 31.

2. A. Trader began stock-taking for the year ending June 30 on that date. He did not complete the stock-taking until the close of business on July 4, when he ascertained the value of stock at cost price as £7 250.

The following information is available for the period July 1 to July 4:

	£
Purchases included in stock figure	£460
Sales of goods not included in stock figure	£725

Goods invoiced to a customer on June 30 at £120, but held in the factory pending instructions as to delivery, were included in the stock figure at cost price. The margin of gross profit on sales is calculated at 25 per cent.

Draw up a statement to show the correct value of stock at cost price on June 30.

3. R. Marshall did his stock-taking on Sunday December 27, although the financial year did not end until December 31. He valued his stock at that date at £12 725. Records for the last few days of December were as follows:

	£
Sales in cash	895
Stock received from suppliers at cost	1 055
Sales on credit	585
Returns by customers (at selling price)	60
Returns to suppliers (at cost price)	48
A 250-litre drum of paraffin oil leaked in a shed where dried goods were also stored. This stock had to be thrown away. Value (at cost)	128
The proprietor took home stock (cost price)	12

Marshall adds 50 per cent to cost prices to find his selling prices. Calculate the stock figure as at December 31.

4. From the following information calculate the value of R. Butler's stock on September 30:

	£
September 1 stock (at cost)	1 300
Purchases during month	15 000
Sales during month	20 000
Sales returns during month	800
Goods taken by Butler (selling price)	400

Gross profit is 20 per cent on selling price.

5. A. Draper began to take stock at 5 p.m. on Saturday December 28. He used cost price as the most suitable valuation. By the time the shop reopened on Monday December 30, he knew that the value of the stock in hand was £7 280.

On that day and the next day new stock arrived (cost price = £240), and a customer returned goods sold to him in early December (invoice value = £300). Cash sales for the two days were £100 and £80 respectively, and credit sales were £200 and £220 respectively.

Draper always adds 20 per cent to cost price to fix his selling prices.

Adjust the stock-taking figure of £7 280 to allow for the movements of stock on the last two days of the year, and thus find the closing-stock figure for December 31.

19.5 Mental Arithmetic Exercises

1. $375 + 294 + 187 =$
2. $4\,725 \div 5 =$
3. $£385 + £42.50 + £217 =$
4. $0.75 \div 0.25 =$
5. $3\frac{1}{2} + 2\frac{3}{4} + 1\frac{5}{8} =$
6. What is 15 per cent of £2 750?
7. What will 7 metres of French fabric cost at 17.50 francs per metre?
8. What should be the selling price of items costing 50p each, to make a profit of 60 per cent?
9. What number is missing in the following? $2 : 3$ as $? : 12$
10. How many pfennigs are there in 23.54 Deutschemarks?
11. What profit shall I make, if I sell 85 articles which cost me £1.25 each for £1.45 each?
12. What is the average age of six students, four of whom are 16 and the other two are 19 years of age?
13. Change £4.50 to pesetas, if the rate of exchange is 184 pesetas to the pound.
14. What is the simple interest payable on £10 000 for 3 months at 12 per cent per annum?
15. A bed is bought on hire purchase for a deposit of £25 and twelve monthly instalments of £3.75 each. What was the total hire purchase price?

Unit Twenty

Gas and Electricity Charges

20.1 Gas Charges

Gas charges in the United Kingdom are based on the *therm*, a British unit of heat equal to 100 000 British Thermal Units (BTU). The following factors are taken into account when gas bills are calculated:

(*a*) **Tariffs.** Customers may be given a choice of tariff. For example, a family householder, using fairly large quantities of gas for central heating, hot-water system and cooking, might be offered a slightly cheaper tariff than a retirement pensioner in a small flat with very few gas appliances. A third tariff might be offered to an industrial user taking very large supplies. These tariffs are often given 'brand' names like Gold Tariff and Silver Tariff. These vary from region to region.

(*b*) **Consumption.** The quantity of gas used is measured in therms.

(*c*) **Charge per therm.** The price per therm varies from place to place according to the ease of supply, the type of gas available, and so on.

(*d*) **Standing charges.** Most gas boards make a minimum standing charge to customers, whether any gas is used or not. This is really to cover installation and maintenance charges, which can be very high with a product like gas which is explosive and potentially dangerous.

A typical calculation would therefore be:

$$\text{Standing charge (Gold Tariff)} = \pounds4.50$$
$$\text{Number of therms used} = 258$$
$$\text{Charge per therm} = 24.5\text{p}$$
$$\text{Total charge} = \pounds4.50 + (258 \times 24.5)\text{p}$$

$$
\begin{array}{r}
258 \\
\times\ 24.5 \\
\hline
129\ 0 \\
1\ 032\ 0 \\
5\ 160\ 0 \\
\hline
6\ 321.0
\end{array}
$$

$$= \pounds4.50 + \pounds63.21$$
$$= \pounds67.71$$

20.2 Exercises: Gas Charges

1. Work out the sums payable by the following domestic gas users on the Silver Tariff for gas supplied at a price of 24.5p per therm. Some of these customers have had appliances supplied on quarterly hire purchase, or have had services supplied during the quarter, and all pay a standing charge of £8.55 per quarter. (Answers to the nearest penny.)

	Name	Number of therms used	Hire purchase charges	Service charges
(a)	Mr Black	348	£8.52	—
(b)	Mr White	495	—	£4.35
(c)	Mr Green	286	—	£4.85
(d)	Mrs Gray	387	£7.36	—
(e)	Miss Brown	729	£6.42	£5.25
(f)	Mrs Potter	426	£14.25	—
(g)	Mrs Mason	186	—	—
(h)	Miss Smith	725	—	£7.86
(i)	Mr Cooper	129	£13.56	£3.40
(j)	Mr Carter	364	—	£2.50

2. Work out the gas bills for the following Gold Star Tariff customers, whose quarterly standing charge is £5.85 and who pay 27.5p per therm for all gas supplied. In addition, each customer pays the sum of £55.00 per quarter for central heating equipment. (Answers to the nearest penny.)

	Name	Number of therms used		Name	Number of therms used
(a)	Mr Tobin	865	(b)	Mr Troy	325
(c)	Mrs Tyler	473	(d)	Miss Vandyke	628
(e)	Lady Walter	724	(f)	Mr Waterman	524
(g)	Mrs Wass	380	(h)	Miss Webster	721
(i)	Mr Gooch	624	(j)	Mr Bryant	529

20.3 Electricity Charges

Electricity charges in the United Kingdom are based on the kilowatt-hour—the amount of electricity used by a one-kilowatt appliance run for one hour—usually called the unit of electricity.

Again, a variety of tariffs is available to suit the needs of different classes of customers. Generally speaking, the large user gets his electricity more cheaply, and the 'off-peak' consumer, who uses equipment like night storage heaters at times when the demand is small, is also given favourable rates.

Most kinds of domestic electrical equipment are sold by electricity boards on hire purchase terms, the quarterly instalments being added to the bill for electricity supplied. Similarly installation, re-wiring and service charges are usually added to the quarterly bill to avoid rendering separate accounts for small services. A standing charge is also levied on all supplies made. A typical calculation would therefore be:

$$\text{Number of units} = 2\ 846 \text{ at normal tariff (4.5p per unit)}$$
$$\text{plus } 7\ 255 \text{ at off-peak tariff (2.5p per unit)}$$

$$\text{Charge for units used} = (2\ 846 \times 4.5) + (7\ 255 \times 2.5)$$

```
          2 846
        ×   4.5
        ───────
        1 423 0
       11 384 0
       ────────
       12 807.0

          7 255
        ×   2.5
        ───────
        3 627 5
       14 510 0
       ────────
       18 137.5
```

$$= £128.07 + £181.38$$
$$= £309.45$$
$$\text{Add standing charge} = \quad £5.85$$
$$\text{Add hire purchase charges} = \quad £16.48$$
$$\text{Total charge} = £331.78$$

20.4 Exercises: Electricity Charges

1. Calculate the electricity charges for the following five customers, who are all on flat-rate charges of 4.5p per unit of electricity, after paying a standing charge of £6.50. Some of them also have hire purchase charges.

Name	Units used	Hire purchase charges
(a) R. Lucas	4 372	—
(b) P. Watt	2 856	£4.45
(c) M. Volta	1 972	£14.50
(d) M. Argent	3 814	£10.85
(e) P. Silver	6 528	£11.70

2. Calculate the electricity charges (to the nearest penny) for the following ten customers, each of whom pays on a dual-rate basis. The day-time units used are charged at a flat rate of 4.5p per unit, while those used at night are charged at a special off-peak rate of 2.65p per unit. There is a standing charge to all users of £8.25.

Name	Flat-rate units used	Off-peak units used	Hire purchase charges
(a) Mr Bennett	846	2 712	—
(b) Mrs Brahms	524	3 814	£4.50
(c) Mr Bentall	654	4 295	£12.85
(d) Mrs Bentham	726	2 368	£7.24
(e) Mr Bridge	814	7 165	—
(f) Mr Britton	1 916	8 194	—
(g) Mr Brooks	2 734	7 125	—
(h) Mr Brown	5 816	8 326	£9.25
(i) Mr Bray	2 972	4 271	£11.75
(j) Mrs Brabham	3 814	5 280	—

3. Calculate the electricity charges for the following heavy industrial users, who pay a fixed basic charge and then pay 2.5p per unit for an agreed quota of units. Electricity supplied over and above the quota is charged at 1.5p per unit.

Name of firm	Basic charge	Agreed quota	Total units used
(a) Bargains Ltd.	£42	10 000	72 000
(b) Dawes Chemical Ltd.	£56	15 000	48 000
(c) Hobsons Ltd.	£108	48 000	136 280
(d) Shaw and Son	£84	30 000	72 550
(e) Peters Ltd.	£72	72 000	126 000

Unit Twenty-one

Rates

21.1 Rateable Values

Rates are taxes paid by the residents of a district for services rendered by their local authority. These services include road repairs, drainage, sewerage, refuse collection, education and many others.

Rates are levied upon *fixed property* in the area — that is, upon houses, factories, shops, cinemas, offices and so on. The amount payable depends on the size of the property, its position and the services available. To decide the value of a property for rating purposes, the Inland Revenue Valuation Officer assesses the likely rent of the property should it be let by the owner at a given base date. This figure—the *gross value*—is up-dated every few years to ensure that it is representative of current prices for accommodation. The gross value is then reduced by a sum which represents the likely annual cost of repairs and redecorations payable by the owner, and the resulting figure is called the *rateable value*. A typical example might be

Dwelling-house with 3 bedrooms, 2 reception rooms, kitchen and bathroom:
Gross value   £375 per annum
Repairs   £90 per annum
Rateable value £285 per annum

The householder or other property owner has a right to appeal to a rates tribunal if he considers this figure unfair. If the tribunal agrees with him it may reduce the assessment, or it may over-rule his objection and confirm the valuation. From that time onwards the rateable value fixed will become the basis for the calculation of the rates payable on the property.

21.2 The Calculation of Rates Payable

Rates are fixed each year by the local authority on the basis of 'so many pence in the pound'. For example, the house mentioned in Section 21.1 which has a rateable value of £285 will bring in £2.85 if a 1p in the pound rate is levied, and a rate of 2p in the pound will cost its owner or occupier £2.85 × 2 = £5.70.

Example

A householder whose property has a rateable value of £285 is told that he must pay a rate of 41p in the pound. How much must he pay?

A rate of 1p in the pound will cost him £2.85
A rate of 41p in the pound costs £2.85 × 41

$$
\begin{array}{r}
2.85 \\
\times \quad 41 \\
\hline
2\,85 \\
114\,00 \\
\hline
\end{array}
$$

= £116.85   116.85

Sometimes a rate is more than £1 in the pound. The same householder, if a rate of £1.27 was levied, would have to pay as follows:

A rate of 127p in the pound costs £2.85 × 127

$$
\begin{array}{r}
2.85 \\
\times \quad 127 \\
\hline
19\,95 \\
57\,00 \\
285\,00 \\
\hline
361.95
\end{array}
$$

= £361.95

Local authorities know the total rateable value of properties in their areas. They can thus calculate what a penny rate will bring in from residents. The figures to be handled are often very large, but the calculation is simple.

Example

The property in Casterbridge is valued at £2 784 960. What will a penny rate bring in?

$$£2\,784\,960 \times \frac{1}{100}$$

$$= £27\,849.60$$

21.3 Exercises: Simple Rate Calculations

1. What will a rate of 1p in the pound cost the occupiers of the following properties?

   (a) House rated at £240   (b) Flat rated at £180
   (c) House rated at £385   (d) Shop rated at £520
   (e) Shop rated at £585   (f) Office rated at £620
   (g) Office rated at £680   (h) Factory rated at £2 750
   (i) Factory rated at £3 868   (j) Factory rated at £4 825

2. What will a rate of 42p in the pound cost each of the following ratepayers?

   (a) Householder whose house is rated at £420
   (b) Householder whose house is rated at £515
   (c) Retailer whose shop is rated at £625
   (d) Garage owner whose garage is rated at £1 150
   (e) Factory owner whose premises are rated at £4 360

3. Work out the rates payable on each of ten properties, if the rateable values and current level of rates are as follows:

(a) £270; 25p in the pound
(b) £320; 36p in the pound
(c) £485; 42p in the pound
(d) £650; 38p in the pound
(e) £720; 29p in the pound

(f) £1 425; £1.47 in the pound
(g) £1 864; £1.52 in the pound
(h) £1 750; £1.48 in the pound
(i) £2 380; £1.64 in the pound
(j) £2 650; £1.72 in the pound

4. Work out the yield of a penny rate in each of ten local authorities which have total property in their areas rated as follows:

(a) Capital City: £24 264 721
(b) Newtown: £13 495 840
(c) Freetown: £15 816 724

(d) Casterbridge: £18 724 368
(e) Benbow City: £16 328 527

5. Work out the total yield from the following towns whose aggregate rateable values are as shown, and whose rates are levied at the figures given in the second column.

(a) £14 472 650; 27p in the pound
(b) £17 565 480; 36p in the pound
(c) £26 815 540; 42p in the pound

(d) £38 727 660; 58p in the pound
(e) £55 494 720; 64p in the pound

21.4 Raising the Money for Services

Local government officers regularly need to calculate the rate necessary to finance a particular facility or service.

Example

A local authority has a proposal before it to build a municipal swimming pool at a cost of £450 000. The pool will then cost £10 000 per year to run, over and above any money collected as admission charges. This deficit must be found from the rates; the aggregate rateable value of all the property in the city is £22 500 000.

(a) What rate will be necessary to finance the building of the pool?

(b) What rate will be necessary each year to operate the pool?

The yield of a 1p rate is £22 500 000 ÷ 100

= £225 000

Rate necessary to provide the pool = $\dfrac{£450\ 000}{£225\ 000}$ (dividing the cost of the pool by the yield of a 1p rate)

= 2p rate

Rate necessary to operate the pool = $\dfrac{£10\ 000}{£225\ 000}$

= $\dfrac{2}{45}$p

= 0.044p

$$
\begin{array}{r}
0.044 \\
45\ )\overline{2.00} \\
1\ 80 \\
\hline
200
\end{array}
$$

Example

A local authority in a district where the aggregate rateable value of all properties is £48 516 200 authorizes services and new facilities at a total cost of £5 726 420. What rate must be levied (to the nearest 0.1p) to raise the necessary money?

$$\text{Rate to be levied} = \frac{\text{cost of services, etc.}}{\text{yield of 1p rate}}$$

$$= \frac{£5\ 726\ 420}{£485\ 162}$$

```
                    11.80
        485 162 ) 5 726 420
                  4 851 62
                   874 800
                   485 162
                   389 638 0
                   388 129 6
                     1 508 40
```

$$= 11.8\text{p in the pound}$$

21.5 Exercises: The Cost of Services

1. What rate in the pound will be necessary to build the following facilities?

	Facility	Cost of facility	Yield of 1p rate
(a)	Swimming pool	£210 000	£10 500
(b)	Buildings	£3 000	£150 000
(c)	Clinic	£21 750	£72 500
(d)	School	£108 000	£48 000
(e)	Town hall	£4 550 000	£650 000

2. What rate in the pound will be necessary to buy the following pieces of equipment, if the local authority area has an aggregate rateable value of £7 480 000?

   (a) Earth-mover costing £37 400
   (b) Muck-scraper costing £33 660
   (c) Dust cart costing £14 960
   (d) Sewage-treatment works costing £897 600
   (e) Coach costing £22 440

3. The following table lists sums of money which five local authorities have to raise, together with the yield of a penny rate for each authority. What rate in the pound must be fixed by each authority?

	Sum required	Yield of 1p rate
(a)	£640 000	£32 000
(b)	£3 680 000	£46 000
(c)	£680 000	£8 500
(d)	£1 512 000	£12 600
(e)	£292 400	£17 200

4. In a certain town a penny rate yields £47 256. What will a rate of 55p in the pound bring in? What rate must be levied (correct to 0.01p) to build a library costing £84 726?

5. A new bridge is estimated to cost £5 480 000. Half the cost is to be paid out of the city rates and the rest will be financed by a toll on vehicles using the bridge. What rate (to the nearest 0.1p) must be levied to pay for it, if the rateable value of property in the city is £26 500 000?

6. In a certain borough a penny rate raises £29 276. The rate for the year is 55p in the pound. How much will the council have altogether to spend on its services? A new branch library is to cost £84 250. What rate (to the nearest 0.1p) is needed to raise this amount?

7. In a rural area a penny rate raises £42 120. Rates are fixed at 65p in the pound. How much will the council raise? What rate (to the nearest 0.1p) is needed to buy a fleet of 5 dust carts at £18 270 each?

8. In a certain borough a penny rate raises £42 850. The rate for the year is 31p in the pound. How much will the council have altogether to spend on its services? The cost of a recreation ground is estimated to be £185 500. What rate (to the nearest 0.1p) is needed to raise this amount?

Unit Twenty-two

Depreciation

22.1 What is Depreciation?

Depreciation is the reduction in value of a piece of property or equipment which results from 'fair wear and tear'. It is an everyday experience: anyone who owns a motor vehicle knows that he is lucky if it will last longer than a few years of steady use. As time goes on it will begin to become unreliable; it will no longer be as safe as it should be, and the cost of repairs will soar. Eventually he will replace it by a new machine.

In business it is usual to *write down* the value of all assets year by year, that is, to reduce their value on the book-keeping records so that the decline is recorded as a loss suffered by the business.

There are two chief methods of writing off depreciation of equipment. These are:

(a) the *equal-instalment method* (sometimes called the *straight-line method*), and

(b) the *diminishing-balance method*.

22.2 The Equal-instalment Method

As the name of this method implies, the same amount of money is written off the value of the asset every year.

The sum to be written off each year, the *annual depreciation charge*, depends on the cost of the asset when bought, the length of its useful life and its *residual value*, that is, the amount for which it can be sold when it is no longer of use to the business. This charge is calculated by the use of a formula:

$$Annual\ depreciation\ charge = \frac{cost\ price\ of\ the\ asset\ -\ residual\ value}{estimated\ lifetime\ in\ years}$$

Example

A machine costs £10 000, and a further £2 500 is needed to erect it into position and to install access facilities for the raw materials it is to process. It is estimated that it will have a working life of ten years, and that at the end of that time it will have a scrap value of £1 500. Using the formula, we have

$$Annual\ depreciation\ charge = \frac{£12\ 500\ -\ £1\ 500}{10} = £1\ 100$$

Over the years the value of the machine will decrease as follows:

		£
Year 1:	Machine cost	10 000
	Installation, etc.	2 500
		12 500
	Depreciation	1 100
Year 2:	Value at start	11 400
	Depreciation	1 100
		10 300
	and so on over the years until	
Year 10:	Value at start	2 600
	Depreciation	1 100
		£1 500

22.3 Exercises: Depreciation by the Equal-instalment Method

1. Calculate the annual depreciation charge for each of the following assets, using the equal-instalment method:

	Asset	Cost price	Scrap value	Working life (years)
(a)	Motor car	£6 800	£800	4
(b)	Heavy lorry	£22 500	£5 500	5
(c)	Typewriter	£520	£120	8
(d)	Drilling machine	£2 380	£175	15
(e)	Scraping machine	£4 750	£500	10
(f)	Bulldozer	£38 000	£5 000	8
(g)	Road tanker	£45 800	£7 500	5
(h)	Tug	£286 000	£36 000	8
(i)	Computer	£15 000	£1 500	5
(j)	Container crane	£750 000	£5 000	20

2. Mills Ltd. purchased a machine for £1 500 on January 1 19 . . Its probable working life was estimated at ten years and its probable scrap value at the end of that time as £200. It was decided to write off depreciation by equal instalments over the ten years. Show the calculation of the annual instalment of depreciation.

3. Thompson Ltd. purchased a machine for £2 800 on January 1 19 . . Its probable working life was estimated at eight years and its probable scrap value at the end of that time as £400. It was decided to write off depreciation by equal instalments over the eight years. Calculate the annual instalment and show how the machine fell in value over the first three years of its life.

4. T. Brown started business on January 1 19 .. and on that date purchased machinery for £36 000. He decided to close his books each year at December 31 and to depreciate machinery on the fixed-instalment method, assuming a scrap value of nil at the end of the life of the machines, which is estimated to be ten years.

On July 1 of the following year he purchased another machine for £5 600. Show the amounts written off at the end of the first year, and at the end of the second year.

5. Some new machinery in a factory was purchased for £284 600. In addition it cost £10 400 to erect into position. Its estimated life is 15 years and its residual value £35 000. Calculate the annual depreciation charge, based on the equal-instalment method, correct to the nearest £1.

22.4 The Diminishing-balance Method

Under the diminishing-balance method a fixed percentage is written off each year from the value of the asset at the start of that year. For example, the depreciation percentage might be agreed at 20 per cent and one-fifth of the diminishing value of the asset would then be written off each year. This is a much larger percentage of the value of the asset than is at first written off under the equal-instalment method. The actual deductions, however, only come to about the same amount over the full lifetime of the asset, because the percentage deduction is being made only on the diminishing balance, and consequently the actual sum written off gets less every year.

If we consider the example discussed in Section 22.2, and apply the diminishing-balance method, assuming a 20 per cent depreciation each year, we have:

		£
Year 1:	Machine cost	10 000
	Installation, etc.	2 500
		12 500
	Depreciation at 20% $(=\frac{1}{5})$	2 500
Year 2:	Value at start	10 000
	Depreciation	2 000
Year 3:	Value at start	8 000
	Depreciation	1 600
		6 400
	and so on over the years until	
Year 10:	Value at start	1 678
	Depreciation	336
		£1 342

One argument in favour of this method of calculating depreciation is that the fall in the depreciation deducted from the asset is offset by the rise in the cost of repairs as the asset wears out, so that the annual cost of both to the business is about even, taking one year with another.

22.5 Exercises: Depreciation by the Diminishing-balance Method

In these exercises, carry out your calculations to the nearest £1.

1. Show the depreciation each year on the diminishing-balance method, and the value at the end of each year, for the first three years of the life of each of the following assets:

	Cost on January 1, Year 1	Rate of depreciation
(a)	£800	20%
(b)	£2 500	25%
(c)	£4 800	25%
(d)	£6 650	$33\frac{1}{3}\%$
(e)	£7 280	40%

2. The assets in the following table were not purchased at the start of the financial year, which begins on January 1, and only a fair proportion of the depreciation is therefore to be deducted in the first year. Then in subsequent years a full year's depreciation will be deducted. Show the calculation for the depreciation, and the annual value of the asset on December 31 after depreciation, for each of the first three years for each asset.

	Date of purchase, Year 1	Cost price	Rate of depreciation
(a)	July 1	£800	20%
(b)	July 1	£1 600	25%
(c)	October 1	£4 500	25%
(d)	October 1	£7 000	$33\frac{1}{3}\%$
(e)	April 1	£12 500	40%

3. On January 1 19.. Marshall Bros. bought furniture and fittings for £1 200 and on April 1 19 . ., one year later, the same firm bought additional furniture for £400. At the end of each year depreciation is provided for at the rate of 25 per cent per annum by the diminishing-balance method. Show the Furniture and Fittings calculation for the first two financial years.

4. On January 1, 19.. P. Walker Ltd. bought a machine for £1 800. It was decided to write off depreciation by the diminishing-balance method, at 25 per cent per annum. Show the Machinery calculation for the first two years.

5. John Mainway started business as a haulage contractor on January 1, 19 . . and the same day he bought a new lorry for £22 000. His business expanded, and on July 1 of the *following* year he purchased a second lorry for £24 500. On October 1 of the next year (year three) he purchased a third lorry, also for £24 500. Show the calculation for depreciation and the value of the lorries on his books at December 31 for each year of his first three years in business. The rate of depreciation is 20 per cent on the diminishing-balance method.

Unit Twenty-three
Simple Transport Calculations

23.1 Running a Car

Practically every business depends to some extent on motor transport, and the money spent on running a fleet of vehicles is a very important part of business costs.

The chief costs of a transport department are the cost of buying the vehicles and their tyres, fuel and oil, and the necessary maintenance charges. There are also certain important taxes, particularly the Road Fund licence charges, Value Added Tax on vehicles and spares and on all maintenance services, and the tax on new private cars. By law, a driver must be insured against injury to other people (including his passengers) and damage to other people's property: this is the so-called *third-party insurance*. *Comprehensive insurance* policies offer wider cover, including also injury to the driver himself and loss of or damage to his own vehicle.

Example

At the beginning of the year a businessman bought a car for £5 800. The tax for the year was £70 and the insurance premium was £145. Petrol cost 35p per litre and the car (which averaged 10 kilometres per litre) was driven a total of 25 000 kilometres during the year. It used 1 litre of oil (costing £1.10) per 1 000 kilometres and servicing charges were £168. At the end of the year the car was sold for 25 per cent less than it cost. Calculate (a) the total cost of the year's motoring, and (b) the average cost per kilometre, correct to the nearest 0.1p.

		£
(a) Original cost of car		5 800
Tax		70
Insurance		145

$$\text{Petrol} = \frac{25\ 000}{10} \times 35 \text{ pence}$$

		£
= 2 500 × 35 pence = £25 × 35 =		875
Oil = 25 × £1.10 = £25 + £2.50 =		27.50
Servicing charges		168
	Total cost	7 085.50
Less money recovered on sale of vehicle		
= £5 800 − £1 450 =		4 350
	Cost for year's motoring	£2 735.50

(b) Cost per kilometre $= \dfrac{£2\,735.50}{25\,000}$

$\qquad\qquad\qquad\quad = \dfrac{£2.7355}{25}$

$\qquad\qquad\qquad\quad = \dfrac{273.55}{25}$ pence

$\qquad\qquad\qquad\quad = 10.94$ pence

$\qquad\qquad\qquad\quad = 10.9$p per kilometre

23.2 Exercises: Motor Vehicle Expenses

1. At the beginning of the year, a businessman bought a car for £5 610. The tax for the year was £70 and the insurance premium was £162. Petrol cost 35p per litre and the car (which averaged 12 kilometres per litre) was driven a total of 18 000 kilometres during the year. It used 1 litre of oil (costing £1.08) per 1 000 kilometres. At the end of the year the car was sold for $33\frac{1}{3}$ per cent less than it cost. Calculate (a) the total cost of the year's motoring, and (b) the average cost per kilometre, correct to the nearest 0.1p.

2. At the beginning of the year, a businessman bought a car for £7 600. The tax for the year was £70 and the insurance premium was £135. Petrol cost 36p per litre and the car (which averaged 8 kilometres per litre) was driven a total of 20 000 kilometres during the year. It used 1 litre of oil (costing £1.12) per 1 000 kilometres. At the end of the year the car was sold for 25 per cent less than it cost. Calculate (a) the total cost of the year's motoring, and (b) the average cost per kilometre, correct to the nearest 0.1p.

3. The expenses of running a car for one year were as follows:
   (i) tax £70
   (ii) insurance £154
   (iii) depreciation £685
   (iv) maintenance £185
   During the year the owner travelled 18 400 kilometres with an average petrol consumption of 8 kilometres per litre. If the cost of petrol was 34.5 pence per litre calculate (a) the total cost of the year's motoring, and (b) the average cost per kilometre in pence correct to one tenth of a penny.

(RSA adapted)

4. The expenses of running a car for one year were as follows:
   (i) tax £70
   (ii) insurance £148
   (iii) depreciation £980
   (iv) maintenance £188

During the year the owner travelled 25 000 kilometres with an average petrol consumption of 10 kilometres per litre. If the cost of petrol was 38 pence per litre calculate (*a*) the total cost of the year's motoring, and (*b*) the average cost per kilometre in pence correct to one tenth of a penny.

(RSA adapted)

5. Certain annual expenses of owning a motor car are listed below:

	£
Road fund licence	70.00
Insurance	158.00
Servicing and repairs	165.20
Petrol	574.20
Garage rent	156.00

(*a*) Express the insurance figure above as a percentage of the total listed expenses (correct to 1 decimal place).

(*b*) If the petrol costs 36 pence per litre how many litres are used per year?

(*c*) The Servicing and Repairs expenses are in the ratio 4 : 3. How much was spent on repairs?

(RSA adapted)

23.3 Speed, Time and Distance

Many business calculations involve problems of speed, time and distance. We may need, for example, to plan journeys, by road, rail, sea and air. We may have to draw up timetables of arrivals and departures, or to calculate turn-round times for ships and aircraft.

The basis of many of these calculations is the simple relationship between speed, time and distance:

Distance travelled = the speed of travel multiplied by the time taken

This is usually written as $D = S \times T$, or simply

$$D = ST$$

For example, if I travel at 40 kilometres per hour for 2 hours I shall cover a distance of

$$D = ST$$
$$= 40 \times 2$$
$$= 80 \text{ kilometres}$$

We can put this relationship in another way by saying that

speed = the distance travelled divided by the time taken

or

$$S = \frac{D}{T}$$

For example, if an aircraft flies from London to Gibraltar, a distance of 1 800 kilometres, in 2 hours its speed is given by

$$S = \frac{1\ 800}{2}$$

$$= \underline{900 \text{ kilometres per hour}}$$

We have still another alternative: we can say that

the time taken on a journey = the distance travelled divided by the speed

or

$$T = \frac{D}{S}$$

For example a motor car will travel 300 kilometres at a speed of 50 kilometres per hour in a time given by

$$T = \frac{D}{S}$$

$$= \frac{300}{50}$$

$$= \underline{6 \text{ hours}}$$

In each of these three statements of the relationship the value of the speed S refers to the *average* speed, since there are very few journeys which are completed at the same speed from start to finish.

Example

An aeroplane flies a distance of 1 800 kilometres in $2\frac{1}{2}$ hours. (*a*) What is its speed in kilometres per hour? (*b*) What is its speed in metres per second?

(*a*)

$$S = \frac{D}{T}$$

$$= \frac{1\ 800}{2\frac{1}{2}}$$

$$= \frac{\cancel{1\ 800}^{360} \times 2}{\cancel{5}_1}$$

$$= \underline{720 \text{ kilometres per hour}}$$

(*b*) To change the units of this speed to metres per second is simple. First we change the kilometres to metres—which means we must multiply by 1 000. Then we change the hours to seconds, which means we must divide by 60 × 60 (60 minutes in 1 hour and 60 seconds in 1 minute). So

$$\text{Speed in metres per second} = \frac{\cancel{720}^{12} \cancel{20}^{20} \times 1\ 000}{\cancel{60}_1 \times \cancel{60}_1}$$

$$= \underline{200 \text{ metres per second}}$$

Example

A motorist travels 250 kilometres at 60 km/h and then a further 150 kilometres at 80 km/h. (*a*) How long did the whole journey take? (*b*) What was his average speed for the whole journey?

(Answer correct to nearest kilometre per hour.)

(*a*) Part 1 of the journey: $T = \dfrac{D}{S} = \dfrac{250}{60} = 4\frac{1}{6}$ hours

Part 2 of the journey: $T = \dfrac{D}{S} = \dfrac{150}{80} = 1\frac{7}{8}$ hours

$$
\begin{aligned}
\text{Total time} &= 4\tfrac{1}{6} + 1\tfrac{7}{8} \text{ hours} \\
&= 5\frac{4 + 21}{24} \text{ hours} \\
&= 5\frac{25}{24} \text{ hours} \\
&= 6\frac{1}{24} \text{ hours} \\
&= 6 \text{ hours } 2\tfrac{1}{2} \text{ minutes}
\end{aligned}
$$

(*b*) Average speed for whole journey $= \dfrac{D}{T} = \dfrac{400}{6\frac{1}{24}}$ km/h

$$= \frac{\cancel{400}^{80}}{\cancel{145}_{29}} \times 24$$

$$= \frac{1\,920}{29}$$

$$= 66 \text{ km/h}$$

$$
\begin{array}{r}
66.2 \\
29\,\overline{)\,1\,920} \\
1\,74 \\
\hline
180 \\
174 \\
\hline
60
\end{array}
$$

23.4 Exercises: Speed, Time and Distance

1. An aeroplane flies a distance of 3 840 kilometres in 6 hours. What is its average speed (*a*) in kilometres per hour, and (*b*) in metres per second? (Answer correct to the nearest metre.)

2. An aeroplane flies a distance of 2 700 kilometres in $4\frac{1}{2}$ hours. What is its average speed (*a*) in kilometres per hour, and (*b*) in metres per second? (Answer correct to the nearest metre.)

3. A cyclist travelled for $4\frac{1}{2}$ hours at an average speed of 16 km/h and then for $3\frac{1}{2}$ hours at an average speed of 20 km/h. Find (*a*) the total distance he covered, and (*b*) his average speed for the whole journey.

4. A motorist travelled for $2\frac{1}{2}$ hours at an average speed of 50 km/h. He then joined the motorway and for $3\frac{1}{2}$ hours averaged 92 km/h. Find (*a*) the total distance covered, and (*b*) the average speed for the whole journey.

5. A cyclist travelled 126 kilometres at an average speed of 36 km/h, and a further 80 kilometres at an average speed of 24 km/h. Find his average speed for the whole journey in kilometres per hour. Give the answer correct to one decimal place. (RSA)

6. A cyclist travelled 204 kilometres at an average speed of 24 km/h, and a further 120 kilometres at an average speed of 30 km/h. Find his average speed for the whole journey in kilometres per hour. Give the answer correct to one decimal place. (RSA)

7. A motor race consists of 2 laps, each lap being 34 kilometres. What is the total race time in minutes of a motorist who completes the first lap at 160 km/h and the second lap at 10 km/h faster? (RSA)

8. A motor race consists of 2 laps, each lap being 54 kilometres. What is the total race time in minutes of a motorist who completes the first lap at 144 km/h and the second lap at 18 km/h faster? (RSA)

Unit Twenty-four

Commission

24.1 What is Commission?

Commission is money paid to an employee or an agent of a business as a reward for services rendered. The commission usually takes the form of a payment based on a certain percentage of the value of the goods sold or purchased or of the value of the services arranged. The following methods of fixing commission payments are the most usual:

(*a*) **Basic salary plus straight commission.** Often used for rewarding an employee salesman, who is paid a basic wage which will offer a bare living, and a commission in addition which is the same for every unit he sells. This will enable him to achieve really substantial earnings if he works hard and builds up a lively connexion with customers.

(*b*) **Quantity commissions and sales commissions.** A quantity commission is paid on the *number* of units sold or orders taken; for instance, a vacuum cleaner salesman might get a commission of £1 on every vacuum cleaner he sells. A sales commission is paid on the *value* of the sales made; thus a confectionery salesman's commission might be fixed at 5 per cent of the value of his sales.

(*c*) **Sales quotas and bonuses.** Many retail organizations pay a basic salary to employees who are then allocated a *quota* of sales which they are expected to achieve each week. If they sell more than this quota they are paid a commission or *bonus* on the extra sales.

(*d*) **Graduated commissions.** A *graduated commission* increases with the quantity sold, so that a really high reward can be earned by the very best salesmen. A freezer salesman might earn a $2\frac{1}{2}$ per cent commission on the first five machines sold, then a 5 per cent commission on the next ten sold and a 10 per cent commission on any further sales.

(*e*) **Brokerage.** A *broker* is someone who arranges services for other people who do not themselves have the necessary expert knowledge. A Lloyd's broker for instance, arranges insurance policies with the underwriters of Lloyd's of London. A stockbroker buys and sells stocks and shares on the Stock Exchange, and metal brokers and wool brokers operate on the metal and wool exchanges. The reward paid for these services is called *brokerage*, and the rate at which brokerage is to be charged is often laid down by the governing body of the institution concerned, for example the Stock Exchange Council (see also Section 27.6).

24.2 Calculating Commission

When an employee is paid a basic salary plus a straight commission—either on each unit sold, or on the value of his sales—the calculation of his earnings is simple.

Example

Mr. Jones is paid a salary of £60 a month plus a 2 per cent commission on sales. In January he sells goods valued at £22 780. What were his earnings for the month?

$$\text{Earnings} = \text{salary} + \text{commission}$$
$$= £60 + (\tfrac{2}{100} \times £22\,780)$$
$$= £60 + £455.60$$
$$= £515.60$$

Where the quota system is used the commission is not payable until the quota has been sold. Accordingly the quota must be deducted from the total sales and the commission is calculated on the remainder.

Example

A retailer's assistant is paid a salary of £48.50 weekly, for which he is expected to achieve a sales quota of £85. After selling this quota he receives a commission of 2p in the £1 on all other sales. In a certain week he sold goods valued at £215. What were his total earnings?

$$\text{Earnings} = \text{salary} + \text{commission}$$
$$= £48.50 + (\tfrac{2}{100} \times \text{sales in excess of the quota})$$
$$= £48.50 + [\tfrac{2}{100} \times (£215 - £85)]$$
$$= £48.50 + (\tfrac{2}{100} \times £130)$$
$$= £48.50 + £2.60$$
$$= £51.10$$

Where the commission is a graduated commission, the calculation must take into account the arrangements agreed as to the varying rates of commission.

Example

An auctioneer is to be paid a basic fee of £150 for arranging the sale of a valuable herd of livestock. In addition he will be paid rates of commission as follows:

> on the first £5,000, no commission;
> from £5 000 to £15 000, 5% commission;
> from £15 000 to £35 000, 10% commission;
> above £35 000, 20% commission.

The sale realizes £37 110. What will his total earnings be?

	£
Basic fee =	150.00
Commission on the first £5 000 =	0.00
Commission on £5 000–£15 000 (5% × £10 000) =	500.00
Commission on £15 000–£35 000 (10% × £20 000) =	2 000.00
Commission on £35 000–£37 110 (20% × £2 110) =	422.00
	£3 072.00

24.3 Exercises: Straight and Graduated Commissions

1. Work out the following commissions:
   - (a) 10% on £2 880
   - (b) 10% on £4 250
   - (c) 5% on £4 840
   - (d) 5% on £5 120
   - (e) 5% on £7 860
   - (f) 5% on £9 220
   - (g) $2\frac{1}{2}$% on £3 440
   - (h) $2\frac{1}{2}$% on £1 880
   - (i) $2\frac{1}{2}$% on £5 280
   - (j) $2\frac{1}{2}$% on £1 760

2. Work out the following commissions:
   - (a) £1.50 per unit; 36 units sold
   - (b) £3.25 per unit; 13 units sold
   - (c) £1.40 per unit; 45 units sold
   - (d) £1.85 per unit; 28 units sold
   - (e) £4.50 per unit; 18 units sold
   - (f) 15p per unit; 842 units sold
   - (g) 30p per unit; 4 800 units sold
   - (h) 27p per unit; 955 units sold
   - (i) 21p per unit; 2 755 units sold
   - (j) £1.55 per unit; 61 units sold

3. Each of the staff of a store earns a basic salary plus a commission on all sales above a certain quota. The basic salary, quota and rate of commission fixed for five employees are shown in the following table, together with their actual sales during one particular week. Work out the total earnings of each employee for the week.

	Basic salary	Quota	Commission	Actual sales
(a)	£68.50	£500	5%	£950
(b)	£62.50	£650	5%	£1 250
(c)	£71.80	£1 000	6%	£1 540
(d)	£69.50	£1 500	6%	£1 966
(e)	£64.75	£1 600	10%	£2 380

4. Each of the salesmen in the following table receives a basic wage plus a small commission on sales up to a certain limit, and commission at a higher rate on sales above this limit. What will each salesman earn?

	Basic wage	Rate of commission	Limit	Higher rate of commission	Actual sales
(a)	£35.00	1%	£10 000	3%	£17 000
(b)	£40.00	1%	£8 000	4%	£12 000
(c)	£45.00	$1\frac{1}{2}$%	£12 000	5%	£23 500
(d)	£44.00	2%	£15 000	5%	£28 000
(e)	£48.00	2%	£20 000	5%	£45 000

5. A traveller receives a salary of £4 600 per year plus a commission of $2\frac{1}{2}$ per cent on all sales over £15 000. In addition he receives an extra bonus of $1\frac{1}{4}$ per cent on sales over £100 000. If his sales for a year were £145 600, what was his total income? (RSA adapted)

6. An auctioneer is paid a fee of £100 and a commission of 1 per cent on all sales up to £1 500, after which he earns 2 per cent commission. If sales totalled £17 580, what were his earnings?

7. Miss A receives a weekly wage of £80, plus commission of 5p in the pound on all the cosmetics she sells. Miss B's weekly wage is £65, but her commission is 10p in the pound on her sales.
   (a) Find the total income for each person if each sold £500 of goods in one week.
   (b) Another week Miss B's commission is £40 more than Miss A's commission, although both sold equal amounts of cosmetics. How much did each person sell during that week? (RSA adapted)

Unit Twenty-five

Wages and Wage Systems

25.1 Wages

Wages are the reward for labour. The word 'salary' has exactly the same meaning, but in business life the term *wages* is commonly used to describe money paid to hourly- or weekly-paid employees and *salary* is more usually used for people who are paid each month.

Wages calculations, as far as the individual employee is concerned, are a simple matter; he has only to calculate the amount due to him less any deductions for tax, superannuation, trade union contributions and so on. The employer, however, must not only calculate the amount due to each individual employee, he must also find the total sums due to the Inland Revenue (tax) and National Insurance authorities, to trade unions and charities to which employees contribute and to other bodies.

25.2 The Calculation of Gross Wages

Gross wages are the total earnings of an employee. *Net wages* are the 'clear' or 'clean' wages after all tax, pension and other payments have been deducted. Naturally these deductions vary from time to time and from country to country, so that the information given in this Unit must be adapted by those using this book in countries other than the United Kingdom.

Gross wages require no calculation if the wage payable is fixed as a weekly or monthly sum of money. If payment is made on any other principles, for example on an hourly basis with varying rates of overtime pay, or on a basic-salary-plus-commission basis, then it will be necessary to work out each employee's earnings according to his contract of service. Very often this will involve the calculation of hours worked by the employee from a *clock card* (Fig. 25.1) which he has punched on each arrival and departure.

Example

Using the employee's card shown in Fig. 25.1 calculate the gross wages for employee No. 172, Mr G. Morris, for the week commencing April 27. His rate of pay is £1.70 per hour and his normal working day is $7\frac{1}{2}$ hours.

The total hours worked each day must be calculated from the times stamped on the card: these have been already written in on Fig. 25.1. The hours of overtime are calculated by subtracting the normal daily hours from the hours actually worked: for instance, on Tuesday

$$9 \text{ hours } - 7\frac{1}{2} \text{ hours } = 1\frac{1}{2} \text{ hours overtime}$$

Name: G. Morris				Week no. 4		
No. 172				Commencing: 27 April		

Day		In	Out	In	Out	Total	Extra overtime hours
Monday	a.m.	8.30				$7\frac{1}{2}$	
	p.m.		12.30	1.30	5.01		
Tuesday	a.m.	8.30				9	$\frac{3}{4}$
	p.m.		12.31	1.31	6.30		
Wednesday	a.m.	6.30				$10\frac{1}{2}$	$1\frac{1}{2}$
	p.m.		12.30	1.30	6.00		
Thursday	a.m.	8.00				$8\frac{1}{2}$	$\frac{1}{2}$
	p.m.		12.30	1.31	5.30		
Friday	a.m.	8.30				8	$\frac{1}{4}$
	p.m.		12.30	1.30	5.30		
Saturday	a.m.	8.00				6	6
	p.m.		2.00				
Sunday	a.m.					$2\frac{1}{2}$	$2\frac{1}{2}$
	p.m.			2.00	4.30		
Overtime at rate of		Total				52	$11\frac{1}{2}$
Weekday $1\frac{1}{2}$		Add overtime				$11\frac{1}{2}$	
Weekends 2							
		Grand total				$63\frac{1}{2}$	

Fig. 25.1 A clock card

As the clock card states in the lower left-hand corner, weekday overtime is paid at the rate of 'time and a half', so we can count an extra $1\frac{1}{2} \times \frac{1}{2} = \frac{3}{4}$ hour for Tuesday's overtime. Weekend working is paid at 'double time'; for the 6 hours worked on Saturday, therefore, we count an additional 6 hours.

Adding up all the working hours, and the extra overtime hours, the total hours to be paid for are $63\frac{1}{2}$ as the card shows, and this will mean that the gross wages are

$$63\frac{1}{2} \times £1.70$$

```
         1.70
  ×        63
      ─────────
         5 10
       102 00
      ─────────
       107.10
  +      .85  (½ of £1.70)
      ─────────
      £107.95
```

$= £107.95$

25.3 A Ready-reckoner

In wages calculations it is often convenient to use a ready-reckoner. This is a book which contains the results of thousands of calculations. For example Table 25.1 shows the kind of page that would be found in any ready-reckoner, calculating £1.70. The wages clerk working out Mr Morris's earnings in the last example would not do the arithmetical calculation but would turn to this page, which shows that $63 \times £1.70 = £107.10$. Payment for the odd half-hour would be 85p. The total would therefore be £107.95, which is the same result as that of our calculation.

25.4 Exercises: Wages Calculations

1. Calculate the gross wages for the ten staff whose hours of work, extra hours of overtime and rates of pay are as follows:

(Overtime is paid at normal rates.)

	Name	Normal hours worked	Hours of overtime worked	Rate per hour (pence)
(a)	Mr A	54	$10\frac{1}{2}$	185
(b)	Mr B	44	2	195
(c)	Mrs C	$37\frac{1}{2}$	—	155
(d)	Mr D	56	12	165
(e)	Miss E	48	6	180
(f)	Mr Z	38	—	135
(g)	Mr Y	44	3	280
(h)	Mr X	62	18	172
(i)	Mrs W	48	5	165
(j)	Miss V	42	2	160

2. Calculate the gross pay of the ten employees whose working hours and rates of pay are as follows:

	Name	Normal hours	Overtime hours	Overtime rate	Normal pay rate (pence)
(a)	Mr K	$37\frac{1}{2}$	$5\frac{1}{2}$	Time and a half	180
(b)	Mr L	40	6	Double time	185
(c)	Miss M	40	4	Time and a half	165
(d)	Miss N	40	—	—	155
(e)	Mrs O	$37\frac{1}{2}$	$7\frac{1}{2}$	Double time	280

	Name	Normal hours	Overtime hours	Overtime rate	Normal pay rate (pence)
(f)	Miss P	35	15	Double time	190
(g)	Mr Q	38	22	Double time	185
(h)	Mr R	40	20	Time and a half	145
(i)	Mr S	40	16	Double time	165
(j)	Mr T	38	8	Double time	280

3. The following table shows the hourly rates of pay for three workmen together with the number of hours of overtime worked by each of them in one week. The normal working week is 40 hours and overtime is paid at time plus a quarter. Calculate the total amount payable to each of the three men.

	Hourly rate	Hours overtime
A	172p	6
B	168p	8
C	160p	7

(RSA COS)

4. Using the ready-reckoner page shown in Table 25.1, calculate the gross wages of each of ten employees, paid at a rate of £1.70 per hour, who worked the following hours:

(a) 42 hours

(b) 46 hours

(c) 58 hours

(d) 72 hours

(e) $39\frac{1}{2}$ hours

(f) $47\frac{1}{2}$ hours

(g) $53\frac{1}{4}$ hours

(h) $65\frac{1}{4}$ hours

(i) $77\frac{1}{4}$ hours

(j) $81\frac{1}{2}$ hours

25.5 Deductions from Wages

In most countries deductions of some sort are made from wages. There are three main types of deduction. *Statutory deductions* are deductions required by law. The chief of these are tax deductions, usually made (in the United Kingdom) under the Pay As You Earn (PAYE) income tax scheme, and the National Insurance contributions which employees pay in order to provide certain allowances such as retirement pensions, sickness and unemployment benefits and the health services. *Compulsory deductions* are made for contributions towards company pension schemes which employees are obliged to

Table 25.1 A page from a ready-reckoner

(0.588 = 1£)   **£1.70**

1	1.70	41	69.70	81	137.70	121	205.70	161	273.70
2	3.40	42	71.40	82	139.40	122	207.40	162	275.40
3	5.10	43	73.10	83	141.10	123	209.10	163	277.10
4	6.80	44	74.80	84	142.80	124	210.80	164	278.80
5	8.50	45	76.50	85	144.50	125	212.50	165	280.50
6	10.20	46	78.20	86	146.20	126	214.20	166	282.20
7	11.90	47	79.90	87	147.90	127	215.90	167	283.90
8	13.60	48	81.60	88	149.60	128	217.60	168	285.60
9	15.30	49	83.30	89	151.30	129	219.30	169	287.30
10	17.00	50	85.00	90	153.00	130	221.00	170	289.00
11	18.70	51	86.70	91	154.70	131	222.70	171	290.70
12	20.40	52	88.40	92	156.40	132	224.40	172	292.40
13	22.10	53	90.10	93	158.10	133	226.10	173	294.10
14	23.80	54	91.80	94	159.80	134	227.80	174	295.80
15	25.50	55	93.50	95	161.50	135	229.50	175	297.50
16	27.20	56	95.20	96	163.20	136	231.20	176	299.20
17	28.90	57	96.90	97	164.90	137	232.90	177	300.90
18	30.60	58	98.60	98	166.60	138	234.60	178	302.60
19	32.30	59	100.30	99	168.30	139	236.30	179	304.30
20	34.00	60	102.00	100	170.00	140	238.00	180	306.00
21	35.70	61	103.70	101	171.70	141	239.70	181	307.70
22	37.40	62	105.40	102	173.40	142	241.40	182	309.40
23	39.10	63	107.10	103	175.10	143	243.10	183	311.10
24	40.80	64	108.80	104	176.80	144	244.80	184	312.80
25	42.50	65	110.50	105	178.50	145	246.50	185	314.50
26	44.20	66	112.20	106	180.20	146	248.20	186	316.20
27	45.90	67	113.90	107	181.90	147	249.90	187	317.90
28	47.60	68	115.60	108	183.60	148	251.60	188	319.60
29	49.30	69	117.30	109	185.30	149	253.30	189	321.30
30	51.00	70	119.00	110	187.00	150	255.00	190	323.00
31	52.70	71	120.70	111	188.70	151	256.70	191	324.70
32	54.40	72	122.40	112	190.40	152	258.40	192	326.40
33	56.10	73	124.10	113	192.10	153	260.10	193	328.10
34	57.80	74	125.80	114	193.80	154	261.80	194	329.80
35	59.50	75	127.50	115	195.50	155	263.50	195	331.50
36	61.20	76	129.20	116	197.20	156	265.20	196	333.20
37	62.90	77	130.90	117	198.90	157	266.90	197	334.90
38	64.60	78	132.60	118	200.60	158	268.60	198	336.60
39	66.30	79	134.30	119	202.30	159	270.30	199	338.30
40	68.00	80	136.00	120	204.00	160	272.00	200	340.00

join as a condition of service. *Voluntary deductions* are those desired by the employee. These may include trade union or sports club subscriptions, charitable donations, regular savings contributions and so on.

Many simple systems for keeping wages records have been introduced and we shall look at two of the best known: the Simplex and the Kalamazoo.

25.6 The Simplex Wages System

A sheet from a Simplex wages book is shown in Fig. 25.2, and explained fully below. This system is used for up to twenty-six employees.

25.7 Exercises: The Simplex Wages System

Rule up some sheets of paper similar to the one shown in Fig. 25.2. Use these to complete the wage records for three small firms, using the data shown in Table 25.2 on page 180 and remembering to record the totals at the bottom of each sheet.

25.8 The Kalamazoo Wages System

Over three million people in the United Kingdom are paid weekly by the Kalamazoo Wages System. Each of them receives in his pay packet a wage slip or *wage advice note* which shows exactly how his wages for the week have been calculated, arranged in such a way that both the wages slip and the amount of money can be checked before the envelope is opened. This wage advice note has been prepared by a system known as *simultaneous records*, because the slip has been prepared at the same time as two other records, the PAYE individual pay record and the payroll. The *individual pay record* sets out an employee's wages for 52 weeks (or 12 months for a monthly-paid worker) and the payroll records the sums being paid to all the workers in the business this week, so that the total pay to be drawn from the bank can be calculated.

The three-in-one system is illustrated in Figs. 25.3 and 25.4. Fig. 25.3 shows clearly how the three records are prepared simultaneously, ten sets at a time, in the following way:

(a) Ten tear-off wage advice notes (see Fig. 25.4) are placed on the copywriter, where a row of studs hold the papers firm.

(b) The wage advice notes are covered with a sheet of carbon paper, and over this is positioned the payroll form, which has ten columns plus a 'total' column on the right.

(c) The payroll form is covered with a second sheet of carbon paper, and each employee's individual pay record is positioned in turn on the studs so as to bring the next clean column on the pay record over the next blank column on the payroll form and the next blank wage advice note.

Name	National Insurance Number	Contribution Table Letter	Overtime			Wage for Week	Gross Wage for Week	Compa Pensi Schem
			Hours	Rate	Pay			
1	2	3	4	5	6	7	8	9
F. JONES	YY 01 02 03 B	A	-	-	- -	84 00	84 00	4
K. SMITH	22 01 02 03 B	A	2	1·60	3 20	96 00	99 20	4
F. FELLOWS MRS	XX 01 02 03 A	A	9	1·75	15 75	72 00	87 75	4
R. LARGE MISS	YY 10 24 86 D	A	3	1·30	3 90	64 00	67 90	3
P. FINCH	XZ 37 39 08 C	A	5	1·80	9 00	85 00	94 00	4
J. MARSTON	VT 56 21 24 A	A						

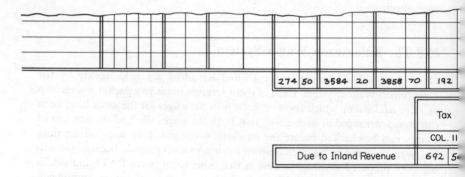

All figures shown are merely for example purposes. Actual deductions should be made by reference to current information from the Inland Revenue and Department of Health and Social Security

| | 274 50 | 3584 20 | 3858 70 | 192 |

	Tax
	COL. 11
Due to Inland Revenue	692 5

Notes on Fig. 25.2

The employee's name is written in box 1.

The national insurance number of the employee is required as part of his records and is recorded in box 2.

The letter in box 3 denotes the class of contribution which is to be deducted from the employee's pay for National Insurance. This varies for different employees.

Boxes 4, 5 and 6 denote the number of overtime hours worked, the rate of overtime pay and the total overtime pay to which the employee is entitled.

Box 7 shows the weekly basic wage payable.

Box 8 shows the gross wage, including overtime.

Where a company runs an approved pension scheme, the employee's contribution may be deducted from the gross wages, to give the taxable pay. The contribution is shown in box 9 and the taxable pay in box 10.

Taxable Pay 10	Tax 11	Primary Class 1 12	Charity 13	S.A.Y.E. 14	Total Deductions 15	Net Wage 16	Secondary Class 1 17	18
79 80	17 70	6 18	10	5 –	28 98	50 82	10 93	
74 24	20 40	7 30	10	10 –	37 80	56 44	12 91	
83 36	20 70	6 46	10	5 –	32 26	51 10	11 42	
64 50	3 00cr	5 00	10	3 –	5 10	59 40	8 84	
89 30	21 00	6 92	10	5				

Note: (Cr) denotes a
refund of tax
to the employee

65 77	692 50	284 09	7 60	106 00	1105 14	2560 63	502 21	

imary ass1 COL.12	COL.13	Secondary Class1 COL.17	COL.18			TOTAL
4 09		502 21				1478 80

Boxes 11, 12, 13 and 14 show the other statutory and voluntary deductions. The words 'Primary Class 1' refer to the particular kind of National Insurance contribution paid by the employee. Box 13 is available for any other statutory deduction which may be authorized in future, or it may be altered to a voluntary deduction of some sort. Box 14 has been used in this example for a SAYE deduction. Box 15 then gives the total deductions from the taxable pay in box 10, to give the net wage (box 16).

Box 17 shows the employer's contribution to National Insurance.

At the bottom of the page the columns are totalled to give the figures for total pay, total tax (due to the Inland Revenue) and total National Insurance payments.

Schools and colleges wishing to purchase pages like this one for use in the classroom should address inquiries to George Vyner Ltd. at the address shown at the beginning of this book.

Table 25.2

Name	National Insurance number	Contribution Table letter	Overtime Hours	Overtime Rate	Wages for week	Company pension contribution	Tax	National Insurance contributions Primary Class 1	National Insurance contributions Secondary Class 1
1. Mr A	XY 22 17 50 B	A	3	2.10	112.00	7.98	17.25	8.52	15.07
Mr B	ZZ 13 16 58 C	A	4	2.30	88.00	5.83	15.00	7.05	12.47
Mr C	YZ 29 72 44 D	A	$8\frac{1}{2}$	1.88	78.00	5.64	—	6.82	12.06
2. Mr P	AB 13 76 28 B	A	$5\frac{1}{2}$	2.30	95.00	6.46	18.50	7.82	13.83
Mr Q	CD 48 62 71 C	A	6	2.20	86.00	5.95	21.25	7.21	12.74
Mr R	EF 52 65 84 D	A	$4\frac{1}{2}$	2.80	106.00	7.12	18.25	8.60	15.21
3. Mr X	PQ 37 21 14 B	A	4	2.30	104.00	6.79	12.75	8.21	14.52
Mr Y	LM 16 24 19 C	A	$6\frac{1}{2}$	1.90	98.50	6.65	3.56	8.06	14.25
Mr Z	ST 19 27 18 D	A	11	2.10	87.50	6.63	14.25	8.06	14.25

(d) Entries made on the individual pay record also appear on both the payroll and the wage advice note. Finally the completed wage advice notes are torn off, and folded to go into the pay packets, together with the money due to the employee.

The final result is that the individual's pay record carries a full record of his wages from week to week, while the wages advice note (Fig. 25.4) shows the same information. This is as follows:

(a) The date, that is, Week 1 beginning on April 11.

(b) A, B and C are different kinds of earnings, perhaps salary, commission and bonus.

(c) Contributions to company pensions are deducted before tax is calculated.

(d) Gross pay to date for the year is the same as this week's pay, since this is the first week in the year.

(e) Tax and (f) National Insurance contributions are found from the Inland Revenue tax tables and the DHSS *Employer's Guide* respectively.

(g) Net pay is found by subtracting the total deductions from the gross pay.

(h) These lines can be used for sums of money which are not really pay, such as travel allowances.

(i) The 'total amount payable' is the sum which is to be put into the pay packet. It is followed by full details of National Insurance contributions.

After completion each individual pay record is returned to a special storage file, from which it can be taken out at any time if the employee concerned complains that he has not been paid correctly. When ten wage advice notes have been prepared the payroll is removed and totalled, so that the necessary money can be collected from the bank, while the ten pay slips are separated and put into the wage packets ready for the cashier to add the appropriate amounts of money.

25.9 Exercises: The Kalamazoo Wages System

These exercises cannot be carried out without proper stationery. Schools and colleges who wish to train students on actual documents can purchase a supply from Kalamazoo Ltd. at the address given at the beginning of this book. They will also need sets of tax tables, obtainable from the local Inland Revenue office, and copies of the *Employer's Guide to National Insurance Contributions* published by the Department of Health and Social Security.

If special stationery and tax tables are not available, you could draw up a few wage advice notes as shown in Fig. 25.4 and record on these the details given in the following examples, but you will not be able to work out the tax payable without tax tables or the insurance contributions without an *Employer's Guide*, and you will have to use imaginary figures for these.

The exercise envisages a small firm of five employees. You are required to draw up individual pay records for these five people from the information supplied in Table 25.3 on page 185. To do this, you should lay out (a) a

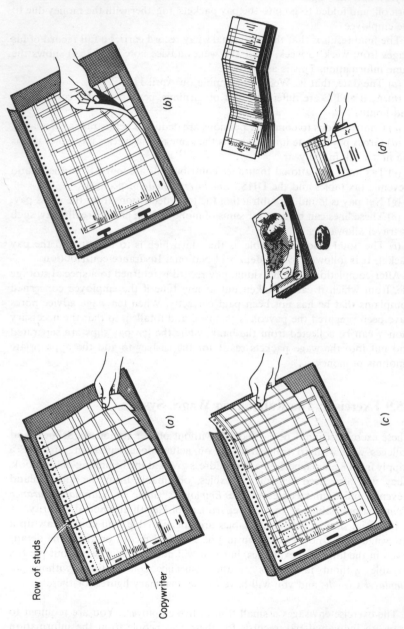

Row of studs

Copywriter

Fig. 25.3 The Kalamazoo wages system

PAY ADVICE

Kalamazoo
18203 11 J 3

Week or Month No.	Date	1	11/4	(a)

Details		

Earnings	A	Basic	96 =
	B	Overtime (b)	3 20
	C		
	D		
	E		
	Gross Pay		99 20

| Superannuation | 4 96 | (c) |

Gross Pay for Tax Purposes	94 24	(d)
Gross Pay to Date for Tax Purposes	94 24
Tax Free Pay	25 60
Taxable Pay to Date	68 64
Tax Due to Date	20 40

Tax Refund

Deductions	Tax		20 40	(e)
	*N.I. Contribution (Employee)		7 30	(f)
	0	Dr. Barnardo's	10
	1	SAYE	10 =
	2		
	3		
	4		
	5		
	6		
	Total Deductions		37 80

Net Pay	56 44	(g)
F (h)	
G	

Total Amount Payable	56 44	(i)
N.I. Contribution (Employer)	12 91
N.I. Total (Employer & Employee)	20 21
H	
*Contracted-out Contribution included above	

YOUR PAY IS
MADE UP AS
SHOWN ABOVE   K. Smith

Fig. 25.4 A Kalamazoo wage advice note

set of ten wage advice notes, (b) a sheet of carbon paper on top, (c) a payroll sheet, (d) another sheet of carbon paper and (e) the individual pay record of each employee, positioned in turn over the first, second, third, fourth and fifth blank columns on the payroll. The information about wages earned in Week 1 can then be entered on the simultaneous records. After completing the five sets of entries, you should tear off the wage advice notes, total the payroll for the week and put away the five individual pay records in a suitable storage envelope.

A day or so later try Week 2's records, and so on for each of the five weekly sets of records. When you have done this you should have grasped the idea of the system, and even be ready to undertake work as a Kalamazoo wages clerk, though you will probably need some help initially from an experienced member of your firm.

Week 1

Earnings are as stated in the individual pay records, except for M. Carey (overtime £3). Don't forget that Thomas's 5 per cent pension contribution is deducted from his gross pay each week.

Use the tax tables from the Inland Revenue office to decide 'tax-free pay' and 'taxable pay to date'; you can then find 'tax due to date'. The earnings-related NHI contributions for both the employee and the employer are found in the booklets *Contracted-out Contributions* and *Not-contracted-out Contributions*, associated with the *Employer's Guide to National Insurance Contributions*. Don't forget the other deductions, such as union and social club subscriptions.

Week 2

Earnings are as stated in the individual pay records, except for M. Carey (overtime £3) and D. Cecil (overtime £3). Don't forget that gross pay to date for tax purposes includes Week 1 and Week 2.

Use the tax tables to decide 'tax-free pay' and 'taxable pay to date', and then calculate 'tax due to date'. Now find the tax payable this week by deducting Week 1's tax payment from the tax due to date.

Week 3

Earnings are as before, except for M. Carey (overtime £3 again) and J. Thomas (fee for special services £50.00).

Week 4

Earnings are as before, except for M. Carey (overtime £3) and B. Peters, who has been awarded a merit-grading increase in pay to £162 per week; make the necessary alteration at the top of his individual pay record card.

Week 5

Earnings as before (but don't forget B. Peters' increase of the previous week) except for M. Carey (overtime £3) and D. Cecil (overtime £3). Also J. Chalmers' PAYE code alters to 148 after a multiple birth in his family.

Table 25.3 Individual pay records details

No.	Name	Address	National Insurance number	Date of birth	Married or single	Rate of pay	PAYE code as at 6/4	NHI letter	Position and/or trade	Payments details
1	Peters, Brian	22 Hill Street, Oxbridge	YP 30 15 78 B	31.7.21	M	£135 per week	128 H	A	Foreman Fitter	Deduct union 55p Social club 25p
2	Chalmers, John	37 College Lane, Oxbridge	XC 40 17 36 C	14.5.36	M	£105 per week	100 H	A	Fitter	Deduct union 55p Social club 25p
3	Carey, Maureen	12 Erasmus Towers, Oxbridge	YC 29 58 75 D	27.12.58	S	£73.50 per week	67 L	A	Typist	Deduct social club 15p
4	Cecil, Deborah	137 Chester Street, Grantaville	MC 71 38 62 D	14.11.58	S	£69.50 per week	67 L	A	Clerk-typist	Deduct social club 15p
5	Thomas, James	19 Parker Place, Camford	ZT 81 49 72 C	19.11.19	M	£165 per week	227 H	A	Manager	Pays 5% of gross salary to pension scheme Social club 50p

25.10 Mental Arithmetic Exercises

1. $32 + 49 + 78 + 26 =$
2. $725 - 387 =$
3. $4\,129 \times 5 =$
4. £27.50 + £37.09 + £4.27 =
5. £625.73 − £381.29 =
6. $3\frac{3}{4} \times \frac{2}{5} =$
7. Share £4 200 in the proportions of $3 : 2$.
8. Change $\frac{17}{40}$ to a percentage.
9. Three students are 16 years old and two are 21 years old. What is their average age?
10. £1 is worth 4.18 Deutschemarks. How many Deutschemarks will a British tourist receive for £50?
11. How many seconds are there in $4\frac{1}{2}$ minutes?
12. What will be the profit on 60 items purchased for £3.50 each and sold for £5.30 each?
13. What is the simple interest on £450 for 3 years at 8 per cent per annum?
14. Buying a car costing £4 500 on hire purchase requires a £900 deposit and 36 instalments of £130. How much is to be paid in interest altogether?
15. What wages are payable to a man who works for 54 hours at £1.95 per hour?

Unit Twenty-six

Compound Interest

26.1 Simple Interest and Compound Interest

In Unit 13 we discussed *interest* which is paid whenever money is borrowed, as a reward to the lender for the use of his funds. We considered in particular *simple interest*, which is paid regularly to the lender throughout the period of the loan.

If money is lent at *compound interest*, on the other hand, the interest falling due at the end of each year is not paid over to the lender. Instead, the sum is added to the amount of the original loan and counted as an extra loan; interest for the following year is calculated on the new total.

Suppose, for instance, that I borrow £100 at 10 per cent per annum compound interest. The interest payable to the lender at the end of the first year will be £10, but instead of paying him this sum I add it to the loan, so that I owe him £110. At the end of the second year the interest will be 10 per cent of £110, which is £11, and I add that £11 to the £110 so that I now owe him £121.

Money invested at compound interest quickly builds up to very considerable sums, and that is why compound interest has become so very important: most of our savings, such as life assurance policies, pension funds and so forth, are partly built up from the compound interest they earn during our working lives to provide a substantial sum for our retirement.

A Good Compound Interest Story

Most readers will have heard of the island of Manhattan, 56 square kilometres of what is now New York City, which was purchased from its Red Indian owners by the early settlers for 60 Dutch guilders, about 24 dollars. This purchase has always been regarded as a particularly shameful piece of business, and has been held up as an example of the bad treatment accorded to the Red Indians. Some Americans have resented this slur upon their ancestors, and one recently calculated that if the Red Indians had prudently invested the 24 dollars at a fair rate of compound interest, the investment would now be worth more than the total value of all the land, buildings and other installations on the island of Manhattan today, so that the Red Indians might not have had such a bad deal after all. Most of us will sympathize with them nevertheless (see also Section 26.5).

Example

What will a loan of £500 amount to in three years at 5 per cent per annum compound interest?

Compound interest, like simple interest, is calculated year by year as a percentage of the outstanding principal. One easy way to do this is to work out first what interest would be payable if the rate were 1 per cent per annum—which merely involves moving the number two places to the right through the decimal point—and then to use this result to work out what the rest of the interest will be. This example concerns a 5 per cent interest rate, so we will work out for each year what 1 per cent interest will be, and hence what is 4 per cent. Adding these together gives total interest for the year.

	£
Principal borrowed at start of year 1	500.00
1% interest for year 1 $= $	5.00
4% interest (to make 5% in all) $= $	20.00
Amount at end of year 1 $= $	525.00
1% interest for year 2 $= $	5.25
4% interest (to make 5% in all) $= $	21.00
Amount at end of year 2 $= $	551.25
1% interest for year 3 $= $	5.512 5
4% interest (to make 5% in all) $= $	22.050 0
Amount at end of year 3	578.812 5

So in three years £500 grows to £578.81 at a rate of compound interest of 5 per cent per annum.

Interest at any rate can be calculated by this method: for example, $11\frac{1}{8}\%$ would be calculated at $1\% + 10\% + \frac{1}{8}\%$.

26.2 Exercises: Easy Compound Interest Calculations

1. Calculate what the following loans will amount to in 2 years at 5 per cent per annum compound interest:

   (a) £200   (b) £450
   (c) £500   (d) £750
   (e) £1 000   (f) £1 500
   (g) £8 000   (h) £9 550
   (i) £15 000   (j) £33 500

2. Calculate (to the nearest penny) what the following loans will amount to in 3 years at $8\frac{1}{2}$ per cent per annum compound interest:
   (a) £400   (b) £650
   (c) £800   (d) £950

(e) £1 000   (f) £1 750
(g) £5 500   (h) £8 850
(i) £17 500   (j) £42 550

3. The principal, interest and period of ten loans at compound interest are listed in the following table. Calculate the amount to be repaid (to the nearest penny) at the end of each loan.

	Principal	Rate of interest (per annum)	Number of years
(a)	£500	4%	2
(b)	£600	$3\frac{1}{2}\%$	2
(c)	£800	$8\frac{1}{2}\%$	3
(d)	£1 500	$10\frac{1}{2}\%$	3
(e)	£850	$11\frac{1}{8}\%$	3
(f)	£1 650	$12\frac{1}{2}\%$	3
(g)	£2 250	$11\frac{1}{4}\%$	3
(h)	£3 250	$7\frac{3}{4}\%$	3
(i)	£4 500	$8\frac{1}{2}\%$	4
(j)	£9 250	$6\frac{1}{2}\%$	4

4. If £2 500 is invested at $8\frac{1}{4}$ per cent compound interest for 3 years, the interest being added at the end of each year, calculate how much the investment will amount to at the end of the period. (Give the answer to the nearest £10.)   (RSA)

5. If £3 500 is invested at $8\frac{1}{2}$ per cent compound interest for 3 years, the interest being added at the end of each year, calculate how much the investment will amount to at the end of the period. (Give the answer to the nearest £10.)   (RSA)

6. Find, to the nearest penny, the difference between the simple and compound interest on £800 for three years at 17 per cent per annum.

(RSA adapted)

7. Find, to the nearest penny, the difference between the simple and compound interest on £1 500 for three years at 18 per cent per annum.

(RSA adapted)

8. On January 1, Year 1, and on each subsequent January 1, I invested £4 000 in a building society giving $14\frac{1}{2}$ per cent per annum compound interest, the interest being added annually. How much, to the nearest £10, was there in my account at the end of Year 4?   (RSA adapted)

9. A man borrows £6 000 at $15\frac{1}{2}$ per cent per annum compound interest on January 1. At the end of the year he repays £1 000; at the end of the 2nd year he repays £2 000, and at the end of the 3rd year he repays a further £2 500. How much will still be owing? (Answer to the nearest pound.)

(RSA adapted)

10. A man borrows £8 000 at $12\frac{1}{2}$ per cent per annum compound interest. At the end of the first year he repays £2 000; at the end of the 2nd year he repays £2 000, and at the end of the 3rd year he repays a further £2 500. How much will still be owing? (Answer to the nearest pound.)

(RSA adapted)

26.3 Compound Interest by the Formula Method

When we have to calculate compound interest payable for a large number of years, the method described in Section 26.1 becomes very laborious. However, instead, we can use a formula for calculating A, the total amount of a loan of a principal P over n years at compound interest at R per cent per annum:

$$A = P \times \left(1 + \frac{R}{100}\right)^n$$

The small figure n means that the number inside the brackets must be multiplied by itself n times: $(1.05)^3$, for example is $1.05 \times 1.05 \times 1.05$.

Example

What will an investment of £5 000 amount to in 6 years at 8 per cent per annum compound interest?

$$A = P \times \left(1 + \frac{R}{100}\right)^n$$

$$= £5\,000 \times (1 + \tfrac{8}{100})^6$$
$$= £5\,000 \times (1.08)^6$$

It would be very time-consuming to work out 1.08 multiplied by itself 6 times, that is, $1.08 \times 1.08 \times 1.08 \times 1.08 \times 1.08 \times 1.08$. For this kind of calculation it is almost essential to use either an electronic calculator or a method based on seven-figure logarithms. Using either of these the working is straightforward.

$$A = £5\,000 \times (1.08)^6$$
$$= £7\,934$$

Example

What will an investment of £4 850 amount to in 21 years at $7\frac{1}{2}$ per cent compound interest per annum?

$$A = P \times \left(1 + \frac{R}{100}\right)^n$$

$$= £4\ 850 \times (1.075)^{21}$$

$$= \underline{\underline{£22\ 147}}$$

26.4 Exercises: Compound Interest by the Formula Method

You will need to use either an electronic calculator or logarithm tables for these exercises.

1. Using the formula method calculate the amount that will accumulate in each of the following investments:

	Principal	Rate of interest (per annum)	Number of years
(a)	£2 000	8%	4
(b)	£2 500	10%	5
(c)	£4 000	$6\frac{1}{2}\%$	8
(d)	£6 500	$7\frac{1}{2}\%$	10
(e)	£10 000	10%	12

2. Using the formula method calculate the amount that will accumulate with each of the following investments:

	Principal	Rate of interest (per annum)	Number of years
(a)	£1 420	$7\frac{1}{2}\%$	5
(b)	£2 560	8%	5
(c)	£3 320	$6\frac{1}{2}\%$	6
(d)	£4 475	$12\frac{1}{2}\%$	6
(e)	£6 236	$13\frac{1}{2}\%$	6

26.5 How Much Did the Dutch Pay for the Island of Manhattan?

To conclude this story, let us look again at the purchase of the island of Manhattan, and use the formula for compound interest to work out how much the Red Indians' 24 dollars selling price for the island would now be worth if they had invested the money at compound interest. The sale took place in 1625 which, let us say, is 350 years ago. America was a rather risky place to invest in at that time, so 10 per cent was probably a fair rate of interest. Then

$$A = P \times \left(1 + \frac{R}{100}\right)^n$$

$$= 24 \times (1 + \tfrac{10}{100})^{350} \text{ dollars}$$
$$= 24 \times (1.10)^{350} \text{ dollars}$$
$$= 7\,416\,000\,000\,000\,000 \text{ dollars}$$

This must certainly be more than the value of the properties on Manhattan Island today, but as few Red Indians at that time were familiar with investing in the 'ten per cents', and as they were actually paid in trade goods rather than in cash, we may still perhaps reserve our sympathies for them. Certainly the calculation emphasizes the fact that compound interest over very long periods of time produces some astonishingly large figures.

26.6 Mental Arithmetic Exercises

1. $4\,756 - 2\,483 =$
2. $3\,819 \div 19 =$
3. $4.5 \times 0.2 =$
4. $\frac{1}{2} + \frac{2}{3} + \frac{5}{6} =$
5. $1\frac{2}{5} \div \frac{7}{10} =$
6. What discount at 5 per cent shall I receive on goods priced at £145?
7. What is the cost of 5 kilograms of beef at 9.50 francs per kilogram?
8. Electricity costs 3p per unit. What is the charge for 650 units?
9. What is the average age of five students aged respectively 18, 19, 20, 21 and 27?
10. What is 30 per cent of £1 800?
11. What commission will a salesman earn on sales of £8 500, if he is paid 2 per cent on the first £5 000 and 4 per cent on the rest?
12. What will be the wages earned per week of a man paid £1.95 per hour for 42 hours?
13. How fast does a train travel on average if it covers 456 kilometres in 3 hours?
14. What will be the value at stock-taking of 2 800 cases of whisky at £41 a case?
15. In a certain town the rate is fixed at £1.10 in the pound. How much will a householder have to pay if the rateable value of his property is £250?

Unit Twenty-seven

Stocks and Shares

27.1 What are Stocks and Shares?

Stocks and shares are securities issued to people who subscribe capital to companies, or lend money to companies, public authorities or local and central governments. It is simpler to start with an explanation of 'shares'.

Shares are certificates issued to people who subscribe capital to a company, thus purchasing an interest in that company. When first issued shares are sold at an issue price chosen by the company, called the *par value*. This is often £1, but shares valued at 50 pence, 25 pence or 10 pence are commonly issued. The value of a share does not stay at this par value for very long. If the company is profitable the shares will rise in value. If the company is making losses on its activities the shares will fall below par.

To understand why this is so, let us take an example of a £1 share sold to a member of the public, Mr Smith, by a firm called Metal Employers PLC, who are looking for nickel in a developing country. Suppose Mr Smith's contribution, together with many similar contributions totalling £100 000, enables the company to buy up mineral rights in an area of the country concerned. Within a few weeks a large deposit of nickel is discovered there, worth £1 000 000. The costs of extracting the nickel will amount to £500 000, but the rest will be profit and will belong to the shareholders. Clearly the £1 share Mr Smith owns will now be worth more than £1, for the £100 000 investment in the company has led to the discovery of nickel of a net value of £500 000. Mr Smith certainly would not sell his £1 share *at par*, that is for its par value of £1. On the other hand, if no nickel had been discovered Mr Smith's share would fall in value on the Stock Exchange, for any buyer would take into account the poor chances of a future discovery of nickel now that a good deal of exploration had proved unfruitful.

At the end of the financial year, the directors of a company decide how much of the year's profits should be distributed among the shareholders; that is, what should be the year's *dividend*. Dividends are sometimes quoted in terms of a fixed sum of money per share held, and sometimes as a percentage of the par value of the shares, irrespective of how much the shareholder actually paid for them. This means that if a 10 per cent dividend is to be paid on the £1 shares of a company, each shareholder will receive 10p dividend on every share he holds even though the shares may have been purchased at very different prices. A shareholder who buys a share at par on the day they are issued will receive 10p dividend on his investment of £1. Suppose the same shareholder bought some more shares later when the shares had risen in price, and paid £2 for each £1 share. On dividend day he would receive 10p for the dividend on each of these shares, even though they cost him twice as much.

Stocks are securities very similar to shares. In the past they were often created by consolidating shares into stock usually in £100 blocks. This brought certain advantages when it came to transferring the securing from one person to another. Stocks are issued today when money is loaned to companies, public corporations of various types and to the Government. For instance, a name like *Treasury 9% 1995 Stock* indicates that the original money was lent to the Treasury at 9% per annum interest and will be repaid in 1995. Some stocks are undated, and will not be repaid on any specific date. The most famous undated stock is Old Consols, issued in 1745. At that time all the United Kingdom Government debts were consolidated into a single undated stock, at $2\frac{1}{2}$ per cent interest. At the time of writing, £100 of Old Consols stock is worth £18.375—well below par.

Government stocks are often called gilt-edged stocks, because they were recorded in former times in a special gilt-edged ledger. They are of undoubted security. If they are repayable they will certainly be repaid in full on the due date, although in modern times inflation may eat into the value of the money that is repaid.

27.2 Simple Share Calculations

Example

A man buys 500 £1 shares in Unigold PLC at par. Later he sells them at 83p per share. What loss did he suffer? As he bought each share for £1 and sold it for 83p, he lost 17p per share.

$$\text{Total loss} = 500 \times 17\text{p}$$
$$= £85.00$$

In practice he would also have to pay certain charges, but we will disregard these at present (see also Section 27.6).

Example

A man buys 500 £1 shares at a price of £1.17 each and sells them at £1.38 each. What profit does he make?

$$\text{His profit on each share} = £1.38 - £1.17$$
$$= 21\text{p}$$
$$\text{Total profit} = 500 \times 21\text{p}$$
$$= £105.00$$

Example

An investor buys 500 £1 shares at 50p each and 200 £1 shares at £4 each. The first lot of shares pays a dividend of 9 per cent and the second group pays 42 per cent.

(a) What is the total dividend? (b) What yield (correct to one decimal place) does he receive on his total investment? (The *yield* on an investment is the effective rate of interest it earns.)

(a) The 500 shares pay him £9 per £100 (par value), making $5 \times 9 = £45$ dividend.

The 200 shares pay him £42 per £100 (par value), making $2 \times £42 = £84$ dividend.

$$\text{Total dividend} = £45 + £84$$
$$= £129$$

(b) The 500 £1 shares cost him £250.

The 200 £1 shares cost him £800.

$$\text{Total investment} = £250 + £800$$
$$= £1\,050$$

Rate per cent earned (yield) on investment

$$= \frac{£129}{£1\,050} \times 100$$

```
                    12.28
          105 ) 1 290.
                1 05
                 240
                 210
                 300
                 210
                  900
                  840
```

$$= 12.3\%$$

27.3 Exercises: Simple Share Calculations

1. Find the cost of the following lots of shares:

    (a) 500 £1 shares at £1.30 each   (b) 300 £1 shares at £1.17 each
    (c) 400 £1 shares at 57p each   (d) 800 50p shares at 48p each
    (e) 2 000 £1 shares at £1.63 each   (f) 1 500 £1 shares at 75p each
    (g) 4 500 25p shares at 18p each   (h) 2 800 £1 shares at £4.25 each
    (i) 3 600 £1 shares at 84p each   (j) 7 200 £1 shares at £4.85 each

2. Calculate the dividends paid each year to the holders of the following shares:

    (a) 500 £1 shares paying 8%   (b) 300 50p shares paying 20%
    (c) 250 £1 shares paying 16%   (d) 850 25p shares paying 20%
    (e) 1 250 £1 shares paying $11\frac{1}{2}\%$ (f) 4 500 £1 shares paying 8%
    (g) 6 500 £1 shares paying $2\frac{1}{4}\%$ (h) 7 200 £1 shares paying 18%
    (i) 3 800 £1 shares paying $5\frac{1}{2}\%$ (j) 6 700 £1 shares paying $7\frac{1}{2}\%$

3. For each of the following investors, calculate (i) the total dividend received, and (ii) the percentage return on his total investment (i.e. the yield) correct to 1 decimal place:

   (a) Mr *A* buys 400 £1 shares at 60p each (paying a 10 per cent dividend) and 500 £1 shares at £1.25 each (paying a 15 per cent dividend).

   (b) Mr *B* buys 1 000 25p shares at par (they pay a dividend of 4p per share) and 2 500 £1 shares at £2.50 each (they pay a 30 per cent dividend).

   (c) Mr *C* buys 200 £1 shares at £1.50 (they pay a $12\frac{1}{2}$ per cent dividend) and 500 £1 shares at 80p each (they pay a 15 per cent dividend).

   (d) Mr *D* buys 5 000 50p shares at 55p each (they pay a dividend of 7p per share) and 2 000 £1 shares at £1.75 (they pay a 40 per cent dividend).

   (e) Mr *E* buys 2 000 £1 shares at £4.50 each (they pay an 80 per cent dividend) and 1 500 £1 shares at 75p each (they pay a 10 per cent dividend).

27.4 Simple Stock Calculations

It is best in simple stock calculations to visualize £100 of stock, although in real life they can be bought or sold in any amounts. Like shares, stocks can fluctuate in value above and below the original value (called the *nominal value*) so that £100 stock might change hands at any price. The rate of interest payable is always calculated on the nominal value, so that £100 of $6\frac{1}{2}\%$ stock gives an interest payable of £6.50 per year, whatever it cost the owner when he bought it.

The chief types of calculation met with are illustrated in the examples which follow.

Example

What will an investor pay for £5 000 of Treasury Stock at $89\frac{1}{4}$?

$$£5\ 000 \text{ stock is } 50 \times £100 \text{ stock.}$$
$$\text{Each } £100 \text{ is selling at } £89\frac{1}{4}$$
$$\text{Cost to investor} = 50 \times £89.25$$

$$
\begin{array}{r}
89.25 \\
\times \quad 50 \\
\hline
4\ 462.50
\end{array}
$$

$$= \underline{\underline{£4\ 462.50}}$$

Example

An investor spends £990 on $2\frac{1}{2}$ per cent Old Consols at $£16\frac{1}{2}$. (a) What will he receive as interest in each year? (b) What yield does he receive on his investment? (Answer correct to 1 decimal place.)

(a) First we must calculate how much stock he can buy for £990.

For every £16½ he receives £100 of Old Consols

$$\text{Total stock received} = \frac{£990}{16\frac{1}{2}} \times 100$$

$$= \frac{£990 \times 100 \times 2}{33}$$

$$= £6\,000 \text{ stock}$$

Interest = £2½ on every £100 stock

Total interest = $60 \times 2\frac{1}{2}$

$$= £150$$

$$\begin{array}{r} 60 \\ \times\ 2\frac{1}{2} \\ \hline 120 \\ 30 \\ \hline 150 \end{array}$$

(b) Yield on investment $= \dfrac{150^5}{990_{33}} \times 100$

$$\begin{array}{r} 15.15 \\ 33)\overline{500.} \\ 33 \\ \hline 170 \\ 165 \\ \hline 50 \\ 33 \\ \hline 170 \\ 165 \end{array}$$

$$= 15.2\%$$

27.5 Exercises: Simple Stocks Calculations

1. Find the cost to the investor of the following stocks:
   (a) £500 Victory 4% Loan Stock at £98.50
   (b) £800 Exchange 5% Stock at £85.50
   (c) £1 200 5½% Funding Stock at £78.25
   (d) £4 800 Transport 4½% Stock at £42¼
   (e) £6 000 2½% Consols at £16¾

2. An investor makes five purchases of stock. Use the following table to find how much stock he receives in each deal:

	Cash invested	Price per £100 of stock
(a)	£95	£47½
(b)	£148¾	£42½
(c)	£10 750	£21½
(d)	£442	£110½
(e)	£3 112.50	£103¾

3. In each of the deals in the following table find (i) how much stock the investor receives for his money, (ii) how much interest he will receive in each year, and (iii) what yield he actually earns on his money. (Answer correct to one decimal place.)

Name of stock	Cash invested	Price per £100 of stock
(a) 6% Transport Stock	£311$\frac{1}{2}$	£44$\frac{1}{2}$
(b) 10% Funding Stock	£1 020	£102
(c) 8$\frac{1}{2}$% Loan Stock	£4 250	£85
(d) 2$\frac{1}{2}$% Consols	£680	£17
(e) 3% Investment Stock	£310	£15$\frac{1}{2}$

27.6 More Stocks and Shares Calculations

Investors frequently change the investments they hold, as the shares or stocks rise and fall in value on the market. They are trying either to make a gain on their capital investment or to earn a higher yield by changing their holdings. This usually involves some expense in the form of broker's commission (sometimes called brokerage). This may be as low as $\frac{1}{4}$ per cent, but it is usually more on shares.

Example

Find the change in income when £2 700 of 8 per cent stock is sold at 96$\frac{1}{4}$ and the proceeds invested in 9$\frac{1}{4}$ per cent stock at 107$\frac{3}{4}$. In both deals brokerage is $\frac{1}{4}$ per cent.

The £2 700 of stock is sold at 96$\frac{1}{4}$. The broker will retain $\frac{1}{4}$ per cent as his commission.

$$\text{Proceeds of sale} = 27 \times £96$$

$$\begin{array}{r} 96 \\ \times\ 27 \\ \hline 672 \\ 1\ 920 \\ \hline 2\ 592 \end{array}$$

$$= £2\ 592$$

This sum will be spent on 9$\frac{1}{4}$ per cent stock at 107$\frac{3}{4}$.
This time the broker's commission must be added.

Cost of new stock = £108 for each £100 stock

$$\text{Amount of stock received} = \frac{£2\ 592}{108} \times 100$$

$$\begin{array}{r} 2\ 400 \\ 108\ \overline{)259\ 200} \\ 216 \\ \hline 43\ 2 \\ 43\ 2 \\ \hline \cdots \end{array}$$

$$= £2\ 400$$

Income from first stock $= £27 \times 8$

$\qquad\qquad\qquad\qquad = £216$

Income from second stock $= £24 \times £9\frac{1}{4}$

$$
\begin{array}{r}
24 \\
\times\ \ 9\frac{1}{4} \\
\hline
216 \\
6 \\
\hline
222
\end{array}
$$

$\qquad\qquad\qquad\qquad = £222$

So the change in income $= £222 - £216$

$\qquad\qquad\qquad\qquad = £6$

27.7 Exercises: More Stocks and Shares Calculations

1. Find the change in income when £5 400 of $3\frac{7}{8}$ per cent stock is sold at $96\frac{1}{4}$ and the proceeds invested in $5\frac{1}{4}$ per cent stock at $107\frac{3}{4}$. Brokerage $\frac{1}{4}$ per cent on each deal. (RSA)

2. Find the change in income when £850 of 5 per cent stock is sold at $60\frac{1}{4}$ and the proceeds invested in 9 per cent stock at $101\frac{3}{4}$. Brokerage $\frac{1}{4}$ per cent on each deal. (RSA)

3. A man sold £1 250 of a $4\frac{1}{2}$ per cent stock at $64\frac{1}{4}$ and invested the proceeds in a building society at $7\frac{1}{2}$ per cent per annum. What was the change in his annual income? The broker's commission on the sale was $\frac{1}{4}$ per cent.

4. An investor bought £500 of 5 per cent stock at $103\frac{3}{4}$ and 800 25p shares at $71\frac{1}{2}$p each. Calculate (a) the amount of capital invested and (b) the income in one year from the stocks and shares if the dividend payable on the shares was 18 per cent. Broker's commission was $\frac{1}{4}$ per cent on the stock and $1\frac{1}{2}$p per share on the shares. (RSA)

5. A man bought £800 of 7 per cent stock at $126\frac{3}{4}$ and 500 £1 shares at £1.33$\frac{1}{2}$ each. Brokerage was $\frac{1}{4}$ per cent on the stock and $1\frac{1}{2}$p per share. Calculate (a) the amount of capital invested and (b) the income in one year from the stocks and shares if the dividend payable on the shares was 16 per cent. (RSA)

6. £1 500 of an $11\frac{1}{2}$ per cent stock is sold at 88 and £550 of a $13\frac{1}{2}$ per cent stock is sold at 80 and the proceeds reinvested at $12\frac{1}{2}$ per cent. Find the change in income received. Ignore broker's commission. (RSA adapted)

7. £300 of a $14\frac{1}{2}$ per cent stock is sold at 116 and £450 of a $10\frac{1}{2}$ per cent stock is sold at 136 and the proceeds invested at $12\frac{1}{2}$ per cent. Find the change in income received. Ignore broker's commission. (RSA adapted)

8. A woman buys £1 800 of $13\frac{1}{2}$ per cent stock at $114\frac{1}{4}$ and £2 700 of $11\frac{1}{4}$ per cent stock at $96\frac{3}{4}$. Brokerage is $\frac{1}{4}$ per cent in each case. Find (a) the total cost and (b) the income obtained. (RSA adapted)

9. A woman buys £300 of $15\frac{1}{2}$ per cent stock at $124\frac{3}{4}$ and £4 800 of $11\frac{1}{2}$ per cent stock at $46\frac{3}{4}$. Brokerage is $\frac{1}{4}$ per cent in each case. Find (a) the total cost and (b) the income obtained. (RSA adapted)

10. A man holds 20 £5 shares which are paying a dividend of 24 per cent. He sells them when the shares are at £6.75 each and reinvests this cash in £1 shares at £1.12$\frac{1}{2}$ each. (a) How many £1 shares does he buy? (b) If the new shares pay a dividend of 12$\frac{1}{2}$ per cent, what will be the change in his income? Ignore broker's commission. (RSA adapted)

Unit Twenty-eight

Areas, Perimeters and Volumes

28.1 Lengths and Areas

When we measure any solid object we have three dimensions or measurements to consider: *length, breadth* and *height*. Sometimes we may need to deal only with length and breadth, for instance, if we want to know the size of a floor in order to decide how much carpet we should buy to cover it. When the height of an object is very small compared with its other dimensions we speak of its *thickness* rather than its height: a plank of wood is an example. In measuring these dimensions the metre and the centimetre are probably the most common units used, although millimetres are often used to measure thickness, particularly of sheet metal.

In this unit we shall consider *rectangles*—shapes which have four straight sides and four right angles—and rectangular solids, called *cuboids*. If the four sides of a rectangle are of equal length we have a special kind of rectangle called a *square*. If all six faces of a cuboid are squares, we call the solid a *cube*.

To calculate the area of a rectangle we use the formula

$$area = length \times breadth$$
or
$$area = l \times b$$

If we measure the length and breadth in metres, the area will be in *square metres* (written m^2).

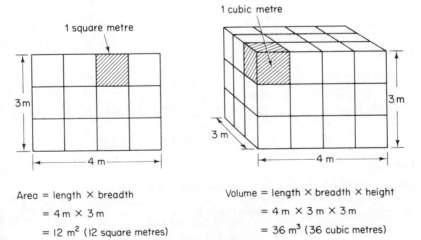

Area = length × breadth

    = 4 m × 3 m

    = 12 m^2 (12 square metres)

Volume = length × breadth × height

    = 4 m × 3 m × 3 m

    = 36 m^3 (36 cubic metres)

Fig. 28.1 Areas of rectangles and volumes of cuboids

Table 28.1 Table of square measure

100 square millimetres = 1 square centimetre
100 square centimetres = 1 square decimetre
100 square decimetres = 1 square metre
100 square metres = 1 are
100 ares = 1 hectare
100 hectares = 1 square kilometre

In abbreviated form this reads

$$100 \text{ mm}^2 = 1 \text{ cm}^2$$
$$100 \text{ cm}^2 = 1 \text{ dm}^2$$
$$100 \text{ dm}^2 = 1 \text{ m}^2$$
$$100 \text{ m}^2 = 1 \text{ a}$$
$$100 \text{ a} = 1 \text{ ha}$$
$$100 \text{ ha} = 1 \text{ km}^2$$

28.2 Areas of Rectangles

Areas of rectangles are easily calculated using the formula given in Section 28.1.

Example

What is the area of a flower bed $5\frac{1}{2}$ m long and $3\frac{1}{2}$ m broad?

$$\text{Area} = l \times b$$
$$= 5\frac{1}{2} \text{ m} \times 3\frac{1}{2} \text{ m}$$
$$= \frac{11}{2} \times \frac{7}{2} \text{ m}^2$$
$$= \frac{77}{4} \text{ m}^2$$
$$= 19\frac{1}{4} \text{ m}^2$$

Example

What is the area of a football pitch 120 m long and 90 m broad?

$$\text{Area} = l \times b$$
$$= 120 \text{ m} \times 90 \text{ m}$$
$$= 10\ 800 \text{ m}^2$$
$$= 1 \text{ ha } 8 \text{ a (1 hectare 8 ares)}$$

Example

What is the area of an oak panel 25 cm long and 6 cm broad?

$$\text{Area} = l \times b$$
$$= 25 \text{ cm} \times 6 \text{ cm}$$
$$= 150 \text{ cm}^2$$
$$= 1 \text{ dm}^2 50 \text{ cm}^2$$

28.3 Exercises: Areas of Squares and Other Rectangles

1. Calculate the areas of squares which have sides of the following lengths:
   (a) 7 cm
   (b) 42 cm
   (c) $1\frac{1}{2}$ m
   (d) $2\frac{1}{4}$ m
   (e) 15 m
   (f) 75 m
   (g) 100 m
   (h) 125 m
   (i) 500 m
   (j) $1\frac{1}{2}$ km

2. Find the areas of rectangles which have the following dimensions:

	length	breadth		length	breadth
(a)	25 cm	7 cm	(b)	42 cm	12 cm
(c)	50 cm	40 cm	(d)	85 cm	50 cm
(e)	$2\frac{1}{2}$ m	$1\frac{1}{2}$ m	(f)	$3\frac{1}{2}$ m	$2\frac{1}{2}$ m
(g)	12 m	8 m	(h)	$14\frac{1}{2}$ m	10 m
(i)	160 m	85 m	(j)	125 m	110 m

3. Find the areas of rectangular rooms which have the following dimensions:

	length	breadth		length	breadth
(a)	7.5 m	4.25 m	(b)	3.65 m	2.5 m
(c)	8.65 m	5.25 m	(d)	4.72 m	3.35 m
(e)	4.75 m	4.3 m	(f)	5.95 m	3.85 m
(g)	5.28 m	3.35 m	(h)	8.72 m	4.7 m
(i)	6.43 m	3.8 m	(j)	9.38 m	6.55 m

4. Find the area (in hectares) of a playing field which measures 150 m by 240 m.

5. Find the area (in hectares) of a recreation ground 140 m long and 120 m wide.

28.4 Areas of Irregular Figures

Many rooms, such as entrance halls, and plots of ground are of irregular shape and their areas cannot be found directly by a simple calculation. Often this can be overcome by dividing the shapes into two or more rectangles. The area of each separate piece is found as usual, and then the results are added together to give the total area.

In Fig. 28.2, for instance, the irregular figure can be divided very easily into the two areas labelled X and Y.

The area of $X = l \times b$
$$= 3.5 \text{ m} \times 3.2 \text{ m}$$

$$
\begin{array}{r}
3.5 \\
\times\ 3.2 \\
\hline
70 \\
10\ 50 \\
\hline
11.20
\end{array}
$$

$$= 11\ 2 \text{ m}^2$$

The length of one side of Y is marked on the diagram, 1 m 50 cm. The other, dimension, CD, has to be worked out. FE = 4 m 80 cm and AB opposite is 3 m 50 cm. Clearly CD is the difference between FE and AB, that is,

$$4 \text{ m } 80 \text{ cm} - 3 \text{ m } 50 \text{ cm} = 1 \text{ m } 30 \text{ cm}$$
$$\text{So the area of } Y = l \times b$$
$$= 1.5 \text{ m} \times 1.3 \text{ m}$$

$$
\begin{array}{r}
1.5 \\
\times\ 1.3 \\
\hline
45 \\
1\ 50 \\
\hline
1.95 \\
\end{array}
$$

$$= 1.95 \text{ m}^2$$

The area of the whole figure $= 11.2 \text{ m}^2 + 1.95 \text{ m}^2$
$$= 13.15 \text{ m}^2$$

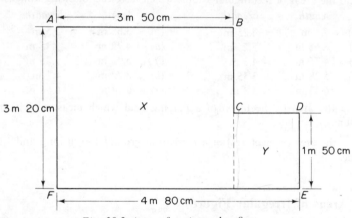

Fig. 28.2 Area of an irregular figure

In Fig. 28.3, we can find the area of the garden path in two ways:

(a) we can find the area of both rectangles $ABCD$ (the garden) and $EFGH$ (the central flower bed) and subtract the area of the flower bed from the total area of the garden; or

(b) we can divide the path itself up into four rectangles, find the area of each and add them together.

Method (a)　　　Area of $ABCD$ = 5.5 m × 4.2 m

$$
\begin{array}{r}
5.5 \\
\times\ 4.2 \\
\hline
1\ 10 \\
22\ 00 \\
\hline
23.10 \\
\end{array}
$$

$$= 23.1 \text{ m}^2$$

Since each path is 1 m wide, we must deduct 2 m from each outside dimension in order to find the dimensions of *EFGH*. Then

Area of *EFGH* = 3.5 m × 2.2 m

$$\begin{array}{r} 3.5 \\ \times\ 2.2 \\ \hline 70 \\ 7\ 00 \\ \hline 7.70 \end{array}$$

= 7.7 m²

Area of path

= 23.1 m² − 7.7 m²

= 15.4 m²

Method (b)   Two of the four rectangles which make up the path each measure 5.5 m by 1 m and the other two each measure 2.2 m by 1 m. Then

Area of path = (2 × 5.5 m × 1 m) + (2 × 2.2 m × 1 m)
= 11 m² + 4.4 m²
= 15.4 m²

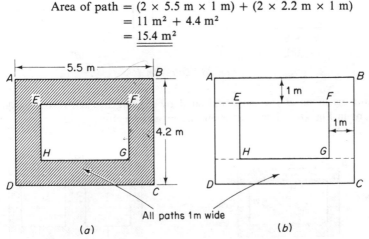

Fig. 28.3 Two ways of finding the area of a garden path

28.5 Exercises: Areas of Irregular Figures

1. Find the areas of each of the figures in Fig. 28.4. The dimensions are given in metres.

2. A carpet 4 m by $3\frac{1}{2}$ m is laid in a room measuring 5 m by $4\frac{1}{2}$ m. Find the area of floor left uncovered.

3. A square bowling green measures 25 m along each edge. Surrounding it is a path 2 m wide, and beyond the path are hedges and flower beds which are 3 m wide all round. What is the area of (*a*) the green itself, (*b*) the paths, (*c*) the flower beds? (Hint: it is always helpful to draw a diagram.)

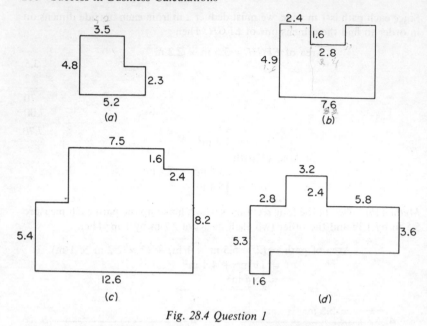

Fig. 28.4 Question 1

4. Find the areas of the paths indicated by shading in each of the garden plans in Fig. 28.5. The dimensions are given in metres.

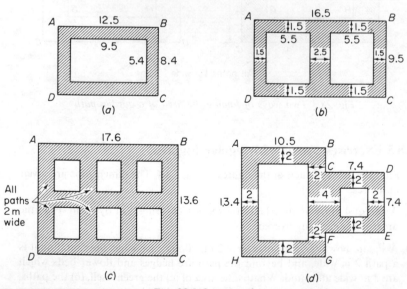

Fig. 28.5 Question 4

5. A church hall floor is $12\frac{1}{2}$ m long by 16 m wide. It is to be stained with a material costing £1.20 per tin. Each tin covers 4 m². (a) How many tins will be needed? (b) What will be the total cost?

6. A courtyard is 40 m long and 36 m wide, and a path 2 m wide runs round the edge of it inside the boundary. What is the area of this path? If it is to be covered with paving stones each with an area of $\frac{1}{4}$ m² how many will be needed?

7. Fig. 28.6 shows the walls of a room, opened out as a flat figure. The dimensions are given in metres. Find the area of the walls, not counting the door and the window.

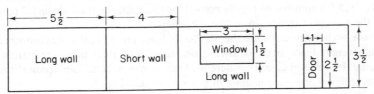

Fig. 28.6 Question 7

8. What will be the area of the walls of a room 4 m long, 3 m wide and $2\frac{1}{2}$ m high if the areas of the doors and windows total $8\frac{1}{2}$ m²?

9. What will be the area of the walls of a room $5\frac{1}{2}$ m long, $4\frac{1}{2}$ m wide and 3 m high if the doors and windows take up 12 m²?

10. Find (a) the area of the walls of a room and (b) the cost of covering them with spray-on wall covering priced at 42p per m² covered. The measurements are: length $4\frac{1}{2}$ m, width 4 m, height 3 m and the areas of the windows and doors total 10 m².

28.6 Perimeters of Rectangles

The *perimeter* of a figure is the distance all the way round its edge. It is often important to know the length of perimeters, for example when fencing fields or gardens, or when framing pictures.

It is very easy to calculate the perimeter of a rectangle. The four sides of a rectangle can be considered as two pairs of opposite sides, and the two members of each pair are the same length. (The four sides of a square, of course, are *all* the same length.) Then

$$\text{Perimeter} = (2 \times \text{length}) + (2 \times \text{breadth})$$

or $\qquad$ *Perimeter* = 2 *(length + breadth)*

Example

What is the length of the perimeter of a garden 56 m long by 24 m wide?

$$\begin{aligned}
\text{Perimeter} &= 2(56 + 24) \text{ m} \\
&= 2 \times 80 \text{ m} \\
&= 160 \text{ m}
\end{aligned}$$

Example

Find the perimeter of a garden 18 m long by 8 m wide. What will it cost to fence it with panels 2 m long, if panels cost £8.50 each and posts cost £3 each? Two of the panels will be replaced by garage gates costing £35, and labour charges are £60. (Ignore the width of posts.)

$$\text{Perimeter} = 2(18 + 8) \text{ m}$$
$$= 2 \times 26 \text{ m}$$
$$= 52 \text{ m}$$

Number of panels to cover whole perimeter = $\frac{52}{2}$ = 26 panels

To find the number of panels needed for the fence, we must deduct 2 panels for the garage entrance: 26 − 2 = 24 panels.

Now we have to calculate the number of fence posts needed. Remember that in a straight fence there is always *one more* post than there are panels of fencing. In a closed circuit—where the fence comes back to join up on the first post—there is the *same number* of posts as panels (Fig. 28.7).

In this example, however, we must allow for the garage gates: one post is left out, the post where the gates meet.

For this fence therefore we shall need:

$$
\begin{aligned}
24 \text{ panels at £8.50 each} &= £204 \\
25 \text{ posts at £3 each} &= £75 \\
\text{Garage gates} &= £35 \\
\text{Labour charges} &= \underline{£60} \\
& \underline{£374}
\end{aligned}
$$

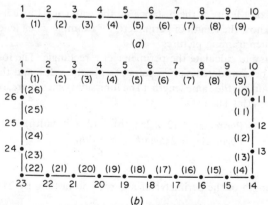

Fig. 28.7 Fences and fence posts: (a) in a straight fence the number of posts is one more than the number of panels; (b) in a closed circuit the number of posts is the same as the number of panels

Example

What is the breadth of a rectangle of area 240 m² and length 20 m?

$$\text{Area} = \text{length} \times \text{breadth}$$

$$\text{So Breadth} = \frac{\text{area}}{\text{length}} \left(\text{and, of course, length} = \frac{\text{area}}{\text{breadth}} \right)$$

In this instance
$$\text{Breadth} = \frac{240}{20} \text{ m}$$
$$= \underline{\underline{12 \text{ m}}}$$

28.7 Exercises: Perimeters of Rectangles

1. Work out the perimeters of the rectangles which have the following dimensions:

	length	breadth		length	breadth
(a)	17 cm	9 cm	(b)	23 cm	15 cm
(c)	14 m	8 m	(d)	17 m	12 m
(e)	56 m	28 m	(f)	38 m	28 m
(g)	100 m	84 m	(h)	120 m	90 m
(i)	1 km	½ km	(j)	1½ km	1 km

2. What will be the cost of fencing each of the rectangular plots of ground listed in the following table, with fencing at £8 per 2-metre panel and posts at £2 each? Each fence must include a gate 2 m wide, costing £25.00. (Ignore the width of posts.)

	length	breadth		length	breadth
(a)	12 m	4 m	(b)	14 m	8 m
(c)	16 m	10 m	(d)	16 m	12 m
(e)	18 m	12 m	(f)	28 m	14 m
(g)	24 m	16 m	(h)	32 m	20 m
(i)	32 m	24 m	(j)	48 m	30 m

3. Find the missing dimensions of the rectangles of which details are given in the following table:

	area	length	breadth
(a)	480 m²	24 m	?
(b)	960 m²	40 m	?
(c)	2 400 m²	120 m	?
(d)	3 000 m²	175 m	?
(e)	5 400 m²	?	45 m
(f)	7 200 m²	?	48 m
(g)	8 000 m²	320 m	?
(h)	24 000 m²	?	135 m
(i)	32 000 m²	?	125 m
(j)	96 000 m²	320 m	?

4. The perimeter of a football field is 360 m, and its length is 100 m. What is the breadth?

5. The perimeter of a rectangular heating panel is 2.6 m. Its length is 0.8 m. What is its breadth? What is its area?

6. The perimeter of a rectangular field is 1 366 m. Its length is 380 m. What is its breadth?

7. The area of a rectangular sports pitch is 10 800 m². Its breadth is 90 m. What is its length? What is its perimeter?

8. The area of a rectangular swimming pool is 1 650 m². Its length is 55 m. What is its breadth? What is its perimeter?

9. The area of a rectangular recreation ground is 25 200 m². Its breadth is 140 m. What is its length? What is its perimeter?

10. The area of a rectangular playing field is 11 550 m². Its length is 110 m. Find (a) its breadth and (b) its perimeter.

28.8 Volumes of Cubes and Cuboids

Volume is a measure of the three-dimensional space occupied by an object. The term *cubic capacity* is sometimes used for the volume of available space inside an object such as a refrigerator, or the combustion chamber of a petrol engine.

To find the volume of a cuboid we use the formula

$$Volume = length \times breadth \times height$$
or $$Volume = l \times b \times h$$

If we measure the dimension of the cuboid in metres the volume will be in *cubic metres* (written m³) but the *cubic centimetre* (cm³) is also commonly used as a unit of volume, and the *cubic decimetre* (dm³) is widely employed, usually under its other name, the *litre* (l).

Example

What is the volume of a packing case with length = 2 m, breadth = 1.5 m and height = 1.2 m?

$$Volume = l \times b \times h$$
$$= 2 \text{ m} \times 1.5 \text{ m} \times 1.2 \text{ m}$$
$$= 3 \text{ m}^2 \times 1.2 \text{ m}$$
$$= 3.6 \text{ m}^3$$

Example

What is the volume of an air-mail packet measuring 17 cm by 13 cm by 9 cm?

$$Volume = 17 \text{ cm} \times 13 \text{ cm} \times 9 \text{ cm}$$
$$= 1 989 \text{ cm}^3$$

Example

How many cubes of dehydrated food measuring 2 cm along the edge can be fitted into a packet 16 cm long, 12 cm wide and 6 cm high?

> The cubes will fit into the packet as follows:
> 8 cubes along the longest side
> 6 cubes along the width
> 3 cubes high
> Number of cubes = 8 × 6 × 3
> = 144 cubes

Example

A container has a volume of $37\frac{1}{2}$ m³. Its length is 6 m and its width $2\frac{1}{2}$ m. How high is it?

$$\text{Volume} = l \times b \times h$$

Therefore
$$h = \frac{\text{volume}}{l \times b}$$

$$= \frac{37.5}{6 \times 2.5} \text{ m}$$

$$= \frac{37.5}{15} \text{ m}$$

$$= 2\frac{1}{2} \text{ m}$$

28.9 Exercises: Volumes of Cubes and Cuboids

1. Find the volumes of the cuboids which have the following dimensions:

	length	breadth	height
(a)	5 cm	3 cm	2 cm
(b)	8 cm	6 cm	4 cm
(c)	10 cm	5 cm	3 cm
(d)	12 cm	8 cm	6 cm
(e)	15 cm	10 cm	8 cm
(f)	3 m	2 m	1 m
(g)	3 m	1.5 m	1.2 m
(h)	4 m	2.8 m	2.4 m
(i)	5.5 m	2.5 m	1.6 m
(j)	8.5 m	3.5 m	1.5 m

2. How many packets each 1 cubic decimetre (1 dm³) can be packed into each of the following crates?

	length	breadth	height
(a)	2 m	1 m	0.5 m
(b)	1.5 m	1.2 m	0.8 m
(c)	1.8 m	1.3 m	1 m
(d)	2.3 m	1.5 m	1.2 m
(e)	2.5 m	1.8 m	1.4 m
(f)	3.2 m	2 m	1.5 m
(g)	4.6 m	2.1 m	1.8 m
(h)	5.0 m	2.2 m	2 m
(i)	5.5 m	3 m	2.2 m
(j)	6.5 m	3.2 m	2.5 m

3. The volume of a box is 3 m³. If the area of the box is 6 m² what is the height of the box?

4. Find the volume of each of the solids shown in Fig. 28.8. The dimensions are given in centimetres. (It will be necessary to divide the irregular shapes into two or more rectangular solids, to find the volume of each and add the volumes together.)

5. What is the area of the base of a box which has a volume of 420 cm³ and is 5 cm high?

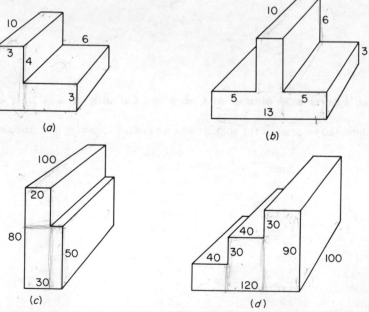

Fig. 28.8 Question 4

28.10 Mental Arithmetic Exercises

1. $200 \times 1\,700 =$
2. $3.6 + 4.25 + 17.19 =$
3. £254.20 − £138.50 =
4. What will 7 tickets at £2.45 each cost altogether?
5. $\frac{3}{4} \times \frac{2}{5} \times \frac{7}{10} =$
6. What is left when 2.75 kilograms is taken from 15.50 kilograms?
7. Divide £200 in the ratio $5 : 2 : 1$.
8. What will be the sale price of an item normally marked at £5.50 but reduced in a sale by 10 per cent?
9. What is the average of 5, 7, 12, 15 and 16?
10. Change £150 to Norwegian krone at the exchange rate of 11.50 k = £1.
11. What is the simple interest on £550 for 4 years at $7\frac{1}{2}$ per cent per annum?
12. An item sold normally at £950 is sold on hire purchase terms over 2 years after a deposit of £50 has been paid. What will be added for interest at 10 per cent per annum?
13. What is the area of a rectangle measuring $4\frac{1}{2}$ m by $3\frac{1}{2}$ m?
14. A container measures 3 m by 4 m by 8 m. What is its volume?
15. What will be the freight charge at £15 per cubic metre for a crate measuring 3 m by 2 m by 2 m?

Unit Twenty-nine

Circles and Cylinders

29.1 The Circumference of a Circle

A circle is a perfectly round plane figure; sometimes the word is used to mean the line enclosing such a figure, every point of which is at the same distance from a fixed point. It is most easily drawn with a pair of compasses, the legs of which may be opened to a suitable dimension, which becomes the *radius* of the circle. The circle is drawn by keeping one leg of the compasses fixed (at the *centre* of the circle) and rotating the other leg, carrying a pencil or other marking material, around it (Fig. 29.1).

Fig. 29.1 A pair of compasses

Fig. 29.2 shows the names of the parts of a circle. There is a constant relationship between the *diameter* and the *circumference* of a circle: no matter how big or how small the circle the circumference will always be roughly $3\frac{1}{7}$ times as large as the diameter. The actual ratio is 1 : 3.141 59; to get over the awkwardness of this figure it is always called π (the Greek letter pronounced *pie*), and in this book its value is taken as $3\frac{1}{7}$ or 3.14.

We may therefore use the following formula in any calculation about the circumference of a circle:

$$\text{Circumference} = \pi \times D,$$

usually written as just πD.

Since the diameter of a circle is twice the radius (look at Fig. 29.2 again), we can say

$$D = 2r$$

and
$$\text{Circumference} = \pi \times 2r \text{ or } 2\pi r$$

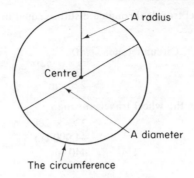

Fig. 29.2 The parts of a circle

We therefore have two formulae for the circumference of a circle:

$$Circumference = \pi D$$
$$Circumference = 2\pi r$$

There are countless occasions when this formula is useful—for example, in calculating how much sheet metal is needed to make a certain number of tins for baked beans, or how many times thread should be wound round a reel if the reel is to carry, say, 100 m of thread.

Example

Find the circumference of a circle of diameter 7 cm.

$$Circumference = \pi D$$
$$= 3\tfrac{1}{7} \times 7 \text{ cm}$$
$$= \tfrac{22}{7} \times 7^1 \text{ cm}$$
$$= 22 \text{ cm}$$

Example

Find the circumference of a circle with radius 21 cm.

$$Circumference = 2\pi r$$
$$= 2 \times 3\tfrac{1}{7} \times 21 \text{ cm}$$
$$= 2 \times \tfrac{22}{7} \times 21^3 \text{ cm}$$
$$= 132 \text{ cm}$$

Example

How far will a wheel travel if its diameter is 70 cm and it rotates 200 times?

Clearly the wheel travels through a distance equal to its own circumference when it rotates once.

$$\text{Circumference} = \pi D$$
$$= \tfrac{22}{7_1} \times \cancel{7}0^{10} \text{ cm}$$
$$= 220 \text{ cm}$$

So in 200 rotations the wheel travels through

$$220 \times 200 \text{ cm}$$
$$= 44\,000 \text{ cm}$$
$$= 440 \text{ m}$$

29.2 Exercises: Finding Circumferences of Circles

1. Find the circumferences of the circles whose diameters are given below. Your answers may involve some simple fractions. (Take $\pi = 3\frac{1}{7}$.)

(a) $3\frac{1}{2}$ cm	(b) 14 cm
(c) 7 cm	(d) 21 cm
(e) $10\frac{1}{2}$ cm	(f) 12 cm
(g) 25 cm	(h) 28 cm
(i) 3 m	(j) 14 m

2. Find the circumferences of the circles whose radii are given below. Your answers may involve some simple fractions. (Take $\pi = 3\frac{1}{7}$.)

(a) 4 cm	(b) 7 m
(c) 14 m	(d) 42 cm
(e) 35 cm	(f) $10\frac{1}{2}$ m
(g) 21 m	(h) 49 m
(i) 56 m	(j) 60 m

3. How far will a vehicle travel if its wheels have a diameter of 63 cm and they rotate 2 000 times? (Take $\pi = 3.14$.)

4. How far will a bicycle travel if its wheels are 70 cm in diameter and they rotate 15 000 times on the journey? (Take $\pi = 3.14$.)

5. How far will a train travel if its wheels have a radius of 42 cm and they rotate 180 000 times on the journey? (Give your answer in kilometres, and take $\pi = 3.14$.)

29.3 The Area of a Circle

The area of a circle, like all other areas, has to be measured in square units, for example, square centimetres or square metres. Clearly this is not easy, since a circle does not divide up into squares. We can, however, demonstrate very simply the probable relationship between the area of a circle and its radius by dividing the circle into portions and re-assembling them in a particular way to produce an approximately rectangular figure. We can then establish the area by using the formula for the area of a rectangle (see Section 28.1):

$$\text{Area of a rectangle} = \text{length} \times \text{breadth}$$

Fig. 29.3(*a*) shows a circle with radius *r*, cut up into eight equal parts. One of these parts has been subdivided into two smaller parts, each of which is therefore one-sixteenth of the original circle. When they are laid out as shown in Fig. 29.3(*b*), the nine parts form a roughly rectangular shape, except that there is a ripple or wavy line along the two long edges.

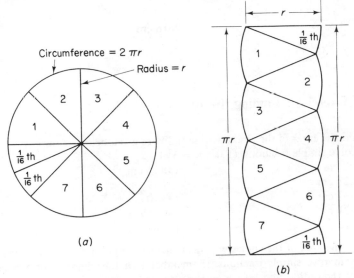

Fig. 29.3 *Finding the area of a circle*

Consider the dimensions of this rough rectangle. Its breadth is *r*, the same as the radius of the circle. Its length is πr, because the entire circumference of the circle is $2\pi r$ and each of the long sides of the rectangle consists of half the circumference. The ripple along the edge can be regarded as of no importance. If we had originally cut the circle into eighty parts instead of eight, the ripple would have been very small indeed. Had we cut it into eight million parts the ripple would have been too tiny to see.

The figure can therefore be regarded as a rectangle with a breadth *r* and a length πr. Clearly, the area of this rectangle is the same as that of a circle with radius *r*.

$$\text{Area} = l \times b$$
$$= r \times \pi r$$

Now $r \times r$ is usually written as r^2, so the formula for calculating the area of a circle is:

$$\textit{Area of circle} = \pi r^2$$

Example

Find the area of a circle radius 14 cm.

$$\text{Area of circle} = \pi r^2$$
$$= 3\tfrac{1}{7} \times 14 \text{ cm} \times 14 \text{ cm}$$
$$= \tfrac{22}{7}_{1} \times 14^{2} \times 14 \text{ cm}^2$$
$$= 44 \times 14 \text{ cm}^2$$
$$= 616 \text{ cm}^2$$

$$\begin{array}{r} 44 \\ \times\ 14 \\ \hline 176 \\ 440 \\ \hline 616 \end{array}$$

29.4 Exercises: Finding the Areas of Circles

1. Find the areas of the circles whose radii are given below. Your answers may involve simple fractions. (Take $\pi = 3\tfrac{1}{7}$.)
   (a) 7 cm
   (b) 14 cm
   (c) 28 cm
   (d) 49 cm
   (e) $3\tfrac{1}{2}$ cm
   (f) 10 cm
   (g) 21 cm
   (h) 25 cm
   (i) 42 cm
   (j) 63 cm

2. Find the area of the circles whose diameters are given below. Your answers may involve simple fractions. (Remember that the diameter of a circle is twice the radius, and take $\pi = 3\tfrac{1}{7}$.)
   (a) 14 cm
   (b) 35 m
   (c) 18 cm
   (d) 42 m
   (e) 56 cm
   (f) 21 m
   (g) 12 cm
   (h) 112 m
   (i) 7 cm
   (j) 273 m

29.5 The Area of a Ring

It is sometimes necessary to work out the area of circular rings, such as the one in Fig. 29.4. Any ring is based on two circles, an inner circle and an outer one. The area of the ring is the difference between the area of the larger circle and the area of the smaller circle. If these have radii of R and r respectively, then

$$Area\ of\ ring = \pi R^2 - \pi r^2$$

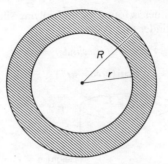

Fig. 29.4 The area of a ring

This is easy to calculate, but it can be made even easier by the help of some simple algebra:

(a) Take out π as a common factor:

$$\text{Area} = \pi(R^2 - r^2)$$

(b) $R^2 - r^2$ is a difference of two squares, and

$$R^2 - r^2 = (R + r)(R - r)$$

So we can say that

$$\textit{Area of ring} = \pi(R + r)(R - r)$$

Find the area of a ring formed by two circles whose radii are 11 cm and 7 cm.

$$\begin{aligned}
\text{Area of ring} &= \pi(R + r)(R - r) \\
&= \tfrac{22}{7}(11 + 7)(11 - 7) \text{ cm}^2 \\
&= \tfrac{22}{7}(18 \times 4) \text{ cm}^2 \\
&= \tfrac{22}{7} \times 72 \text{ cm}^2
\end{aligned}$$

$$\begin{array}{r}
72 \\
\times\ 22 \\
\hline
144 \\
1\,440 \\
\hline
1\,584
\end{array}$$

$$\begin{aligned}
&= \tfrac{1\,584}{7} \text{ cm}^2 \\
&= 226\tfrac{2}{7} \text{ cm}^2
\end{aligned}$$

29.6 The Volume of a Cylinder

A cylinder is a solid with a circular base and parallel sides, so that wherever it is cut across, the cross-section is a circle with the same radius as that of the base. The word comes from the Greek 'to roll'.

The volume of a cylinder is found by multiplying the area of the base (πr^2) by the height of the cylinder (h),

$$\textit{Volume of a cylinder} = \pi r^2 h$$

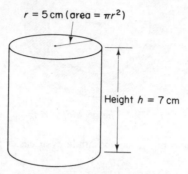

Fig. 29.5 A cylinder

Example

Find the volume of the cylinder illustrated in Fig. 29.4.

$$\text{Volume of cylinder} = \pi r^2 h$$
$$= \tfrac{22}{7} \times 5 \text{ cm} \times 5 \text{ cm} \times 7 \text{ cm}$$
$$= 110 \times 5 \text{ cm}^3$$
$$= 550 \text{ cm}^3$$

29.7 Exercises: Rings and Cylinders

1. Find the areas of the rings made by two circles of radius R and r, if $\pi = 3\frac{1}{7}$ and R and r are as follows:
   (a) $R = 7$ cm and $r = 4$ cm
   (b) $R = 5$ cm and $r = 2$ cm
   (c) $R = 11$ cm and $r = 7$ cm
   (d) $R = 18$ cm and $r = 14$ cm
   (e) $R = 27$ cm and $r = 23$ cm

2. Find the areas of the rings made by two circles of radius R and r, if $\pi = 3.14$ and R and r are as follows:
   (a) $R = 15$ m and $r = 13$ m
   (b) $R = 11$ m and $r = 8$ m
   (c) $R = 7$ m and $r = 5$ m
   (d) $R = 29$ m and $r = 25$ m
   (e) $R = 36$ m and $r = 32$ m

3. Find the volumes of the cylinders of radius r and height h, if $\pi = 3.14$ and r and h are as follows:

(a) $r = 3$ cm and $h = 6$ cm
(b) $r = 5$ cm and $h = 8$ cm
(c) $r = 7$ cm and $h = 10$ cm
(d) $r = 11$ cm and $h = 12$ cm
(e) $r = 14$ cm and $h = 15$ cm

4. Find the volumes of the cylindrical oil-storage tanks whose dimensions are as follows (take $\pi = 3.14$):

(a) radius $= 10$ m and height $= 5$ m
(b) radius $= 12$ m and height $= 7$ m
(c) radius $= 16$ m and height $= 7$ m
(d) radius $= 20$ m and height $= 14$ m
(e) radius $= 30$ m and height $= 14$ m

29.8 Mental Arithmetic Exercises

1. $49\ 752 \div 12 =$
2. $25.55 \div 0.5 =$
3. $3\frac{3}{4} \div 2\frac{6}{7} =$
4. £327.60 $\div 9 =$
5. Round off 638 to the nearest 100.
6. How many days are there from 27 May to 20 July inclusive?
7. $1\ 700 \times 5\ 000 =$
8. $1\ 089 + 134 + 49 + 715 =$
9. How many cubes (each having sides 1 cm long) can be packed into a carton 10 cm long, 8 cm wide and 6 cm high?
10. A factory is rated at £2 400 and rates are fixed at £1.20 in the pound. How much must the owner pay in rates?
11. A retailer marks up all stock by $33\frac{1}{3}$ per cent. An item bought for £48 is then sold in a sale at 10 per cent less than normal prices. What was the selling price?
12. Gas is 27p per therm. What must I pay for 500 therms if a standing charge of £8.50 is also added to the bill?
13. What is the area of a circle of radius 7 cm? (Take $\pi = 3\frac{1}{7}$.)
14. A salesman earns a commission of $1\frac{1}{2}$ per cent on sales of £14 500 plus a basic salary of £50 a month. What were his month's earnings?
15. What is the circumference of a wheel of radius 21 cm? (Take $\pi = 3\frac{1}{7}$.)

Unit Thirty

Simple Business Statistics

30.1 What are Statistics?

The word *statistics* is used in two senses: first, to refer to numerical facts—such as the number of people living in a certain town, or the number of cars using a traffic route each day—and, second, the study of ways of collecting and interpreting these facts.

Statistics starts with the collection of figures, called *data*. In their untreated form this basic statistical material is often called *raw data*. Once collected the raw data can be *processed*. This may be done, as in this Unit, by simple arithmetic, but in many offices the processing is done with the help of computers: this is known as *electronic data processing*. As a result of this processing more useful statistics will be derived from the raw data. Thus we have collections of information called *statistics*, and conclusions drawn from these, which are called *derived statistics*.

Suppose we collect figures about the numbers of families living in a town and the number of private motor cars. We might find that

Number of families = 10 000
Number of private motor cars = 15 000 } *these are statistics*

On average there are $1\frac{1}{2}$ cars per family—*this is a derived statistic*

Every large organization, whether it is a government department or a commercial office, processes data on all important aspects of its work. These may be records of births or deaths, exports, imports, sales of manufactured goods, reliability of different components, and so forth. It is on the basis of deductions made by statisticians from their analysis of data that future policies are largely based.

A number of elementary ideas about statistics are dealt with here, and you will meet examples of their use later in the book.

30.2 Collecting Data

Data can be collected in a number of ways. Many business managers require monthly reports from all their departments on such matters as sales, purchases, capital expenditure, wages paid, staff employed, and so on. These figures can then be used to compare actual performances with planned performances, and adjustments may be made in order to achieve better results.

Student Income and Expenditure Inquiry

Surname .... Initials ....

Age in years .... Course ....

Part 1. This part of the form inquires about your total income for the year. Please estimate the answer to each question as accurately as possible.

How much money do you expect to receive this year (September–August)

£

(a) from official grants?
(b) from your parents?
(c) from part-time or holiday earnings?
(d) from other sources?

Total income for the session   £ _____

Part 2. This part asks you to record your actual financial position for this week (December 6–12 19....)

How much money have you received this week

£

(a) from your parents?
(b) from earnings?
(c) from other sources (savings drawn out, etc.)?   _____

Total income for this week   £ _____

Had you any savings at the start of this week?   Yes/No

If yes, please tick the appropriate box

£5 or less ☐   £20.01–50 ☐
£5.01–10 ☐   £50.01–100 ☐
£10.01–20 ☐   more than £100 ☐

Part 3. This part asks you to state your likely expenditure for this week under certain headings:

£

(a) Rent or lodgings
(b) Board
(c) Other food
(d) Books and materials
(e) Entertainment
(f) Other (please explain)   _____

Total expenditure for this week   £ _____

Fig. 30.1 A questionnaire about student income and expenditure

Other data are collected as the result of a planned inquiry, using forms which are specially designed to obtain the information required.

Figs. 30.1 and 30.2 illustrate two methods of collecting raw data. Fig. 30.1 is a questionnaire designed to obtain information about income and expenditure by teenage students at a Further Education Centre. Fig. 30.2 is part of the record of a traffic census taken from a bridge overlooking a motorway. As each vehicle passed under the bridge, the observer recorded its passage by marking a small stroke under the appropriate heading. For ease of totalling at the end, he has arranged these strokes in groups of five, like little five-barred gates.

Traffic Census   M1 Motorway, A418 overpass

Vehicles travelling north

Date _27 May 19--_   Time _11.45 a.m. - 12.00 noon_

(Private cars)

JHT   JHT   JHT   JHT   JHT
JHT   JHT   JHT   JHT   JHT
JHT   JHT   JHT   JHT   JHT
JHT   JHT   JHT   JHT   JHT
JHT   JHT   JHT   JHT   JHT
JHT   JHT   JHT   JHT   JHT
JHT   JHT   JHT   JHT   JHT
JHT

(Vans and light goods vehicles)

JHT   JHT   JHT   JHT   JHT
JHT   JHT   JHT   JHT   JHT
JHT   JHT   JHT   JHT   JHT
JHT   JHT   JHT   JHT   JHT
JHT   III

(Heavy goods vehicles)

JHT   JHT   JHT   JHT   JHT
JHT   JHT   JHT   JHT   JHT
JHT   JHT   JHT   JHT   JHT
JHT   JHT   JHT   JHT   JHT
JHT   JHT   JHT   JHT   JHT
JHT   JHT   JHT   IIII

(Coaches and buses)

JHT   JHT   JHT   JHT   JHT
JHT   JHT   JHT   JHT   III

Fig. 30.2 A traffic census

30.3 The Presentation of Data: Rounding

Once we have collected the raw data, we must find a way to present them in some meaningful form. Most raw data are so numerous and detailed that the first step has to be to extract essential information and find a way of expressing it in figures which are simple to understand. For example, if we are counting the population of an entire country, some of the details of the statistics will be relatively unimportant. Consider the following raw data:

Population of the United Kingdom, June 19 . .

Males (0–14 years)	6 926 434
Females (0–14 years)	6 572 894
Males (15–65 years)	17 399 146
Females (15–65 years)	17 567 247
Males (65 years and over)	2 756 818
Females (65 years and over)	4 446 899

Look, for instance, at the number of young males in the first line of this table: 6 926 434. Clearly the first four digits of this number are the most significant: compared with the 6 926 thousands, the odd 434 units are not very important. If we leave them out and *round off* the figure to the nearest thousand, writing it simply as 6 926 000, the statistics will be easier to understand, and no great error will be introduced.

When rounding off figures like this, we use the same rule as when we correct up decimal fractions. Anything over halfway *rounds up* the last remaining digit to the next higher number. Anything less than half is disregarded altogether. An exact half rounds to the nearest even number.

Thus 6 926 434 rounds to 6 926 thousands, and 6 926 718 rounds to 6 927 thousands. 6 926 500 *rounds down* to 6 926 thousands (the last figure is an even number) but 6 927 500 *rounds up* to 6 928 thousands (the last figure is therefore an even number).

Example

Round off, to the nearest thousand, the data given above for the population of the United Kingdom.

Population of the United Kingdom June 19 . . ('000s)

Males (0–14 years)	6 926 (rounded down)
Females (0–14 years)	6 573 (rounded up)
Males (15–65 years)	17 399 (rounded down)
Females (15–65 years)	17 567 (rounded down)
Males (65 years and over)	2 757 (rounded up)
Females (65 years and over)	4 447 (rounded up)

30.4 Exercises: Rounding Up and Down

1. An investigation into the life of electric lamps results in the following information (lamp lifetimes in hours):

lamp *A* 177	lamp *B* 293	lamp *C* 212	lamp *D* 104
lamp *E* 597	lamp *F* 239	lamp *G* 414	lamp *H* 426
lamp *I* 89	lamp *J* 437		

   Find the life of each lamp to the nearest 10 hours and present your answers as a table as follows:

   Life of electric lamps (in hours)
   Lamp *A*   . . .
   Lamp *B* etc.   . . .

2. The ages of students on a motor engineering course are as follows:

Mr *A* 17 years 4 months	Mr *B* 18 years 11 months
Mr *C* 19 years 6 months	Mr *D* 27 years 2 months
Mr *E* 24 years 1 month	Mr *F* 45 years 4 months
Mr *G* 18 years 10 months	Mr *H* 19 years 8 months
Mr *I* 24 years 5 months	Mr *J* 17 years 0 months

   Enter these ages, rounded off to the nearest year, into a table headed *Ages of students (in years)*.

3. The population of a borough is given as follows:

Males (over 18)	130 724	Females (over 18)	105 293
Males (14–18)	5 832	Females (14–18)	7 197
Males (under 14)	12 499	Females (under 14)	11 818

   Rewrite this list, rounding off each number to the nearest thousand.

4. A daily train runs from a refinery at Shellhaven to a distribution depot at Reading. The weekly tonnages certified by the Customs authorities are as follows:

Monday 72 509 tonnes	Tuesday 74 296 tonnes
Wednesday 78 112 tonnes	Thursday 58 998 tonnes
Friday 49 759 tonnes	Saturday 84 273 tonnes
Sunday 56 505 tonnes	

   Rewrite these tonnages in a table, rounding off each to the nearest 100 tonnes.

5. The weights of ten recruits to the army are as follows:

A = 58.59 kg	*B* = 67.25 kg	*C* = 49.12 kg	*D* = 71.18 kg
E = 57.56 kg	*F* = 62.35 kg	*G* = 64.79 kg	*H* = 59.75 kg
I = 72.35 kg	*J* = 68.19 kg		

   Rewrite them, rounding each off to the nearest kilogram.

6. (*a*) Add the following numbers and round off the total to the nearest 100:
   5 773, 3 944, 3 449, 5 822, 7 169

(b) Round off each of the above numbers to the nearest 100 and then add them.

(c) Subtract 2 945 from 9 186 and round off the difference to the nearest 100.

(d) Round off 2 945 and 9 186 to the nearest 100 and obtain the difference.

(e) Why do we often round off numbers in statistical work?   (RSA)

30.5 The Presentation of Data: Tabulation

When we have carried out a statistical inquiry we usually find we have acquired an overwhelming mass of chaotic and unclear information. We have to bring it into a more useful form by cutting out some of the unimportant details and emphasizing the most significant items. *Rounding* has already eliminated some of these details. *Tabulation*—presenting the information in the form of a table—will make the picture clearer by grouping together similar items, listing them in classes, and presenting these classes in a form which is easy to read.

It is very important that we choose and define the classes clearly so that we are quite sure of the group in which we should classify any particular item. For example, if we have a group of items costing £5–£10 and another group costing £10–£15, we shall not know into which group to put an item costing exactly £10. In this example, it would therefore be better to make the groups either £5–£9.99 and £10–£14.99, or £5.01–£10 and £10.01–£15.

Example

An investigation into the wages paid to 20 school-leavers during one week found that their wage packets contained the following amounts:

£35.00	£49.50	£36.75	£39.50	£38.80
£50.00	£39.50	£38.50	£36.90	£28.00
£29.50	£41.50	£42.50	£53.60	£32.50
£46.50	£48.20	£52.50	£44.75	£28.50

Tabulate these so that it is clear how many are paid in each of the following classes: under £30, £30—£34.99, £35—£39.99, £40—£44.99, £45—£49.99 and £50 or more.

Sorting out the data we have:

Under £30	/ / /
£30—£34.99	/
£35—£39.99	~~////~~ / /
£40—£44.99	/ / /
£45—£49.99	/ / /
£50 or more	/ / /

The tabulation will therefore be presented as follows:

School-leavers' wages (sample of 20 leavers)

Class	Number
Under £30	3
£30—£34.99	1
£35—£39.99	7
£40—£44.99	3
£45—£49.99	3
£50 or more	3
Total in all classes	20

Derived statistics

Sometimes a table can be improved by the presentation of derived statistics calculated from the collected statistics. Often these take the form of percentages calculated in the usual way.

Thus the traffic census report in Fig. 30.2 can be presented in a table as follows:

Motor traffic on the M1 motorway (15-minute period on May 27 19..)

Private cars	180
Vans and light goods vehicles	108
Heavy goods vehicles	144
Coaches and buses	48
Total number of vehicles	480

Using these raw statistics we can compare the sizes of the various groups of vehicles as percentages of the total traffic, for instance:

$$\text{Percentage of private cars} = \frac{180}{480} \times 100$$
$$= \frac{75}{2}$$
$$= 37\frac{1}{2}\%$$

The other groups may be calculated similarly to give us the following extended table:

Motor traffic on the M1 motorway (15-minute period on May 27 19..)

	Number of vehicles	% of total traffic
Private cars	180	$37\frac{1}{2}$
Vans and light goods vehicles	108	$22\frac{1}{2}$
Heavy goods vehicles	144	30
Coaches and buses	48	10
Total	480	100

30.6 Exercises: Tabulation

1. In the year 19.. expenditure by consumers was given in the *Monthly Digest of Statistics* as follows:

   food £6 968m, drink £2 470m, tobacco £1 692m, housing £4 329m, fuel and light £1 607m, clothing £2 913m, other £14 525m.

   Draw up a table of these items and hence find the total expenditure by consumers in 19..

2. The monthly stocks of potatoes on the farms of the United Kingdom were given (in thousands of tonnes) as follows:

   January 1 663; February 1 183; March 663; April 323; May 102; June 13; July nil; August nil; September nil; October 4 673; November 4 019; December 3 381

   Present these in table form showing the monthly figures in one column and the sales from the farms each month in another column. In the previous December stocks had been 2 154 thousand tonnes. In October, when the crop was harvested, besides the 4 673 thousand tonnes of potatoes taken into stock, the farmers sold 626 thousand tonnes direct to the wholesalers.

3. The following figures show the output of petroleum products (in thousands of tonnes) from United Kingdom refineries in the month of June:

   butane 36; propane 41; aviation spirit 22; motor spirit 930; industrial and white spirit 10; kerosene (paraffin) 535; diesel oil 1 856; fuel oil 3 404; lubricating oil 114; others 22

   Arrange these figures in table form and hence calculate the total output for the month.

4. In the year 19.. United Kingdom reserves of cereals and cereal products (in thousands of tonnes) were as follows:

   wheat 1 075; wheat flour 825; oats 857; milled oats 372; barley 649; ground barley 133

Compile a table of these statistics. Your table should have three rows, for wheat, oats and barley respectively, each having one column for the whole grain and one for the ground cereal (that is flour, milled oats or ground barley). Totals of both rows and columns should be shown and the grand total calculated.

5. The students' union in your College is conducting surveys on (a) students' journeys to and from College, and (b) students' opinions on the College refectory facilities. Design a questionnaire (not more than 8 questions) for *one* of these surveys paying particular attention to the type of student and the ease of reading answers from the forms after completion.   (RSA)

6. The wages (in £s) paid to 50 young people in a factory in a particular week are given as follows:

40.57	41.74	42.44	46.92	44.28
48.64	47.75	42.76	44.71	43.63
44.38	44.44	45.14	44.83	43.84
45.49	43.82	44.38	45.62	42.25
44.77	45.74	45.86	42.15	43.55
44.86	43.11	43.75	44.15	44.74
47.15	44.54	43.61	44.77	44.81
44.32	49.67	46.49	45.32	43.69
42.96	45.81	41.81	43.47	44.94
46.85	44.77	44.85	45.61	48.88

Group the data into 10 classes, using class boundaries £40.00 to 40.99, £41.00 to 41.99, and so on up to £49.00 to 49.99 and present the results in tabular form. Why would it be wrong to use class boundaries £40 to 41, £41 to 42 and so on?   (RSA adapted)

30.7 Exercises: Derived Statistics

1. At the General Election in 19.. the number of votes cast for the Conservative Party was 13 106 905 (46.4 per cent of the total) while for the Labour Party and the Liberals 12 141 676 (43.0 per cent) and 2 109 218 (7.4 per cent) votes respectively were given. A further 900 473 (3.2 per cent) votes were cast for various other candidates. As a result, 330 Conservative, 287 Labour and 6 Liberal Members of Parliament were elected together with 6 other MPs.

Present this information in a suitable table which provides for appropriate totals and for any other calculations you may think necessary.   (RSA)

2. A recent report on housing statistics summarized the figures for 1976–9 as follows:

In the four years from 1976 to 1979, the number of new houses started has declined——338 000 started in 1976, 275 000 in 1977, 272 000 in 1978 and 228 000 in 1979. However, the number of grants approved (for improvements) rose steadily from 236 000 to 305 000 in 1977, 336 000 in 1978 and 406 000 in 1979. Since 1976, starts for new council housing have declined from 149 000 to 107 000 in 1977, to 89 000 in 1978 and 66 000 in 1979.

Tabulate the information and provide additional columns for any secondary statistics you think necessary. (Do not calculate the secondary statistics.)

3. The figures for inland waterway traffic in a four-week period are as follows:
   Total traffic 16 million tonnes; coal 10 million tonnes; iron and steel 4 million tonnes; other traffic 2 million tonnes
   Present this information in a table with three columns headed:

Type of traffic	Weight (in millions of tonnes)	% of total traffic

4. The figures for examination successes in a professional examination for the transport industry were as follows:

   16-year-olds, 25 passes; 17-year-olds, 40 passes; 18-year-olds, 130 passes; 19- and 20-year-olds, 265 passes; over 21, 440 passes

   Present these facts in a table of three columns headed:

Age of entrant	Number of successful candidates	% of total passes

   Give your results correct to 1 decimal place.

5. Passengers from European countries landing at a United Kingdom airport on a single summer's day last year were counted (in thousands) as follows:

   France, 6; Belgium, 2; Holland, 4; Germany, 5; Italy, 5; Spain, 13; Switzerland, 3; Scandinavia, 2; Greece, 2; others, 8

   Show these figures in a table, with three columns headed:

Country	Number of passengers	% of total

   Bring out the total for all countries at the bottom of the table.

6. In England in 1971 there were 16 070 000 dwellings, of these 8 360 000 were owner-occupied, 4 500 000 were rented from local authorities, 2 410 000 were rented from private owners, the remainder were held under other tenures. In Scotland in 1971 there were 1 800 000 dwellings, of these 540 000 were owner-occupied, 940 000 were rented from local authorities, 200 000 were rented from private owners, the remainder were held under other tenures.   Source: *Social Trends*

   Tabulate these data, calculate appropriate derived statistics and include these derived statistics in your tabulation.   (RSA)

7. In the United Kingdom in the financial year 1980–81 the total public expenditure on education was £10 061 million. £5 496 million were spent on schools, £1 144 million on further and adult education, £629 million on student awards, £894 million on universities. The remainder was spent on other educational expenditure. In the financial year 1951–52, £408 million was the total public expenditure on education. The expenditure in millions of pounds on schools, further and adult education, student awards and universities, was 281, 32, 9 and 37 respectively.

Source: *Social Trends* 1982

Tabulate these data, calculate appropriate secondary statistics and include the secondary statistics in your tabulation.   (RSA adapted)

Unit Thirty-one

The Presentation of Data: Pictograms and Charts

31.1 Data in Pictorial Form

Many people find it hard to comprehend information presented to them in number form. Small numbers like one, two or three are easy to understand, but large numbers like one million, two thousand or three hundred seem to be more difficult to grasp. It is therefore often helpful in business to display figures in some sort of picture form, and in this unit we shall discuss some ways in which this can be done.

When presenting information in picture form the following rules are very important:

(a) The presentation must be as striking as possible, ideally using different colours, or different kinds of shading and line thickness to distinguish the pieces of information being conveyed.

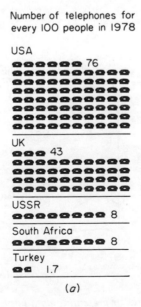

Number of telephones for every 100 people in 1978

USA
76

UK
43

USSR
8

South Africa
8

Turkey
1.7

(a)

Fig. 31.1(a) A pictogram

Hospital in-patient unit costs
(Source : *Department of Health and Social Security*)

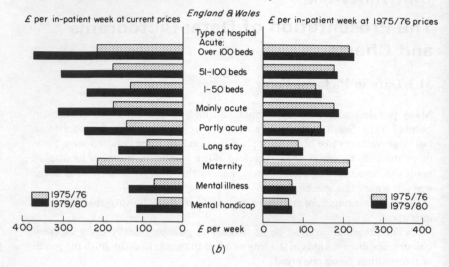

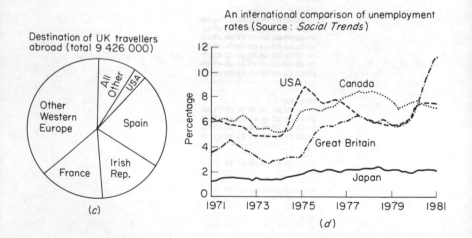

Fig. 31.1 Some ways of presenting data in pictorial form:
(a) a pictogram; (b) a bar chart; (c) a pie chart; (d) a graph
(by courtesy of The Controller, HMSO and 'Barclays Bank Review')

(*b*) There must be a clear title, explaining what the diagram is about.

(*c*) The diagram must be labelled clearly.

(*d*) The units of measurement must be shown, for example, £m (millions of pounds) or m³ (cubic metres).

Fig. 31.2 illustrates these points well, and the choice of a television set as a

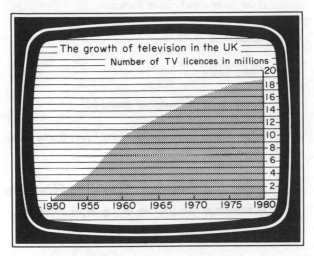

Fig. 31.2 Television data strikingly displayed
(by courtesy of 'Barclays Bank Review')

31.2 Pictograms

A *pictogram* uses little pictures to convey numerical information. Since a typical picture—perhaps a motor car—can hardly be drawn thousands of times on a chart, we often use one picture to represent an agreed number of objects. This must always be indicated on the pictogram; for example, we might say in a pictogram representing data on flight departures from an airport, that 'one aircraft represents 100 flights'. Then half an aircraft would represent 50 flights. Probably no attempt would be made to illustrate fractions of an aircraft smaller than one quarter.

Example

The number of motor car licences issued each year in the United Kingdom rose as follows:

1946	1.8 million
1950	2.1 million
1960	5.6 million
1970	11.8 million
1980	15.4 million

Illustrate this pictorially, choosing a car as the pictogram symbol and rounding off the data to the nearest $\frac{1}{4}$ million.

It is convenient to allow one symbol to represent 1 million licences (Fig. 31.3).

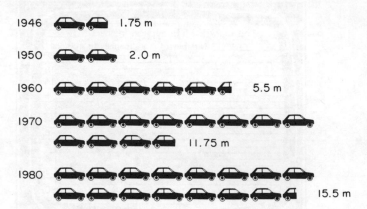

Number of motor car licences issued in the UK
(1 car represents 1 million licences)

1946   1.75 m

1950   2.0 m

1960   5.5 m

1970   11.75 m

1980   15.5 m

Fig. 31.3 A pictogram

31.3 Exercises: Pictograms

Present each of the following sets of data in a pictogram. In each case choose a suitable symbol and label your answer carefully to show the subject matter and the units used.

1. Exports of tuna fish from an East African republic over a four-year period were as follows:

year 1	200 tons
year 2	350 tons
year 3	450 tons
year 4	600 tons

2. Over five years recently, the output of shipyards in a Far Eastern country were as follows:

year 1	20 million tons
year 2	25 million tons
year 3	30 million tons
year 4	40 million tons
year 5	55 million tons

3. The numbers of colour television licences issued in the United Kingdom in the early 1970s were as follows:

1970	273 000
1972	1 635 000
1974	5 558 000
1976	8 628 000
1978	10 983 000

4. The expansion of air services to Swaziland is illustrated by the increasing number of passengers landing at the country's airports:

1965	1 256 passengers
1970	9 560 passengers
1975	17 250 passengers
1980	25 756 passengers

5. The numbers of vehicle tyres produced in the year 19.. in some major manufacturing countries were as follows:

United Kingdom	48 million
France	54 million
Japan	28 million
Italy	32 million
USSR	18 million
Brazil	6 million
Sweden	8 million

31.4 Bar Charts

A *bar chart* is simpler than a pictogram. It relates the information given to the length of a 'bar' or thick line drawn from some given starting point. The bars can be drawn either horizontally or vertically. Fig. 31.1(b) shows a bar chart representing the costs of in-patient provision to the National Health Service, at current and 1975–76 prices. This brings out the effect of inflation—the increased cost in money terms is greater than the increased cost in real terms.

As with all charts and diagrams, we have to choose a suitable scale, deciding, for example, whether 1 centimetre on the bar should represent 100 units of the data, or 1 000 or 1 000 000. Before we can draw the bar chart we must calculate how long to make each bar.

Example

The life expectation of both men and women has risen markedly over the last century. The Registrar-General gives the following information:

| | Expectation of life (years) | |
Year	Men	Women
1840	40	42
1870	41	45
1900	44	48
1930	59	63
1960	68	74

Source: *Digest of Statistics*

Illustrate this information using a suitable diagram.

If we select 1 centimetre as a suitable measure for each 10 years of life, then 1 millimetre will represent 1 year. We shall then draw the 1840 bars 4 centimetres long for men and 4.2 centimetres long for women, and the improving expectation of life in more recent times is represented by the increasing length of the bars for later years (Fig. 31.4).

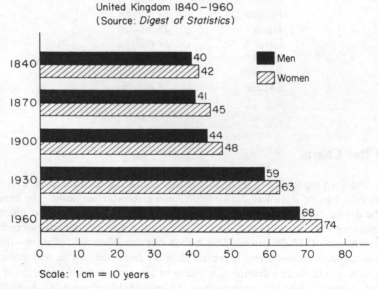

Fig. 31.4 A bar chart

31.5 Exercises: Bar Charts

1. The following information shows the growth in sales of a firm's engineering products in various overseas markets:

| | Foreign sales, Engineering Division (£ million) | |
	1960	1980
Australia	2.5	5.5
Far Eastern countries	3.8	6.5
South Africa	8.2	10.5
West Africa	4.6	14.5
Middle East	3.2	8.6
Europe	10.6	16.6
North America	8.2	12.4

Choose a suitable scale and draw a bar chart to illustrate this information. Be sure to label your diagram properly and give it an appropriate heading.

2. The income of the United Kingdom Government in 1981 was drawn from the following sources:

	£(000 million)
Taxes on income	30.9
Taxes on expenditure	37.3
National Insurance, etc.	14.0
Other receipts	8.8

Source: *National Income and Expenditure*

Choosing a suitable scale, draw a bar chart to illustrate this information. Be sure to label your diagram properly and give it an appropriate heading.

3. The volume of traffic on a road can be measured by finding the number of vehicles per mile. A comparison of traffic densities in a number of countries produced the following results:

Country	Number of vehicles per road-mile
United Kingdom	61
West Germany	51
Netherlands	51
Italy	49
Belgium	36
France	26
Sweden	20

Source: *British Road Federation, Basic Road Statistics*

Choosing a suitable scale, draw a bar chart to illustrate the statistics given. Be sure to label your diagram properly, and give it a suitable heading.

(RSA)

4. Pupils per teacher in secondary schools in England and Wales:

Year	Number of pupils per teacher
1951	20.6
1961	20.4
1971	17.8
1978	16.7

Source: *Social Trends*

Choosing a suitable scale, draw a bar chart to illustrate the statistics given. Be sure to label your diagram properly, and give it a suitable heading.

(RSA COS adapted)

5. Output of oil production platforms for North Sea gas from four platform-building sites is listed in the following table:

	1973	1975	1977	1979
Site 1	1	$1\frac{1}{2}$	$2\frac{1}{2}$	5
Site 2	$\frac{1}{2}$	1	$1\frac{1}{2}$	$3\frac{1}{2}$
Site 3	1	$1\frac{1}{2}$	$2\frac{1}{2}$	4
Site 4	$\frac{1}{2}$	1	2	3

Draw a bar chart for each of these years, showing the four building sites side by side and using a scale of 1 centimetre to represent 1 platform. Devise suitable headings and labels for the charts.

31.6 Pie Charts

A *pie chart* is used to display statistics which give the relative sizes of the components of a total sum: for example, it is a convenient method of showing how a country's exports are made up of manufactured goods, food products, raw materials, fuel and so on. We imagine the whole figure as a round pie, and the various parts of the whole as differently-sized slices of the pie. 'How big a slice of our exports is made up of manufactured goods?' is the sort of question which is often asked by politicians and administrators, and it refers to this useful way of displaying such data.

The size of a slice depends on the angle of the slice at the centre of the pie. The angles of all the slices add up to 360°; if we know the ratio (as a fraction or a percentage) between one part and the whole, we can therefore easily calculate how many degrees to give that slice in the pie chart.

Example

The chief leisure activities of males in the United Kingdom in 1978 are listed in the following table:

Activity	Percentage
Watching television	46
Drink-associated activities	13
Social activities at home	6
Social activities away from home	17
Domestic and other activities	18

Source: *Social Trends*

Prepare a pie chart displaying this information.

We first calculate the angle for the slice representing each activity, for example,

Watching television: angle of slice $= 46\%$ of $360°$
$$= \tfrac{46}{100} \times 360°$$
$$= 46 \times 3.6°$$

$$= 165.6°$$

$$\begin{array}{r} 46 \\ 3.6 \\ \hline 27\,6 \\ 138\,0 \\ \hline 165.6 \end{array}$$

The angles for the other slices, calculated similarly, come to:

Drink-associated activities	46.8°
Social activities at home	21.6°
Social activities away from home	61.2°
Domestic and other activities	64.8°

With this information we can draw the pie chart in Fig. 31.5.

31.7 Exercises: Pie Charts

1. Consumers' expenditure in the United Kingdom in 1979 was made up as shown in the table on page 242.

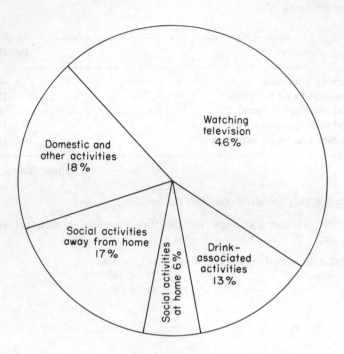

UK males: leisure activities 1978
(Source: *Social Trends*)

Watching
television
46%

Domestic and
other activities
18%

Social activities
away from home
17%

Social activities
at home 6%

Drink-
associated
activities
13%

Fig. 31.5 A pie chart

	Percentage of total
Food	18
Alcohol and tobacco	12
Housing, fuel and light	18
Motor vehicles and travel	10
Clothing, footwear and household goods	14
Other	28

Source: *Social Trends*

Present these data in a pie chart. Give the chart a suitable heading, and state
on it the source of the statistics. Mark each slice of the pie with an appropriate label.

2. The sizes of families in Great Britain in 1980 were as follows:

	Percentage
Families with no dependent children	52
Families with 1 child	18
Families with 2 children	20
Families with 3 children	7
Families with 4 or more children	3

Source: *Social Trends*

Draw a pie chart to illustrate these statistics. Give the chart a suitable heading, and state on it the source of the statistics. Mark each slice of the pie with its appropriate label.

3. The proportions of students in full-time higher education in the United Kingdom in 1977–78 were as follows:

	Males	Females
Colleges of education	7%	18%
Universities	28%	10%
Further education (advanced courses)	65%	72%

Source: *Statistics of Education*

Illustrate this information by means of two separate pie charts. Give each chart a suitable heading, and state the source of the statistics. Mark each slice of the pies with its appropriate label.

4. Public expenditure on social services and housing in 1963–64 and 1979–80 was as follows:

	Expenditure (£ million)	
	1963–64	1979–80
Education	1 330	9 963
National Health Service	1 070	9 362
Social Security benefits	2 040	19 530
Housing	660	6 419
Other	190	2 492
Total	5 290	47 766

Source: *Annual Abstract of Statistics* 1981, amended

(a) Draw a pie chart to illustrate 1963–64 expenditure, using a circle of radius 3 cm.

(b) Draw a pie chart to illustrate 1979–80 expenditure, using a circle of radius 9 cm.

Unit Thirty-two

The Presentation of Data: Graphs

32.1 What are Graphs?

A graph is a diagram which displays a relationship between two variable quantities, one of which is dependent on the other: for example, in a chart showing the changes in the body temperature of a hospital patient, time is the *independent variable* and temperature—which changes as time goes by—is the *dependent variable*. A graph is usually drawn on special paper printed with horizontal and vertical lines forming a grid. You should obtain some of this paper and use it for practice work and for answering the questions given in this Unit.

Before we can begin to *plot* (that is, to lay out or construct) a graph, we always draw two lines, one horizontal and one vertical, as its framework; these are the *axes* of the graph. The horizontal axis, usually called the x-axis, is used to plot the independent variable, and the vertical axis or y-axis, is used for the dependent variable: in a graph showing a firm's sales throughout the year, for instance, we should plot the months of the year horizontally and the values of the monthly sales, which vary as the months go by, would be plotted vertically.

Our next task is to select a suitable *scale* for our graph, according to the data supplied and the size of the paper. We should choose as large a scale as possible because then we can see easily what we are doing. Each axis should be clearly labelled with its scale. The point where the axes meet is the zero of both these scales and is called the *origin* of the graph.

The data are then entered on the graph. Each piece of our information consists of a pair of numbers: a particular value of the independent variable, x, always given first, and the corresponding value of the dependent variable, y. To plot this pair, we first measure along the x-axis a distance corresponding to x and then draw a straight line at right angles to the axis at this point; then we measure a distance y along the y-axis and there draw a second straight line at right angles to the y-axis. We mark the point where these two straight lines meet with a tiny cross: this is the point representing these particular values of x and y (Fig. 32.1). The straight lines drawn to enable us to locate the point will not be needed again, and can be erased.

We plot points representing the rest of the data in exactly the same way, and draw a line to join the points together. This line is the graph which shows how y varies with x.

Finally the graph is given a suitable explanatory title.

Example

Choosing suitable scales and putting in all necessary labels, draw a graph to

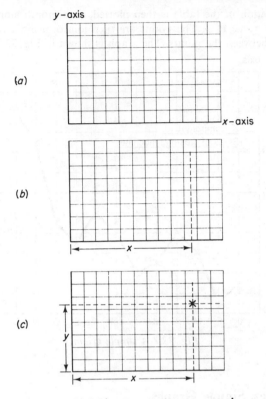

Fig. 32.1 Plotting a point on a graph

illustrate the following monthly sales figures for washing machines by the X Company Ltd.:

January	February	March	April	May	June
£7 500	£6 500	£9 000	£10 000	£8 500	£8 000

July	August	September	October	November	December
£10 000	£11 000	£9 500	£10 500	£14 500	£16 000

First we must choose scales for the axes. We can give the months of the year one large division each along the x-axis; we could not give them two divisions each, because the page is not large enough. To choose a scale for the vertical axis, we look at the data for the largest value of y that we must consider: that is, the December sales figure of £16 000. But we can see too that there is no value of y less than the February figure of £6 000. We can therefore ignore all that part of the y-axis lying below £6 000 and plot only the part lying between £6 000 and £16 000. This saves space and allows us to choose a scale in which one large division represents £1 000 of sales. Both scales are labelled.

The information in the table is then plotted, each month along the x-axis represents one value of x. The points are then joined, using a ruler to draw straight lines between the points. The graph is shown in Fig. 32.2.

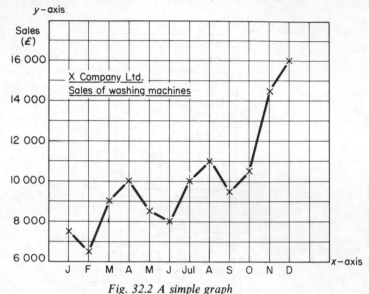

Fig. 32.2 A simple graph

32.2 Exercises: Simple Graphs

1. Choosing suitable scales, record on a graph the following numbers of television sets sold during a certain year:

January	February	March	April	May	June
2 700	2 500	3 100	3 500	3 800	4 000

July	August	September	October	November	December
3 800	3 200	3 600	4 500	4 800	6 000

2. Choosing suitable scales, record the following temperatures (measured on the Fahrenheit scale) on a temperature chart for Mr R. Bristow, a patient admitted to hospital with influenza at 8 a.m. on November 4.

8.00	10.00	noon	14.00	16.00
104°	104.2°	103.8°	103.0°	102.5°

18.00	20.00	22.00	midnight	
102°	102°	101.8°	101.5°	

3. Choosing suitable scales, record on a graph the following numbers of cars sold by a manufacturer during a particular year:

January	February	March	April	May	June
32 000	32 800	34 000	35 000	36 000	28 000

July	August	September	October	November	December
46 000	25 000	30 500	35 500	36 000	38 000

4. Choosing suitable scales, and using different coloured inks if you like, record on a single diagram the following figures for supermarket sales for two branches of a retail chain:

Cambridge branch sales (£):

January	February	March	April	May	June
2 500	2 300	2 600	2 800	3 100	3 300

July	August	September	October	November	December
3 050	3 400	3 700	4 100	4 800	4 950

Huntingdon branch sales (£):

January	February	March	April	May	June
2 000	2 200	2 600	3 000	3 500	3 800

July	August	September	October	November	December
3 900	4 000	4 500	4 800	5 500	6 000

32.3 Straight-line Graphs

Sales graphs like those we have discussed in the previous sections are zig-zag lines or sometimes curves; but some graphs are straight lines. This happens when there is a particular kind of arithmetical relationship between the two sets of data, called *direct variation*. Foreign currency conversions are examples of direct variation: every pound note is worth exactly the same number of Deutschemarks, and two pound notes are worth twice as many. If we plot this relationship on a graph we shall have a straight line. Such a line can be extended indefinitely, and the relationship it represents will be valid whatever the values of the variables. We can use such a graph as a ready-reckoner, reading off values other than the ones plotted, either within the range given (*interpolation*) or outside this range, by extending the straight line (*extrapolation*).

Such a graph can be drawn after plotting only two points, but in practice at least three are usually plotted, to guard against error. Suitably spaced out figures should be used.

Example

A man earns £1.70 per hour. Plot this information on a graph for working weeks up to 60 hours, and hence read off how much he earns for a 48-hour week. How many hours does he need to work to earn £100 in one week?

The wage the man earns depends directly on the hours he works; so we can expect a straight-line graph. Let us plot points for 20 hours, 40 hours and 60 hours a week: these figures are chosen because these are fairly sensible for a week's work. Few people work less than 20 hours or more than 60 hours in a week.

$$\text{Earnings for 20 hours' work} = 20 \times £1.70 = £34.00$$
$$\text{Similarly, earnings for 40 hours' work} = £68.00$$
$$\text{earnings for 60 hours' work} = £102.00$$

We plot working hours on the x-axis and earnings (the dependent variable) on the y-axis. Plotting the three points gives us the graph in Fig. 32.3.

(a) To find the man's earnings for a 48-hour week, we find the point on the x-axis corresponding to 48 hours, and draw a line at right angles to this axis. Where this cuts the graph we draw a second line at right angles to the first. The point where this second line meets the y-axis—that is, the earnings axis—corresponds to the man's earnings for a 48-hour week: it is just below £82.

(b) To read off how long the man must work to earn £100 we carry out the

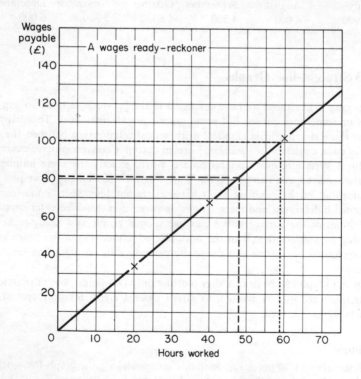

Fig. 32.3 A straight-line graph

reverse process. We draw a line at right angles to the earnings axis at the point corresponding to £100. Where this cuts the graph we draw a second line at right angles to the first: the point where this second line meets the x-axis gives us the hours to be worked in order to earn £100, that is, about 59 hours.

These answers are approximate. Unless the scale of the graph is very large, readings cannot be made to any high degree of accuracy.

32.4 Exercises: Straight-line Graphs

1. A man works for £2.40 per hour. Plot his possible earnings as a graph, using plotting points based on 20 hours', 40 hours' and 60 hours' work. Then use your graph to calculate (a) the wages he earns for working 48 hours, and (b) how many hours he worked in a week when his wage was £134.40.

2. Draw a graph to compare distance travelled (in kilometres) with time taken (in hours up to 6 hours) if the average speed of a vehicle is 75 kilometres per hour. Show clearly on your graph, and state (a) the distance travelled in 5.4 hours, (b) the time required to travel 235 kilometres, (c) the difference in distance between the points reached after 2.4 hours and after 3.7 hours (giving the answers to the nearest kilometre).   (RSA)

3. Draw a graph to compare distance travelled (in kilometres) with time taken (in hours up to 5 hours) if the average speed of a vehicle is 60 kilometres per hour.
Show clearly on your graph, and state
(a) the distance travelled in 4.5 hours;
(b) the time required to travel 210 kilometres;
(c) the difference in distance between the points reached after 1.5 hours and after 2.75 hours (giving the answers to the nearest kilometre).   (RSA)

4. Draw a graph to show the relationship between lb and kg, taking 11 lb = 5 kg.
By using your graph, and not by calculation, show clearly and state (a) the equivalent weight in lb of 27.5 kg, and (b) the equivalent weight in kg of 44 lb.   (RSA)

5. Draw a graph showing the relationship between pounds sterling and dollars, using £100 = $175. Use values between £0 and £1 000 in £100 steps, and use your graph to find: (a) How many £s = $495 and (b) How many $ = £750.   (RSA)

32.5 Straight-line Graphs which Do Not Pass through the Origin

Many straight-line graphs pass through the origin (that is, the point where both variables are zero); in the example illustrated in Fig. 32.3, for instance, the man earns nothing if he has done no work. This is not always true, however. A worker is not paid overtime pay, for example, until his basic working week of, say, 42 hours has been exceeded; in a graph of overtime pay (y) plotted against his working hours (x), therefore, y is zero when x is 42, and the graph cannot pass through the origin. To consider another example: we can draw a straight-line graph relating thermometer readings on the Celsius and Fahrenheit temperature scales, but since 0° Celsius (the freezing-point of water) is 32° Fahrenheit, this graph does not pass through the origin either.

Example

A trainee's weekly wage is £52, and he also earns £1.60 an hour for overtime. Construct a graph showing his total pay when the overtime is any length of time up to 20 hours. Use your graph to find (*a*) the total pay when the overtime is $5\frac{1}{2}$ hours, (*b*) the overtime necessary to produce a pay of £66.80.

(RSA adapted)

We calculate the values of the man's weekly earnings, including payment for 5, 10, 15 and 20 hours overtime, as follows:

Earnings for basic week + 5 hours overtime = £52 + £8 = £60
Earnings for basic week + 10 hours overtime = £52 + £16 = £68
Earnings for basic week + 15 hours overtime = £52 + £24 = £76
Earnings for basic week + 20 hours overtime = £52 + £32 = £84

We plot these four points, and obtain the graph in Fig. 32.4.

(*a*) We can read off the total pay for a basic week plus $5\frac{1}{2}$ hours overtime by the method used in the last example; it comes to about £61.

(*b*) The overtime to be worked to produce a pay of £66.80 is about $9\frac{1}{4}$ hours.

Again, unless the scale is very large, highly accurate readings cannot be made.

32.6 Exercises: More Straight-line Graphs

1. A man's basic salary is £60 per week. To this is added £3 for every £1 000 of goods he sells. Draw a graph showing how his earnings increase while his sales vary between nil and £20 000, using sales of £5 000, £10 000, £15 000 and £20 000 as plotting points. From your graph calculate (*a*) his earnings when sales total £14 000 and (*b*) his sales in a week when he is paid £114.

2. The freezing point of water is 0° Celsius or 32° Fahrenheit, and the boiling point is 100° Celsius or 212° Fahrenheit.

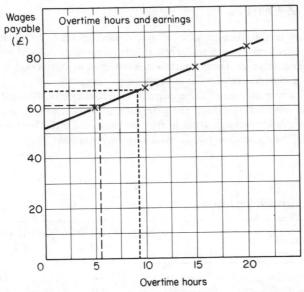

Fig. 32.4 A straight-line graph which does not pass through the origin

Draw a graph for converting these two scales within the range of the freezing point to boiling point of water.

From your graph state: (*a*) the Celsius equivalent of 50° F, and (*b*) the Fahrenheit equivalent of 25° C.   (RSA)

3. A man's weekly wage is £60, and he also earns £2.40 an hour for overtime. Construct a graph showing his total pay when the overtime is any length of time up to 20 hours. Use your graph to find (*a*) the total pay when the overtime is 8 hours; (*b*) the overtime necessary to produce a pay of £91.20; (*c*) how much more he earns for 12 hours' overtime than for 6 hours' overtime.
(RSA)

4. Two motorists plan to drive from *A* to *B*. Car 1 sets off from *A* at 10 a.m. and averages 60 km/h, arriving at *B* at 2 p.m. Car 2 is delayed by engine trouble at the start and cannot leave until 11 a.m. What was its average speed, if it arrived at *B* at the same time as Car 1? (Draw two line graphs on the same diagram, showing one car starting later than the other.)

32.7 The Z Chart

The Z chart is a particular kind of graph used to study the changes in a business's sales from month to month; it gets its name because it looks like a roughly-made letter Z. These charts are often used in business, because they give a very clear picture of what is happening to a firm's sales.

In order to prepare one of these charts it is necessary to collect three lots of figures each month throughout the year: (a) the *current monthly sales*, (b) the *cumulative sales* for the year (that is, the total sales since the beginning of the year) and (c) the *total sales for the preceding twelve months.*

Example

Draw a Z chart for the following data:

	Sales of ABC Company (£ thousands)	
	This year	Last year
January	39	46
February	33	44
March	41	52
April	49	57
May	56	62
June	63	70
July	71	83
August	53	57
September	42	46
October	37	39
November	36	35
December	53	60

(RSA)

This table gives us all the information we need for our Z chart:

(a) the sales for this year are listed month by month;

(b) the cumulative sales for this year are calculated from the monthly sales: for example, February's sales are added to January's sales to give a cumulative figure of 72 thousand pounds for January and February together, and so on for each month in turn;

(c) the total sales for the year ending on the last day of the current month are calculated as follows: on January 31 this total will be the sum of all last year's sales—651 thousand pounds—*minus* those for January of last year *plus* those for January of this year, that is, $651 - 46 + 39 = 644$ thousand pounds.

The completed table looks like this:

| | Sales of ABC Company (£ thousand) | | | |
	This year	Cumulative total	Last year	Running 12-month total
January	39	39	46	644
February	33	72	44	633
March	41	113	52	622
April	49	162	57	614
May	56	218	62	608
June	63	281	70	601
July	71	352	83	589
August	53	405	57	585
September	42	447	46	581
October	37	484	39	579
November	36	520	35	580
December	53	573*	60	573
	573		651	

* This figure is, of course, the same as the total of the first column.

When recorded on a Z chart these figures appear as in Fig. 32.5.

The lowest line of the Z chart shows how ABC Company's sales vary month by month. The top line shows how these variations affect the sales trend: for instance, although sales rose steadily between February and July this year, each month's figures were less than for the same month last year, and the overall trend was downwards. The 'cumulated sales' line climbs towards the year's total, which it eventually reaches in December; this gives the chart its characteristic Z configuration.

32.8 Exercises: Z Charts

1. (a) Draw a Z chart for the data given on page 255:

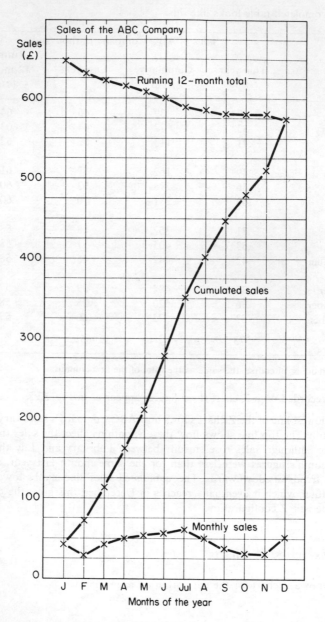

Fig. 32.5 A Z chart

| | Sales of XYZ Company | |
| | This year | Last year |
	(£ thousand)	
January	84	101
February	89	112
March	83	109
April	71	89
May	63	84
June	47	62
July	31	40
August	49	61
September	58	77
October	77	92
November	86	105
December	97	118

(*b*) Comment on your results.   (RSA)

2. (*a*) Draw a Z chart for the following data:

| | Sales of PQR Company | |
| | This year | Last year |
	(£ thousand)	
January	56	66
February	60	64
March	62	61
April	48	58
May	46	59
June	54	63
July	62	67
August	68	72
September	71	84
October	74	91
November	82	106
December	90	110

(*b*) Comment on your results.   (RSA)

3. (a) Draw a Z chart for the following data:

| | Sales of ABC Company | |
| | This year | Last year |
	(£ thousand)	
January	36	28
February	38	32
March	44	36
April	41	40
May	59	71
June	76	76
July	82	78
August	85	75
September	33	24
October	38	36
November	48	38
December	52	31

(b) Comment on the chart.

Unit Thirty-three

More About Averages—Mean, Median and Mode

33.1 Averages in Statistics

Any statistical investigation results in a mass of data. Each item of the data is interesting, but what we wish to see is the *general* picture. For example, in an inquiry about the reliability of motor cars there is sure to be one car that broke down before the unfortunate owner got it home from the showrooms. This is of course a true statistic, but how representative is it of motor cars in general? We cannot conclude from it that all cars break down after only one day. Clearly, we are interested in the average reliability of motor cars. If we are to draw conclusions from the statistics we collect, we shall need to summarize the data by averaging them in some way. It may then help us to see how the actual data are *dispersed around the average.*

Consider the performance of two car models used by XYZ Ltd's sales staff. The weeks of trouble-free running before a major breakdown are as follows:

Model A: 2, 1, 26, 23, 18, 294, 42   Total = 406 weeks
Model B: 44, 56, 73, 69, 76, 45, 43   Total = 406 weeks

The simple average running time before breakdown of both models is
$$406 \div 7 = 58 \text{ weeks}$$

When we look at the way these data are dispersed around the average, we see that the pattern is very different:

		Average	
Model A:	1, 2, 18, 23, 26, 42	(58)	294
Model B:	43, 44, 45, 56	(58)	69, 73, 76

Model B is a reliable performer and provided there were regular maintenance checks after about 40 weeks, would appear to give no trouble to XYZ Ltd. Model A is rather more erratic. On most occasions its performance is poor or moderate, but on one occasion it proved marvellously reliable.

Averages help us to see the general picture, and since they stress a central figure and reduce the significance of extreme values to one side or the other, they are called *measures of central tendency*. The three most commonly used measures of central tendency are:

(a) the arithmetic mean
(b) the median
(c) the mode

Unit 10 of this book deals with simple averages, and it might be useful for readers who need to revise elementary ideas on averages to read through that Unit again before proceeding to a more detailed consideration of these measures of central tendency.

33.2 The Arithmetic Mean from Simple Data

The *arithmetic mean* is the simple average already discussed in Unit 10. In any statistical collection the raw data are observations of a *variable*. For a numerical variable the arithmetic mean is found by adding the values of the observations together, and dividing by the number of observations. It is convenient to use symbols in mathematics to save constantly repeating phrases such as 'arithmetic mean', 'sum of the observations', etc. A value of the variable is usually called x. The number of measurements or observations made is called n. The symbol for the arithmetic mean is $\bar{x}$ (x with a short line over the top) called x-bar and 'the sum of' is designated by Σ, the Greek letter sigma. The formula for the arithmetic mean is therefore:

$$\bar{x} = \frac{\Sigma x}{n}$$

The arithmetic mean is often simply called the *mean*.

Example

An investigation into the takings of a small grocer's shop gives the following results:

	£
	£
January	2 794
February	1 986
March	2 325
April	3 654
May	3 726
June	3 985
July	6 574
August	7 384
September	5 259
October	3 265
November	4 381
December	5 286
	£ 50 619

What is the arithmetic mean of the monthly takings?

$$\bar{x} = \frac{\Sigma x}{n} \quad \left(= \frac{\text{The sum of the observations}}{\text{The number of the observations}} \right)$$

$$= \frac{£50\,619}{12}$$

$$= £4\,218.25$$

33.3 The Arithmetic Mean of a Frequency Distribution

Sometimes data are not presented in detail, with every statistic separate from other statistics, but in the form of a *frequency distribution*. A stadium ticket office might report ticket sales as follows:

Price of ticket	Number sold
£1.50	284
£2.50	232
£4.50	376
£6.50	320

To find the arithmetic mean value of tickets sold we must now take account of the numbers of each type sold—in other words, the *frequency* with which a particular price ticket was sold. Our formula for the arithmetic mean now becomes

$$\bar{x} = \frac{\Sigma f x}{n}$$

where $\bar{x}$ is the arithmetic mean; x is a value of the variable; f is the frequency with which the value x occurs; Σ is 'the sum of' and n is the total number of observations, i.e. the sum of the frequencies. Arranged in a table we have:

Value of ticket (x)	Number sold (f)	Total value in £ (fx)
1.50	284	426
2.50	232	580
4.50	376	1 692
6.50	320	2 080
	$n = 1\ 212$	$\Sigma f x = 4\ 778$

$$\bar{x} = \frac{4\ 778}{1\ 212}$$

```
                              3.942
                     1 212)4 778.0
                           3 636
                           1 142 0
                           1 090 8
                              51 20
                              48 48
                               2 720
```

$$= £3.94$$

You will recognize that we are working out a weighted average as in Section 10.6 but, to conform with standard statistical practice, we are using the term *frequency* rather than weighting to denote the number of times a particular value of x occurs.

33.4 Exercises: The Arithmetic Mean

1. Find the arithmetic mean of each of the following sets of numbers.

   (a) 121; 136; 724; 385; 614
   (b) 2 758; 3 816; 2 742; 4 820
   (c) 27 246; 38 259; 71 634
   (d) 272; 163; 594; 725; 687; 724; 681; 384
   (e) 56 248; 72 386; 74 721; 48 256

2. Students in a class were aged as follows: 17, 17, 17, 18, 18, 18, 18, 18, 18, 18, 19, 19, 19, 21, 21, 21, 22, 23, 25, 27, 34, 46, 53, 72, 76. Find the mean age.

3. Scores out of 100 in an examination were as follows from the 50 candidates. Find the mean score, out of 100.

1 scored 95	4 scored 67	2 scored 53
3 scored 82	3 scored 64	1 scored 51
5 scored 75	11 scored 63	1 scored 50
1 scored 71	1 scored 61	3 scored 44
6 scored 70	5 scored 60	2 scored 39
		1 scored 15

4. The timber from a thinning programme in a forest yielded pitprops as follows:

Length of pitprop in metres	Number produced
1	440
1.25	580
1.5	730
1.75	640
2	320

   Find (a) the total length of pitprop material produced; (b) the mean length of a pitprop. (Answer correct to 2 decimal places.)

33.5 The Median

Many collections of statistics can be arranged in order of size, from the smallest to the biggest. Such an arrangement is called an *array*. If we now look at the central item in that array, we shall be looking at another type of average. This average is called the *median*.

   The median is defined as the value of the central item in an array of statistics.

   Consider the two sets of data on cars considered earlier, arranged in ascending order of size.

   Model A: 1, 2, 18, 23, 26, 42, 294
   Model B: 43, 44, 45, 56, 69, 73, 76

The value of the median item in each of these arrays will be the fourth item, since it will have three items below it and three above it. The values of the median items therefore are

Model A: 23 weeks
Model B: 56 weeks

We can see at once that the median can give a very different 'average' from the arithmetic mean, which was 58 in each case. The median is nowhere near the mean in the case of Model A, but it is quite close for Model B. The explanation is that if an array has a few extreme items, such as 294 in the case of Model A, it will affect the mean, but not the median. In the case of Model A, the median does give a much better idea of the average performance of the model, for it usually is rather poor. By disregarding altogether its very occasional brilliant performance it leaves us with the general idea that Model B is the better car.

Finding the median

The median is the *value* of the middle item in the array. In the example above we have seven items of which the fourth one is the middle item. With an odd number of items the middle item will always be a distinct item. To find it we have a simple formula:

$$\text{Middle item} = \frac{n + 1}{2}\text{th item}$$

Thus in a series of 19 items:

$$\text{Middle item} = \frac{19 + 1}{2}\text{th item}$$

$$= \frac{20}{2}\text{th item}$$

$$= \underline{\underline{10\text{th item}}}$$

The tenth item will be the middle item—with nine items below it and nine items above it.

When there is an even number of items in the array we cannot find an actual item whose value is the median value. For example, with eight items in the array:

$$\text{Middle item} = \frac{8 + 1}{2}\text{th item}$$

$$= \underline{\underline{4\tfrac{1}{2}\text{th item}}}$$

We cannot find a $4\tfrac{1}{2}$th item in the array, and must find the arithmetic mean of the fourth and fifth items.

Note It is wrong to say that because 4 is half of 8 the median must be the value of the fourth item. In an array of eight numbers the fourth item is not central, it has three below it and four above it. For example:

Item   : 1   2   3   4   5   6   7   8
Value of observation: 1   3   6   9   11   12   13   15

$$\text{Median} = \frac{8 + 1}{2}\text{th item} = \frac{9}{2}\text{th item} = 4\tfrac{1}{2}\text{th item}$$

Median value = mean of 4th and 5th items

$$= \frac{9 + 11}{2}$$

$$= \underline{\underline{10}}$$

We must always remember to add one to the number of observations before we divide by 2.

Example

The monthly salaries of twenty bank employees after tax are shown in the following table. Find the median take-home pay of these employees.

Take-home pay of employees, in January (£):

250.60	402.50	360.85	430.25
780.30	385.60	340.25	318.50
640.25	720.42	800.00	714.60
187.50	203.50	260.00	256.30
320.65	250.80	705.30	194.90

Arranged in ascending order of size these become:

Start here	*continued*
187.50	360.85
194.90	385.60
203.50	402.50
250.60	430.25
250.80	640.25
256.30	705.30
260.00	714.60
318.50	720.42
320.65	780.30
340.25	800.00

$$\text{Middle item} = \frac{20 + 1}{2}\text{th item}$$

$$= \underline{\underline{10\tfrac{1}{2}\text{th item}}}$$

The median will therefore be the arithmetic mean of the 10th and 11th items.

$$\text{Median} = \frac{£340.25 + £360.85}{2}$$

$$= \frac{£701.10}{2}$$

$$= £350.55$$

The median monthly pay of bank employees is therefore £350.55. (If you work out the *mean* take-home pay of these employees you will find that it is considerably higher (£426.15) than the median. This is because the few large salaries inflate the value of the mean, but do not affect the median.)

33.6 Exercises: The Median

1. (*a*) Define the median.
    (*b*) Find the median age of the members attending a motor vehicle maintenance course. Their ages are as follows: 16, 17, 20, 32, 17, 19, 15, 28, 47, 62, 18, 17, 20, 21, 23.

2. Find the median life of sparking plugs tested to destruction as follows:
    10 200 km,   7 350 km,   5 680 km,   2 100 km,   14 286 km,
    7 362 km,   4 985 km,   3 426 km,   4 175 km

3. A herd of Friesian cows gives milk yields (in litres) as follows during the year 19 . .. Find the median output.

Cow *A*	10 124	Cow *E*	7 348	Cow *I*	7 675
Cow *B*	7 245	Cow *F*	5 295	Cow *J*	4 259
Cow *C*	9 850	Cow *G*	11 105	Cow *K*	8 249
Cow *D*	8 975	Cow *H*	9 386	Cow *L*	7 368

4. Sales staff paid on a commission basis have earnings as follows. What is the median income?

	£		£
Mr *A*	385	Miss *F*	324
Mrs *B*	540	Miss *G*	478
Miss *C*	630	Mrs *H*	595
Mr *D*	490	Mr *I*	620
Mr *E*	430	Mr *J*	384

33.7 The Mode

The mode is the value of a variable that corresponds to its most frequent occurrence. If we dress *à la mode*, we choose the garments which are all the rage today—the fashions which everyone is wearing. To find the mode in statistics we have only to find the observation which occurs with the greatest frequency.

Example

An inquiry into the number of bedrooms in houses in a seaside town gives the following results:

Number of bedrooms	Number of houses so constructed
1	321
2	524
3	1 793
4	1 425
5	386
6	27
7	14
More than 7	53

The greatest frequency, 1 793, is for houses with 3 bedrooms. The modal house in the town is therefore a 3-bedroom house.

It is possible to have a *bimodal* series, where more than one type is found with the same frequency. Had there been 1 793 houses with 4 bedrooms this would have been a bimodal series.

33.8 Exercises: The Mode

1. A survey in Smalltown, Ohio, reveals that in July adult males are wearing the following types of trousers:

Shorts	321
Jeans	1 726
Corduroys	428
Jodhpurs	17
Flannels	326
Worsteds	925

What is *à la mode* in Smalltown?

2. A basketball team made the following scores in a season:

68, 72, 76, 73, 58, 68, 74, 68, 66, 72, 58, 64, 72, 68

What was its modal score?

3. In one week the weights (in tonnes) of containers passing through a certain port were as follows:

27	32	27	32	32
32	28	32	25	18
31	31	26	27	16
15	32	28	32	15
14	30	29	32	27
16	17	32	32	27

Form a frequency distribution using the five-barred gate system (see Fig. 30.2) and hence find the modal weight for containers.

4. Shoppers invited to state their favourite meat recorded the following preferences:

Beef	Lamb	Beef	Lamb
Chicken	Beef	Chicken	Beef
Rabbit	Chicken	Lamb	Lamb
Lamb	Pork	Beef	Pork
Beef	Lamb	Beef	Lamb
Pork	Beef	Lamb	Beef
Beef	Lamb	Rabbit	Pork
Chicken	Lamb	Beef	Lamb

Which type of meat was the modal preference?

33.9 A Comparison of Averages

Which is the best average to choose when describing a certain set of statistics? A summary of their features is given below.

The arithmetic mean

(a) It is easily understood.
(b) It is fairly easy to calculate.
(c) It takes account of all the data collected.
(d) It can be manipulated mathematically.

but

(a) It rarely comes out to a whole number—so, for example, we might find that on average families have 2.63 children or cats have 1.97 ears.
(b) Sets of data with extreme items, which distort the arithmetic mean, are not truly represented by it.

The median

(*a*) It is easy to calculate.
(*b*) It is always either an actual value in the data, or an average of two adjacent values at the centre of the data. It is therefore easy to understand.
(*c*) It ignores extreme values altogether.

but

(*a*) It is not fully representative of all the data.
(*b*) It is not amenable to mathematical manipulation.

The mode

(*a*) It is easy to determine.
(*b*) It is always an actual value—the most frequently occurring actual value.
(*c*) It ignores extreme items, unless these are the most commonly occurring values.
(*d*) The variable need not be numerical. (See Section 33.8, questions 1 and 4.)

but

(*a*) It is not fully representative of all the data.
(*b*) It is not amenable to mathematical manipulation.
(*c*) Some series have no mode at all. For example, the set of data 17 hours, 43 hours, 221 hours and 19 hours has no mode.
(*d*) Some series are bimodal, or even trimodal, as for example the set of numbers:

2, 3, 4, 7, 2, 3, 5, 8, 2, 2, 7, 5, 6, 9, 7, 1, 5, 3, 4, 4, 6, 6, 3, 7

In general, we use the arithmetic mean for most situations, and where this is not appropriate the median is the second choice.

33.10 Mental Arithmetic Exercises

1. What is the simple average of 17, 25 and 33?
2. What is the simple average of 11, 13, 19 and 25?
3. What is the simple average of 9, 13, 17, 19 and 27?
4. What is the median value of 17, 25, 27, 33?
5. What is the median value of 36, 39, 45, 49, 73?
6. What is the median value of 14, 16, 17, 22, 25, 26?
7. What is the modal value of 2, 5, 7, 5, 6, 3, 4, 5?
8. What is the modal value of 2, 3, 4, 7, 2, 4, 6, 5, 8?
9. What is the arithmetic mean of 207, 224 and 262?
10. What is the arithmetic mean of 12 706, 12 802 and 12 901?

Answers to Exercises
(where appropriate)

Unit 2

2.5 *1.* (a) 1 694; (b) 2 296; (c) 2 050; (d) 2 488; (e) 7 950; (f) 11 523; (g) 2 219 624; (h) 1 384 978.

   2. (a) 29; (b) 105; (c) 712; (d) 2 409; (e) 7 032; (f) 5 709.

   3. (a) 3 339; (b) 49 097; (c) 215 400; (d) 496 640; (e) 29 597 477.

   4. (a) 7 728; (b) 7 655; (c) 85 235; (d) 63 615; (e) 74 507; (f) 60 295.

2.9 *1.* (a) 4; (b) 4; (c) 8; (d) 8; (e) 8; (f) 19; (g) 16; (h) 18; (i) 46; (j) 30.

   2. (a) 135; (b) 581; (c) 79; (d) 119; (e) 225; (f) 1 151; (g) 845; (h) 6 294; (i) 419; (j) 8 739; (k) 20 343; (l) 80 897; (m) 246 429; (n) 134 039; (o) 179 609.

   3. (a) 493; (b) 2 741; (c) 5 225; (d) 6 831; (e) 6 107; (f) 68 827; (g) 21 231; (h) 92 760; (i) 117 235; (j) 597 726.

2.14 *1.* (a) 11 123; (b) 74 024; (c) 8 190; (d) 44 232; (e) 8 564; (f) 50 498; (g) 47 044; (h) 46 926; (i) 57 210; (j) 138 456.

   2. (a) 50 336; (b) 189 051; (c) 72 296; (d) 215 118; (e) 68 706; (f) 403 678; (g) 56 335; (h) 289 192; (i) 130 734; (j) 148 683.

   3. 5 008 books.

   4. 32 959 litres.

   5. 55 486 books.

   6. 8 628 packs.

   7. 107 463 tickets.

2.18 *1.* (a) 59; (b) 262; (c) 1 229; (d) 1 455; (e) 551; (f) 1 094; (g) 888; (h) 989; (i) 814; (j) 712.

   2. (a) 310 remainder 6; (b) 2 406 remainder 1; (c) 544 remainder 4; (d) 489 remainder 4; (e) 818 remainder 3; (f) 1 494 remainder 3; (g) 1 053 remainder 2; (h) 1 389 remainder 3; (i) 1 145 remainder 5; (j) 648 remainder 4.

2.20 *1.* (a) 212 remainder 5; (b) 235 remainder 2; (c) 343 remainder 15; (d) 492 remainder 13; (e) 1 020 remainder 7; (f) 177 remainder 9; (g) 210 remainder 11; (h) 549 remainder 7; (i) 1 032 remainder 1; (j) 1 723 remainder 4.

   2. (a) 379 remainder 39; (b) 462 remainder 53; (c) 1 022 remainder 14; (d) 997 remainder 39; (e) 3 988 remainder 14; (f) 21 remainder 119; (g) 91 remainder 27; (h) 157 remainder 120; (i) 1 189 remainder 96; (j) 609 remainder 4.

   3. 317 pennies.

   4. 75 casual customers.

   5. 9 coaches.

   6. 1 505 men.

2.21 *1.* (a) 49; (b) 381; (c) 47; (d) 1 988; (e) 595; (f) 14 780; (g) 192; (h) 62; (i) 302; (j) 91.

   2. (a) 217; (b) 548; (c) 146; (d) 2 322; (e) 931; (f) 5 047; (g) 251; (h) 102; (i) 172; (j) 121 remainder 3.

   3. (a) 169; (b) 944; (c) 80; (d) 1 905; (e) 750; (f) 5 888; (g) 640; (h) 31; (i) 218; (j) 44.

   4. (a) 28; (b) 59; (c) 692; (d) 13; (e) 166; (f) 119; (g) 243; (h) 680; (i) 3 408; (j) 2 remainder 5; (k) 62 remainder 1; (l) 11; (m) 13 162; (n) 390; (o) 5.

   5. (a) 34; (b) 216 metres; (c) 24 sheets; (d) 1 620; (e) 40; (f) the quotient; (g) 263 garments; (h) 25; (i) 12 000; (j) 5 000; (k) £17 000; (l) 22; (m) 973; (n) 460; (o) 8 000 trees.

Unit 3

3.3 *1.* (*a*) 85.12; (*b*) 154.49; (*c*) 278.26; (*d*) 162.063; (*e*) 2 418.66; (*f*) 2 980.266; (*g*) 678.242; (*h*) 8 581.450 9.

2. (*a*) 12.72; (*b*) 20.3; (*c*) 51.43; (*d*) 16.68; (*e*) 117.934; (*f*) 25.772; (*g*) 514.073; (*h*) 397.47; (*i*) 44.939; (*j*) 388.513; (*k*) 23.675; (*l*) 350.945.

3.5 *1.* (*a*) 11.34; (*b*) 15.228; (*c*) 14.144; (*d*) 22.425; (*e*) 242.73; (*f*) 103.74; (*g*) 147.81; (*h*) 363.032; (*i*) 123.808; (*j*) 747.62.

2. (*a*) 4.59; (*b*) 18.24; (*c*) 14.63; (*d*) 33.366; (*e*) 16.649 1; (*f*) 1 158.08; (*g*) 193.555 2; (*h*) 28 573.9; (*i*) 306.085 5; (*j*) 21.174 35.

3.7 *1.* (*a*) 276.5; (*b*) 42.75; (*c*) 4 295; (*d*) 45 967; (*e*) 3 785.6; (*f*) 4 583; (*g*) 4 972.5; (*h*) 725 610; (*i*) 8 697 000; (*j*) 386 560.

2. (*a*) 4.765; (*b*) 0.495; (*c*) 2.758 4; (*d*) 2.476 5; (*e*) 0.003 816 7; (*f*) 0.012 736; (*g*) 2.976 5; (*h*) 18.965; (*i*) 0.472 563 6; (*j*) 0.002 785 6.

3.9 *1.* (*a*) 2; (*b*) 3; (*c*) 2.2; (*d*) 11.6; (*e*) 43; (*f*) 30.3; (*g*) 52; (*h*) 0.234; (*i*) 1.09; (*j*) 23.4.

2. (*a*) 45.1; (*b*) 10.23; (*c*) 11.9; (*d*) 0.27; (*e*) 13.7; (*f*) 16.47; (*g*) 27; (*h*) 0.121; (*i*) 191; (*j*) 14.9.

3.11 *1.* (*a*) 9.5; (*b*) 31.1; (*c*) 29.0; (*d*) 15.0; (*e*) 7.8; (*f*) 14.5.

2. (*a*) 28.69; (*b*) 35.10; (*c*) 455.95; (*d*) 258.25; (*e*) 138.67; (*f*) 4 426.23.

3. (*a*) 136.07; (*b*) 51.5; (*c*) 139.8; (*d*) 22; (*e*) 17.44; (*f*) 218.086.

Unit 4

4.4 *1.* (*a*) £15.94; (*b*) £26.73; (*c*) £46.21½; (*d*) £43.02½; (*e*) £43.36½; (*f*) £64.48½; (*g*) £1.054.89; (*h*) £1 368.68; (*i*) £2 211.93; (*j*) £1 321.12.

2. Weekly gross takings = £1 110.22½.

3. Takings for the whole year = £476 354.

4.6 *1.* (*a*) £7.50; (*b*) £56.40; (*c*) £120.86; (*d*) £28.55; (*e*) £159.02; (*f*) £99.70.

2. (*a*) 83p; (*b*) £1.14; (*c*) £2.87; (*d*) £13.70; (*e*) £66.75; (*f*) £87.15.

3. (*a*) £26.22; (*b*) £30.78; (*c*) £136.42; (*d*) £186.58; (*e*) £404.22½; (*f*) £2 143.48½.

4. Mr *A*, £102.74; Mrs *B*, £40.00; Mr *C*, £65.22; Miss *D*, £46.32; Mr *E*, £74.13; Mr *F*, £58.15.

4.8 *1.* (*a*) £109.80; (*b*) £381; (*c*) £75.57; (*d*) £753; (*e*) £1 232; (*f*) £116.77½.

2. Shop A, £424.65; Shop B, £673.90; Shop C, £1 055.30; Shop D, £1 520.80; Shop E, £3 883.85.

3. £2 134.35.

4. £10 670.40.

5. £218.55.

6. Yes, he will gain £445 per year.

7. £320.10.

8. £2 972.

4.10 *1.* (*a*) £5.50; (*b*) £23.04; (*c*) £78.02½; (*d*) £55.07; (*e*) £138.97; (*f*) £362.81.

2. (*a*) £172.59; (*b*) £42.65; (*c*) £72.57; (*d*) £127.56; (*e*) £716.28; (*f*) £586.72.

3. £101.20 each.

4. £207.50 each.

5. £2.30 each.

6. £2 917 and £5 834.

7. £9 750 and £19 500.

4.11 *1.* 219. *2.* 88. *3.* 4 113. *4.* 727. *5.* £1 319.73. *6.* £55. *7.* £342. *8.* £70. *9.* £69. *10.* 455 seconds. *11.* 16 years 7 months. *12.* 0.02. *13.* 23.025. *14.* 89.7. *15.* £7.35.

Unit 5

5.3   *1.* (a) $1\frac{1}{4}$; (b) $1\frac{5}{8}$; (c) $1\frac{5}{12}$; (d) $1\frac{1}{24}$; (e) $1\frac{1}{5}$ (f) $\frac{29}{30}$; (g) $1\frac{11}{12}$; (h) $2\frac{2}{7}$; (i) $1\frac{5}{8}$; (j) $1\frac{37}{40}$; (k) $1\frac{23}{40}$; (l) $1\frac{13}{14}$.

  2. (a) $8\frac{1}{8}$; (b) $10\frac{3}{5}$; (c) $13\frac{4}{5}$; (d) $11\frac{1}{6}$; (e) $8\frac{7}{8}$; (f) $17\frac{13}{15}$; (g) $12\frac{3}{5}$; (h) $7\frac{7}{8}$; (i) $12\frac{13}{15}$; (j) $14\frac{17}{20}$; (k) $9\frac{5}{24}$; (l) $9\frac{59}{60}$.

5.5   *1.* (a) $\frac{1}{6}$; (b) $\frac{1}{8}$; (c) $\frac{3}{10}$; (d) $\frac{4}{15}$; (e) $\frac{11}{21}$; (f) $\frac{1}{6}$; (g) $\frac{5}{12}$; (h) $\frac{7}{30}$; (i) $\frac{1}{12}$; (j) $\frac{7}{30}$.

  2. (a) $2\frac{1}{6}$; (b) $3\frac{1}{20}$; (c) $1\frac{1}{40}$; (d) $4\frac{1}{6}$; (e) $3\frac{29}{30}$; (f) $4\frac{22}{35}$; (g) $3\frac{5}{6}$; (h) $6\frac{37}{70}$; (i) $3\frac{29}{60}$; (j) $6\frac{43}{60}$; (k) $13\frac{23}{24}$; (l) $12\frac{31}{40}$.

5.7   *1.* (a) $\frac{1}{2}$; (b) $\frac{1}{6}$; (c) $\frac{3}{14}$; (d) $\frac{3}{4}$; (e) $\frac{1}{6}$; (f) $\frac{11}{24}$; (g) $\frac{8}{15}$; (h) $\frac{4}{9}$; (i) $\frac{3}{5}$; (j) $\frac{1}{4}$.

  2. (a) $\frac{5}{18}$; (b) $\frac{1}{8}$; (c) $\frac{1}{12}$; (d) $\frac{5}{12}$; (e) $\frac{1}{2}$; (f) $\frac{1}{4}$; (g) $\frac{3}{8}$; (h) $\frac{1}{5}$; (i) $\frac{1}{10}$; (j) $\frac{8}{45}$; (k) $\frac{3}{8}$; (l) $\frac{1}{2}$.

5.9   *1.* (a) 2; (b) 3; (c) 6; (d) 7; (e) 4; (f) 4; (g) $4\frac{1}{2}$; (h) 12; (i) 24; (j) $16\frac{1}{2}$.

  2. (a) $12\frac{3}{5}$; (b) $11\frac{1}{4}$; (c) $23\frac{1}{3}$; (d) $10\frac{1}{8}$; (e) $23\frac{4}{5}$; (f) $22\frac{1}{2}$; (g) $13\frac{3}{4}$; (h) 8; (i) 11; (j) $7\frac{4}{5}$; (k) 18; (l) 9.

5.11   *1.* (a) 2; (b) $3\frac{1}{2}$; (c) 6; (d) $1\frac{4}{5}$; (e) $\frac{6}{9}$; (f) $\frac{5}{6}$; (g) $1\frac{13}{15}$; (h) $1\frac{1}{2}$; (i) $2\frac{1}{4}$; (j) $1\frac{7}{15}$.

  2. (a) 2; (b) 6; (c) $2\frac{2}{5}$; (d) 6; (e) $\frac{9}{14}$; (f) 5; (g) $1\frac{11}{14}$; (h) $3\frac{3}{4}$; (i) $2\frac{2}{3}$; (j) $1\frac{4}{5}$.

5.12   *1.* 464. *2.* 89. *3.* 18 920. *4.* 704. *5.* 4.7. *6.* 2. *7.* 2.375. *8.* 9. *9.* $\frac{5}{6}$. *12.* $3\frac{5}{8}$. *11.* $2\frac{1}{10}$ *12.* £288. *13.* 4 hours 35 minutes. *14.* $\frac{9}{?}$. *15.* 15.

Unit 6

6.3   *1.* (a) 1, 2; (b) 7; (c) 3, 11; (d) 5; (e) 13; (f) 23; (g) 7, 17, 29; (h) 11, 19; (i) 13; (j) 7.

  2. 1, 2, 3, 5, 7, 11, 13, 17, 19, 23, 29.

  3. 41, 43, 47, 53, 59.

  4. (a) 12, 1, 6, 2, 4, 3; (b) 15, 1, 5, 3; (c) 18, 1, 2, 9, 3, 6; (d) 24, 1, 12, 2, 6, 4, 3, 8; (e) 27, 1, 9, 3; (f) 36, 1, 18, 2, 12, 3, 9, 4, 6; (g) 54, 1, 27, 2, 18, 3, 9, 6; (h) 72, 1, 36, 2, 18, 4, 12, 6, 9, 8, 24, 3; (i) 80, 1, 40, 2, 20, 4, 10, 8, 5, 16; (j) 84, 1, 42, 2, 21, 4, 12, 7, 3, 28, 6, 14.

  5. (a) 3; (b) 7; (c) 2, 4; (d) 2, 4, 8; (e) 5; (f) 2, 3, 4, 6, 12; (g) 2, 3, 6; (h) 2, 4, 8; (i) 17; (j) 2, 4, 8, 16.

  6. (a) 2, 4; (b) 5; (c) 2, 7, 14; (d) 2, 3, 4, 6, 12; (e) 2, 5, 10; (f) 3, 5, 15; (g) 2, 3, 6, 9, 18; (h) 2, 4; (i) 19; (j) 2, 4, 8, 16.

  7. (a) 12; (b) 60; (c) 20; (d) 12; (e) 14; (f) 84; (g) 21; (h) 60; (i) 36; (j) 12.

  8. (a) 35; (b) 10; (c) 15; (d) 36; (e) 75; (f) 30; (g) 100; (h) 42; (i) 30; (j) 12.

6.5   *1.* (a) $\frac{7}{12}$; (b) $1\frac{1}{20}$; (c) $\frac{24}{35}$; (d) $\frac{5}{6}$; (e) $1\frac{1}{3}$; (f) $\frac{23}{30}$; (g) $\frac{17}{20}$; (h) $1\frac{3}{8}$; (i) $1\frac{1}{2}$; (j) $\frac{3}{28}$.

  2. (a) 1; (b) $\frac{23}{24}$; (c) $1\frac{1}{4}$; (d) $\frac{1}{3}$; (e) $\frac{13}{30}$; (f) $\frac{13}{15}$; (g) $1\frac{7}{10}$; (h) $6\frac{1}{2}$; (i) $4\frac{43}{5}$; (j) $10\frac{1}{2}$.

  3. (a) $\frac{5}{8}$; (b) $1\frac{2}{31}$; (c) $2\frac{1}{4}$; (d) $2\frac{11}{31}$; (e) $\frac{7}{8}$; (f) $6\frac{2}{5}$; (g) $2\frac{2}{9}$; (h) $2\frac{11}{14}$; (i) $\frac{1}{3}$; (j) $4\frac{2}{3}$.

6.6   *1.* 164.85. *2.* £103.20. *3.* £2 000 000. *4.* £1 453. *5.* 24 000 bottles. *6.* 7. *7.* 24.5 metres. *8.* $\frac{7}{20}$. *9.* 1 440 minutes. *10.* 6. *11.* 8. *12.* £63.20. *13.* $\frac{3}{8}$ kilometre. *14.* £35 000. *15.* 72.

Unit 7

7.4   *1.* (a) 2.756 km, 275 600 cm, 2 756 000 mm; (b) 3.818 km, 381 800 cm, 3 818 000 mm; (c) 4.265 5 km, 426 550 cm, 4 265 500 mm; (d) 5.872 75 km, 587 275 cm, 5 872 750 mm; (e) 175.650 km, 17 565 000 cm, 175 650 000 mm; (f) 189.265 km, 18 926 500 cm, 189 265 000 mm; (g) 38.565 725 km, 3 856 572.5 cm, 38 565 725 mm; (h) 72.469 585 km, 7 246 958.5 cm, 72 469 585 mm; (i) 0.027 956 km, 2 795.6 cm, 27 956 mm; (j) 0.138 721 km, 13 872.1 cm, 138 721 mm.

2. (a) 2.756 5 kg, 2 756 500 mg; (b) 3.812 5 kg, 3 812 500 mg; (c) 7.256 425 kg, 7 256 425 mg; (d) 8.497 256 kg, 8 497 256 mg; (e) 27.284 3 kg, 27 284 300 mg; (f) 385.625 712 kg, 385 625 712 mg; (g) 0.045 856 kg, 45 856 mg; (h) 0.038 721 kg, 38 721 mg; (i) 0.145 979 kg, 145 979 mg; (j) 0.156 958 kg, 156 958 mg.

3. (a) 2 500 ml, 250 cl, 25 dl; (b) 3 800 ml, 380 cl, 38 dl; (c) 47 500 ml, 4 750 cl, 475 dl; (d) 27 900 ml, 2 790 cl, 279 dl; (e) 8 765 ml, 876.5 cl, 87.65 dl; (f) 9 214 ml, 921.4 cl, 92.14 dl; (g) 385 725 ml, 38 572.5 cl, 3 857.25 dl; (h) 396 321 ml, 39 632.1 cl, 3 963.21 dl; (i) 726 942 ml, 72 694.2 cl, 7 269.42 dl; (j) 459 725 ml, 45 972.5 cl, 4 597.25 dl.

7.6 *1.* 3 040 small packets. *2.* 50 000 cartons. *3.* £90. *4.* 3 000 bags. *5.* 3 110 litres. *6.* 8 970 kg. *7.* 9 500 kg. *8.* 220 kg. *9.* 140 000 cartons. *10.* £16 380. *11.* £82.50. *12.* £10 575.

Unit 8

8.2 *1.* (a) 1 : 20; (b) 1 : 2; (c) 3 : 4; (d) 1 : 4; (e) 1 : 5; (f) 2 : 5; (g) 2 : 5; (h) 1 : 5.
2. (a) 1 : 100; (b) 1 : 20; (c) 1 : 14; (d) 2 : 7; (e) 1 : 400; (f) 1 : 50; (g) 1 : 30; (h) 1 : 48;
3. (a) 1 : 2.67; (b) 1 : 3.75; (c) 1 : 3.70; (d) 1 : 3.43; (e) 1 : 3.17; (f) 1 : 6.92; (g) 1 : 142.86; (h) 1 : 2.67.
4. (a) 1 : 1.7;(b) 1 : 4;(c) 1 : 6;(d) (i) 1 : 1.22, (ii) 1 : 1.23; (e) 1 : 15; (f) 1 : 0.87; (g) 1 : 8; (h) 1 : 8.5.

8.4 *1.* (a) £171 and £114; (b) £220 and £110; (c) £400 and £80; (d) £320 and £240; (e) £400 and £320; (f) £952 and £833; (g) £4 020 and £3 216; (h) £1 076, £807 and £538; (i) £2 012, £2 012 and £1 509; (j) £10 600, £5 300 and £3 975.
2. (a) 210 kg and 140 kg; (b) 354 kg and 118 kg; (c) 291 kg, 194 kg and 97 kg; (d) 2 630 kg, 1 052 kg and 1 052 kg; (e) 1 368 kg, 1 368 kg and 114 kg; (f) 2 500 tonnes, 1 500 tonnes and 1 000 tonnes; (g) 2 058 tonnes, 1 372 tonnes and 1 372 tonnes; (h) 1 300 tonnes, 1 300 tonnes and 650 tonnes; (i) 640 tonnes, 640 tonnes and 480 tonnes; (j) 678 tonnes, 678 tonnes and 226 tonnes.
3. X has £5 250, Y has £2 625 and Z has £875.
4. A has £1 650, B has £1 650, C has £1 100 and D has £550.
5. A receives 5 600 kg, B receives 3 400 kg and C receives 1 800 kg.
6. Question 1 carries 48 marks, Question 2 40 marks and Question 3 32 marks.
7. X has £108, Y has £54 and Z has £36.

8.6 *1.* (a) 10p; (b) 10½p; (c) 21p; (d) 30p; (e) 50p; (f) 54p; (g) £56; (h) £80; (i) £400; (j) £100.
2. (a) £34 300; (b) £1 584; (c) £428.40; (d) £657.90; (e) £3 281.25; (f) £3 840; (g) £76.00; (h) £4.50; (i) £7.80; (j) £166.40.

8.7 *1.* £111.85. *2.* £127.15. *3.* 50 652. *4.* £8 770. *5.* 40 packets. *6.* 150 cm. *7.* 2 750 l. *8.* 46 days. *9.* 9⅝. *10.* $\frac{6}{7}$. *11.* £16.80. *12.* A has £2 000, B has £1 800. *13.* £17.50. *14.* One receives £72, the other £48. *15.* £108.50.

Unit 9

9.4 *1.* (a) 50%; (b) 25%; (c) 20%; (d) 30%; (e) 70%; (f) 15%; (g) 12½%; (h) 37½%; (i) 45%; (j) 87½%; (k) 41⅔%; (l) 75%.
2. (a) 150%; (b) 175%; (c) 162½%; (d) 170%; (e) 215%; (f) 380%; (g) 437½%; (h) 560%; (i) 665%; (j) 233⅓%; (k) 366⅔%; (l) 462½%.
3. (a) 55%; (b) 75%; (c) 36%; (d) 28%; (e) 41%; (f) 58%; (g) 65%; (h) 73%; (i) 85½%; (j) 72½%; (k) 96.4%; (l) 78½%.

9.6   *1.* (a) $\frac{3}{10}$; (b) $\frac{2}{5}$; (c) $\frac{4}{5}$; (d) $\frac{24}{25}$; (e) $\frac{7}{25}$; (f) $\frac{9}{25}$; (g) $\frac{5}{6}$; (h) $\frac{1}{8}$; (i) $\frac{1}{6}$; (j) $\frac{3}{8}$; (k) $\frac{7}{8}$; (l) $\frac{5}{12}$.

     2. (a) $\frac{9}{10}$; (b) $\frac{3}{5}$; (c) $\frac{3}{25}$; (d) $\frac{39}{50}$; (e) $\frac{14}{25}$; (f) $\frac{12}{25}$; (g) $\frac{11}{40}$; (h) $\frac{11}{16}$; (i) $\frac{1}{3}$; (j) $\frac{17}{20}$; (k) $\frac{22}{25}$; (l) $\frac{11}{20}$.

     3. (a) 0.31; (b) 0.36; (c) 0.72; (d) 0.65; (e) 0.455; (f) 0.625; (g) 0.735; (h) 0.858; (i) 0.4135; (j) 0.6535; (k) 0.876; (l) 0.9259.

9.8   *1.* (a) £60; (b) £150; (c) £180; (d) £240; (e) £480; (f) £150; (g) £480; (h) £320.

     2. (a) £100; (b) £150; (c) £110; (d) £117; (e) £1.25; (f) £52.50; (g) £12.50; (h) £300.

     3. (a) £168; (b) £720; (c) £288; (d) £160; (e) £121; (f) £268.80; (g) £244.80; (h) £352.80.

     4. (a) 72 tonnes; (b) 3 300 tonnes; (c) 201.6 kg; (d) 316.8 kg; (e) $9\frac{1}{2}$ km; (f) 70 km; (g) 1 760 l; (h) 68 l.

9.10 *1.* (a) £2.50; (b) £2.00; (c) £24; (d) £1.25; (e) £10.50; (f) £2.00; (g) £5.50; (h) £9.75.

     2. (a) £1.20; (b) £0.90; (c) £1.80; (d) £1.26; (e) £2.39; (f) £1.37$\frac{1}{2}$; (g) £2.12; (h) £4.31$\frac{1}{2}$.

     3. (a) £41.67; (b) £58.33; (c) £26; (d) £35.20; (e) £32.62$\frac{1}{2}$; (f) £87.97$\frac{1}{2}$; (g) £192; (h) £47.11.

     4. £249.37$\frac{1}{2}$.

     5. £122.10.

     6. £152.83.

9.11 *1.* 932. *2.* 118. *3.* 12 950. *4.* 921. *5.* $4\frac{1}{6}$. *6.* 0.21. *7.* £34.50. *8.* £5 500. *9.* £10 : £6. *10.* £12.60. *11.* $\frac{7}{20}$. *12.* £31.50. *13.* 102 days. *14.* £31.50. *15.* 294 km.

Unit 10

10.3 *1.* (a) 6; (b) 8; (c) 6; (d) 12; (e) 9; (f) 8; (g) 5; (h) 9; (i) 469; (j) 405.

     2. (a) 37 kg; (b) 35 kg; (c) 17 hr 55 min; (d) 6 hr 43 min; (e) 24.4 tonnes.

10.5 *1.* (a) 1 691; (b) 3 071; (c) 428; (d) 563; (e) 46 592.

     2. (a) 3.6; (b) 4.35; (c) 15.4; (d) 22.1; (e) 19.05.

     3. 1 527.

     4. 2 926.

     5. 28 970 cars.

10.7 *1.* (a) 220 g; (b) 400 g; (c) 100 g; (d) 58 kg; (e) 4.24 kg.

     2. (a) 59.6 kg; (b) 70.5 kg; (c) 54.8 kg; (d) 69.6 kg; (e) 55.6 kg.

     3. £77.04.

     4. 59%.

     5. 9 min 17.1 s.

     6. 1 min 56.8 s.

     7. 12.3 tonnes.

     8. 21.3 tonnes.

10.8 *1.* 17.8 m. *2.* £13.65. *3.* £213.50. *4.* £19 281. *5.* 7.36. *6.* $4\frac{1}{40}$. *7.* 10. *8.* 24 780 m. *9.* 45p : 40p. *10.* 0.625. *11.* £700. *12.* £4 970. *13.* 16. *14.* 4.68 kg. *15.* £160.

Unit 12

12.4 *1.* 192 \$. *2.* 1 052 fr. *3.* 430 Dm. *4.* 3 370 fr. *5.* 2 280 \$. *6.* 413 000 yen. *7.* 22 210 000 lire. *8.* 5 500 dinars. *9.* 85 100 markka. *10.* 2 750 000 cruz. *11.* 990 \$. *12.* 6312 fr. *13.* 1 404 guilders. *14.* 8 880 k. *15.* 41 724 fr.

12.6 *1.* (a) £1 000; (b) £10 000; (c) £10; (d) £2 000; (e) £20.

     2. (a) £500; (b) £20 000; (c) £5 000; (d) £30 000; (e) £30 000.

     3. (a) £212.77; (b) £146.20; (c) £4.32; (d) £45.54; (e) £7.28.

12.7 *1.* 829. *2.* 237 pence. *3.* 16 475. *4.* 1 527. *5.* $360\frac{5}{12}$. *6.* $6\frac{5}{8}$. *7.* 41 m. *8.* £9. *9.* 2.45. *10.* 425 fr. *11.* 1 500 000. *12.* 2 500 grams. *13.* 217 minutes. *14.* May 30. *15.* 8000.

Unit 13

13.3 *1.* (a) £36; (b) £120; (c) £168; (d) £350; (e) £160; (f) £288; (g) £432; (h) £500; (i) £1 440; (j) £5 880.

2. (a) £100; (b) £84; (c) £275; (d) £204; (e) £78; (f) £460; (g) £150.24; (h) £777; (i) £1 762.50; (j) £980.

3. (a) £421.88; (b) £400.40; (c) £296; (d) £306; (e) £693.75; (f) £541.80; (g) £2 651.25; (h) £3 631.88; (i) £2 887.50; (j) £4 875.

13.5 *1.* (a) £125; (b) £135; (c) £85; (d) £165; (e) £245; (f) £240.50; (g) £178.50; (h) £180; (i) £162; (j) £193.20.

2. (a) £306; (b) £130; (c) £553.50; (d) £312.50; (e) £672.10; (f) £2 972.20; (g) £100.10; (h) £165; (i) £378; (j) £1 462.50; (k) £471.50; (l) £1 125; (m) £1 080; (n) £5 040; (o) £405; (p) £6 720; (q) £6 321.88; (r) £7 875; (s) £36 562.5 (t) £28 875.

13.7 *1.* (a) 5%; (b) 8%; (c) 8%; (d) 6%; (e) 12%.

2. (a) £1 400; (b) £500; (c) £800; (d) £650; (e) £1 550.

3. (a) $2\frac{1}{2}$ years; (b) $3\frac{1}{2}$ years; (c) 5 years; (d) $4\frac{1}{2}$ years; (e) $2\frac{1}{2}$ years.

13.8 *1.* 1 428. *2.* 1 325 pence. *3.* 15 136. *4.* 508. *5.* 960. *6.* $8\frac{5}{24}$. *7.* £150. *8.* 12. *9.* 4.5. *10.* £64. *11.* 200 000. *12.* 1 500 ml. *13.* 407 minutes. *14.* 33 days. *16.* £12 500.

Unit 14

14.3 *1.* (a) £9.17; (b) £7.50; (c) £6; (d) £10; (e) £15; (f) £10.83; (g) £16.25; (h) £5.42; (i) £4.79; (j) £7.67.

2. (a) £9; (b) £17.50; (c) £20.58; (d) £1.15; (e) £8.75; (f) £20.04; (g) £18.23; (h) £33.33; (i) £5; (j) £2.50.

3. (a) £2.60; (b) £2.77; (c) £3.32; (d) £2.65; (e) £5.38; (f) £3.12; (g) £4.33; (h) £7.69; (i) £10.82; (j) £12.55.

Unit 15

15.3 *1.* Cash balance is £112.45.

2. Cash balance is £65.98.

3. Cash balance is £175.85.

4. Cash balance is £230.15.

15.5 *1.* Balance is £258.30.

2. Balance is £370.16.

3. Balance is £835.48.

15.7 *1.* £157.50 overdrawn.

2. £273.20 overdrawn.

15.9 *1.* $6\frac{11}{12}$. *2.* $\frac{13}{20}$. *3.* $\frac{1}{16}$. *4.* $1\frac{1}{14}$. *5.* 4.55. *6.* 13.9. *7.* £5 950. *8.* £28 : £20. *9.* £22.50. *10.* 26. *11.* 98 Dm. *12.* £37.50. *13.* £115.50. *14.* £21 000, £14 000, £7 000. *15.* £750.

Unit 16

16.3 *1.* Balance in hand = £3.74.

2. Balance in hand = £1.91, restored imprest = £23.09.

3. Balance in hand = £2.82.

4. Balance in hand = £7.74, restored imprest = £17.26.

Unit 17

17.2 *1.* (*a*) £1.29; (*b*) £1.35; (*c*) £67.96; (*d*) £18.60; (*e*) £6.16; (*f*) £9.25; (*g*) £4.25; (*h*) £71.60; (*i*) £57.30; (*j*) £28.50.

   2. (*a*) £21.86; (*b*) £2.86; (*c*) £9.75; (*d*) £41.70; (*e*) £232.80½.

   3. (*a*) 117 750 Dm; (*b*) 4 500 000 lire; (*c*) 9 000 fr; (*d*) 15 750 Swiss fr; (*e*) 20 394 guilders; (*f*) 370 000 Dm; (*g*) 3 135 000 guilders; (*h*) 212 500 fr; (*i*) 24 000 k; (*j*) 21 000 k.

17.4 *1.* (*a*) £78.75; (*b*) £137.60; (*c*) £88.80; (*d*) £129.60; (*e*) £87.75.

   2. (*a*) £175.20; (*b*) £89.30; (*c*) £119.34; (*d*) £220.80; (*e*) £78.96.

   3. (*a*) £81.60; (*b*) £51.30; (*c*) £80.96; (*d*) £53.75; (*e*) £8.58.

17.6 *1.* £3 263.85.

   2. £883.72.

   3. £404.88.

   4. £1 386.42½.

17.7 *1.* £21.15. *2.* £3.76½. *3. 3. 4.* 25. *5.* $\frac{3}{8}$. *6.* 7. *7.* 3.25. *8.* 1 150 000. *9.* 746 pieces. *10.* $\frac{9}{40}$. *11.* £246.67. *12.* £70. *13.* £24 000 and £18 000. *14.* 43 000. *15.* £20.

Unit 18

18.2 *1.* (*a*) 50p; (*b*) 75p; (*c*) £1.25; (*d*) £1.62½; (*e*) £1.87½; (*f*) £5.62½; (*g*) £9.75; (*h*) £18.75; (*i*) £40.00; (*j*) £48.12½.

   2. (*a*) £1.40; (*b*) £3.50; (*c*) £6.72; (*d*) £16.80; (*e*) £18.48; (*f*) £21.84; (*g*) £25.20; (*h*) £34.30; (*i*) £49; (*j*) £67.20.

   3. (*a*) £1.25; (*b*) £2.00; (*c*) £3.75; (*d*) £4.50; (*e*) £12.50; (*f*) £38.75; (*g*) £61; (*h*) £112.50; (*i*) £187.50; (*j*) £310.00.

18.4 *1.* (*a*) 30p; (*b*) 90p; (*c*) £2.00; (*d*) £2.20; (*e*) £3.00; (*f*) £2.75; (*g*) £5.00; (*h*) £10.00; (*i*) £12.50; (*j*) £60.00.

   2. (*a*) 72p; (*b*) 58½p; (*c*) £1.04; (*d*) £1.12½; (*e*) £2.16; (*f*) £2.20; (*g*) £2.40; (*h*) £3.78; (*i*) £14.25; (*j*) £25.65.

18.6 *1.* (*a*) £4; (*b*) £8; (*c*) £3; (*d*) £10; (*e*) £8.40; (*f*) £20; (*g*) £1.20; (*h*) £2.10; (*i*) £12; (*j*) £2.40.

   2. (*a*) £5; (*b*) £3; (*c*) £20; (*d*) £4; (*e*) £40; (*f*) £6; (*g*) £10; (*h*) £3; (*i*) £15; (*j*) £2.50.

   3. (*a*) £575; (*b*) £380; (*c*) £60.40; (*d*) £64; (*e*) £15 000 and £10 800; (*f*) £23 500 and £19 740.

18.7 *1.* 1 332. *2.* 0.315. *3.* 8½. *4.* £332.50. *5.* 66⅔%. *6.* £6.80. *7.* 12. *8.* 56 days. *9.* 730 days. *10.* £2.37. *11.* $\frac{9}{40}$. *12.* £1 500. *13.* 57 k.p.h. *14.* £5 000. *15.* £240.

Unit 19

19.2 *1.* (*a*) £26; (*b*) £62.40.

   2. (*a*) £36; (*b*) £84.

   3. (*a*) £27; (*b*) £52.80.

   4. (*a*) £27; (*b*) £70.20.

   5. (*a*) £750; (*b*) £4 218.75.

   6. (*a*) £238 425; (*b*) £286 110.

   7. (*a*) £10 569; (*b*) £14 796.60.

   8. (*a*) £21 240; (*b*) £28 674.

   9. (*a*) £55 644; (*b*) £69 555.

   10. (*a*) £25 160; (*b*) £32 640.

   11. (*a*) £23 355; (*b*) £30 275.

12. (a) £8 763 (b) C$15 598.14.
13. (a) £54 810 (b) A$ 89 888.40.
14. 26.67%.

19.4   1. £2 963.
2. £7 243.75.
3. £12 645.33.
4. £620.
5. £7 270.

19.5   1. 856. 2. 945. 3. £644.50. 4. 3. 5. 7⅞. 6. £412.50. 7. 122.50 fr. 8. 80p. 9. 8.
10. 2 354 pfennigs. 11. £17. 12. 17 years. 13. 828 pesetas. 14. £300. 15. £70.

Unit 20

20.2   1. (a) £102.33; (b) £134.18; (c) £83.47; (d) £110.72; (e) £198.82; (f) £127.17; (g)
£54.12; (h) 194.04; (i) £57.12; (j) £100.23.
2. (a) £298.72; (b) £150.22; (c) £190.92; (d) £233.55; (e) £259.95; (f) £204.95;
(g) £165.35; (h) £259.12; (i) £232.45; (j) £206.32.

20.4   1. (a) £203.24; (b) £139.47; (c) £109.74; (d) £188.98; (e) £311.96.
2. (a) £118.19; (b) £137.40; (c) £164.35; (d) £110.91; (e) £234.75; (f) £311.61;
(g) £320.09; (h) £499.86; (i) £266.92; (j) £319.80.
3. (a) £1 222; (b) £926; (c) £2 632.20; (d) £1 472.25; (e) £2 682.

Unit 21

21.3   1. (a) £2.40; (b) £1.80; (c) £3.85; (d) £5.20; (e) £5.85; (f) £6.20; (g) £6.80; (h) £27.50;
(i) £38.68; (j) £48.25.
2. (a) £176.40; (b) £216.30; (c) £262.50; (d) £483.00; (e) £1 831.20.
3. (a) £67.50; (b) £115.20; (c) £203.70; (d) £247.00; (e) £208.80; (f) £2 094.75;
(g) £2 833.28; (h) £2 590.00; (i) £3 903.20; (j) £4 558.00.
4. (a) £242 647.21; (b) £134 958.40; (c) £158 167.24; (d) £187 243.68;
(e) £163 285.27.
5. (a) £3 907 615.50; (b) £6 323 572.80; (c) £11 262 526.80; (d) £22 462 042.80;
(e) £35 516 620.80.

21.5   1. (a) 20p; (b) 0.02p; (c) 0.3p; (d) 2.25p; (e) 7p.
2. (a) 0.5p; (b) 0.45p; (c) 0.2p; (d) 12p; (e) 0.3p.
3. (a) 20p; (b) 80p; (c) 80p; (d) 120p; (e) 17p.
4. (a) £2 599 080; (b) 1.79p.
5. 10.3p.
6. (a) £1 610 180; (b) 2.9p.
7. (a) £2 737 800; (b) 2.2p.
8. (a) £1 328 350; (b) 4.3p.

Unit 22

22.3   1. (a) £1 500; (b) £3 400; (c) £50; (d) £147; (e) £425; (f) £4 125; (g) £7 660; (h)
£31 250; (i) £2 700; (j) £37 250.
2. £130.
3. £300. Value after 1st year = £2 500, after 2nd year £2 200, after 3rd year
£1 900.
4. At end of 1st year, £3 600; at end of 2nd year, £3 880.
5. £17 333.

22.5

	Year 1	*Year 2*	*Year 3*
1. (a)	$-£160 = £640$	$-£128 = £512$	$-£102 = £410$
(b)	$-£625 = £1\,875$	$-£469 = £1\,406$	$-£352 = £1\,054$
(c)	$-£1\,200 = £3\,600$	$-£900 = £2\,700$	$-£675 = £2\,025$
(d)	$-£2\,217 = £4\,433$	$-£1\,478 = £2\,955$	$-£985 = £1\,970$
(e)	$-£2\,912 = £4\,368$	$-£1\,747 = £2\,621$	$-£1\,048 = £1\,573$
2. (a)	$-£80 = £720$	$-£144 = £576$	$-£115 = £461$
(b)	$-£200 = £1\,400$	$-£350 = £1\,050$	$-£262 = £788$
(c)	$-£281 = £4\,219$	$-£1\,055 = £3\,164$	$-£791 = £2\,373$
(d)	$-£583 = £6\,417$	$-£2\,139 = £4\,278$	$-£1\,426 = £2\,852$
(e)	$-£3\,750 = £8\,750$	$-£3\,500 = £5\,250$	$-£2\,100 = £3\,150$

3. Year 1, $-£300 = £900$; Year 2, $-£300 = £1\,000$.
4. Year 1, $-£450 = £1\,350$; Year 2, $-£338 = £1\,012$.
5. Year 1, $-£4\,400 = £17\,600$; Year 2, $-£5\,970 = £36\,130$; Year 3, $-£8\,451 = £52\,179$.

Unit 23

23.2 1. (a) £2 646.44; (b) 14.7p per km.
2. (a) £3 027.40; (b) 15.1p per km.
3. (a) £1 887.50; (b) 10.3p per km.
4. (a) £2 336; (b) 9.3p per km.
5. (a) 14.1%; (b) 1 595 litres; (c) £70.80.

23.4 1. (a) 640 km/h; (b) 178 metres per second.
2. (a) 600 km/h; (b) 167 metres per second.
3. (a) 142 km; (b) 17.75 km/h.
4. (a) 447 km; (b) 74.5 km/h.
5. 30.1 km/h.
6. 25.9 km/h.
7. $24\frac{3}{4}$ minutes.
8. $42\frac{1}{2}$ minutes.

Unit 24

24.3 1. (a) £288; (b) £425; (c) £242; (d) £256; (e) £393; (f) £461; (g) £86; (h) £47; (i) £132; (j) £44.
2. (a) £54; (b) £42.25; (c) £63; (d) £51.80; (e) £81.00; (f) £126.30; (g) £1 440; (h) £257.85; (i) £578.55; (j) £94.55.
3. (a) £91.00; (b) £92.50; (c) £104.20; (d) £97.46; (e) £142.75.
4. (a) £345; (b) £280; (c) £800; (d) £994; (e) £1 698.
5. £8 435.
6. £436.60.
7. (a) Miss *A* earns £105, Miss *B* earns £115; (b) £800.

Unit 25

25.4 1. (a) £119.32$\frac{1}{2}$; (b) £89.70; (c) £58.12$\frac{1}{2}$; (d) £112.20; (e) £97.20; (f) £51.30; (g) £131.60; (h) £137.60; (i) £87.45; (j) £70.40.
2. (a) £82.35; (b) £96.20; (c) £75.90; (d) £62.00; (e) £147.00; (f) £123.50; (g) £151.70; (h) £101.50; (i) £118.80; (j) £151.20.
3. (a) £81.70; (b) £84.00; (c) £78.00

4. (a) £71.40; (b) £78.20; (c) £98.60; (d) £122.40; (e) £67.15; (f) £80.75; (g) £90.95; (h) £111.35; (i) £131.75; (j) £138.55.

25.7   The answers to these questions cannot be shown here. The student should compare his answer with Fig. 25.2.

25.9   The answers to these questions cannot be shown here.

25.10   1. 185. 2. 338. 3. 20 645. 4. £68.86. 5. £244.44. 6. $1\frac{1}{2}$. 7. £2 520 and £1 680. 8. $42\frac{1}{2}\%$. 9. 18 years. 10. 209Dm. 11. 270 seconds. 12. £108. 13. £108. 14. £1 080. 15. £105.30.

Unit 26

26.2   1. (a) £220.50; (b) £496.12$\frac{1}{2}$; (c) £551.25; (d) £826.87$\frac{1}{2}$; (e) £1 102.50; (f) £1 653.75; (g) £8 820; (h) £10 528.87$\frac{1}{2}$; (i) £16 537.50; (j) £36 933.75.

2. (a) £510.92; (b) £830.24; (c) £1 021.83; (d) £1 213.42; (e) £1 277.29; (f) £2 235.26; (g) £7 025.09; (h) £11 304.01; (i) £22 352.56; (j) £54 348.65.

3. (a) £540.80; (b) £642.74; (c) £1 021.83; (d) £2 023.85; (e) £1 166.42; (f) £2 349.32; (g) £3 098.01; (h) £4 065.70; (i) £6 236.36; (j) £11 899.81.

4. £3 190.

5. £4 470.

6. £73.29.

7. £154.55.

8. £22 700.

9. £3 101.

10. £4 109.

26.4   Note: The accuracy of the answers to this section depends upon the method used.

1. (a) £2 720.98; (b) £4 026.28; (c) £6 619.98; (d) £13 396.70; (e) £31 384.28.

2. (a) £2 038.59; (b) £3 761.48; (c) £4 844.35; (d) £9 072.11; (e) £13 331.57.

26.6   1. 2 273. 2. 201. 3. 0.9. 4. 2. 5. 2. 6. £7.25. 7. 47.50 fr. 8. £19.50. 9. 21 years. 10. £540. 11. £240. 12. £81.90. 13. 152 km/h. 14. £114 800. 15. £275.

Unit 27

27.3   1. (a) £650; (b) £351; (c) £228; (d) £384; (e) £3 260; (f) £1 125; (g) £810; (h) £11 900; (i) £3 024; (j) £34 920.

2. (a) £40; (b) £30; (c) £40; (d) £42.50; (e) £143.75; (f) £360; (g) £146.25; (h) £1 296; (i) £209; (j) £502.50.

3. (a) £115, 13.3%; (b) £790, 12.2%; (c) £100, 14.3%; (d) £1 150, 18.4%; (e) £1 750, 17.3%.

27.5   1. (a) £492.50; (b) £684; (c) £939; (d) £2 028; (e) £1 005.

2. (a) £200 stock; (b) £350 stock; (c) £50 000 stock; (d) £400 stock; (e) £3 000 stock.

3. (a) £700 stock, £42, 13.5%; (b) £1 000 stock, £100, 9.8%; (c) £5 000 stock, £425, 10%; (d) £4 000 stock, £100, 14.7%; (e) £2 000 stock, £60, 19.4%.

27.7   1. £42.75 increase.

2. £2.50 increase.

3. £3.75 increase.

4. (a) £1 104; (b) £61.

5. (a) £1 691; (b) £136.

6. £26.75 decrease.

7.   £29.25 increase.
8.   (a) £4 680; (b) £546.75.
9.   (a) £2 631; (b) £598.50.
10.   (a) 120 £1 shares; (b) £9 decrease.

Unit 28

28.3   1.   (a) 49 cm²: (b) 17 dm² 64 cm²; (c) 2.25 m²; (d) 5.0625 m²; (e) 2 a 25 m²; (f) 56 a 25 m², (g) 1 ha; (h) 1 ha 56 a 25 m²; (i) 25 ha; (j) 2.25 km².

2.   (a) 1 dm² 75 cm²; (b) 5 dm² 4 cm²; (c) 20 dm²; (d) 42 dm² 50 cm²; (e) 3.75 m²; (f) 8.75 m²; (g) 96 m²; (h) 1 a 45 m²; (i) 1 ha 36 a; (j) 1 ha 37 a 50 m².

3.   (a) 31.875 m²; (b) 9.125 m²; (c) 45.412 5 m²; (d) 15.812 m²; (e) 20.425 m²; (f) 22.907 5 m²; (g) 17.688 m²; (h) 40.984 m²; (i) 24.434 m²; (j) 61.439 m².

4.   3.6 hectares.

5.   1.68 hectares.

28.5   1.   (a) 20.71 m²; (b) 32.76 m²; (c) 107.76 m², (d) 52.88 m².

2.   8.5 m².

3.   Green = 625 m²; paths = 216 m²; flower beds = 384 m².

4.   (a) 53.7 m²; (b) 85.25 m²; (c) 166.4 m²; (d) 122.8 m².

5.   (a) 50 tins; (b) £60.

6.   Area = 288 m²; 1 152 paving stones.

7.   59.5 m².

8.   26½ m².

9.   48 m².

10.   (a) 41 m²; (b) £17.22.

28.7   1.   (a) 52 cm; (b) 76 cm; (c) 44 m; (d) 58 m; (e) 168 m; (f) 132 m; (g) 368 m; (h) 420 m; (i) 3 km; (j) 5 km.

2.   (a) £177; (b) £237; (c) £277; (d) £297; (e) £317; (f) £437; (g) £417; (h) £537; (i) £577; (j) £797.

3.   (a) 20 m; (b) 24 m; (c) 20 m; (d) 17.14 m; (e) 120 m; (f) 150 m; (g) 25 m; (h) 177.78 m; (i) 256 m; (j) 300 m.

4.   80 m.

5.   Breadth = 0.5 m, area = 0.4 m².

6.   303 m.

7.   Length = 120 m, perimeter = 420 m.

8.   Breadth = 30 m, perimeter = 170 m.

9.   Length = 180 m, perimeter = 640 m.

10.   Breadth = 105 m, perimeter = 430 m.

28.9   1.   (a) 30 cm³; (b) 192 cm³; (c) 150 cm³; (d) 576 cm³; (e) 1 200 cm³; (f) 6 m³; (g) 5.4 m³; (h) 26.88 m³; (i) 22 m³; (j) 44.625 m³.

2.   (a) 1 000 packets; (b) 1 440 packets; (c) 2 340 packets; (d) 4 140 packets; (e) 6 300 packets; (f) 9 600 packets; (g) 17 388 packets; (h) 22 000 packets; (i) 36 300 packets; (j) 52 000 packets.

3.   0.5 m.

4.   (a) 390 cm³; (b) 570 cm³; (c) 210 000 cm³; (d) 720 000 cm³.

5.   84 cm².

28.10   1. 340 000. 2. 25.04. 3. £115.70. 4. £17.15. 5. $\frac{21}{100}$. 6. 12.75 kg. 7. £125, £50, £25. 8. £4.95. 9. 11. 10. 1 725 krone. 11. £165. 12. £180. 13. 15¾ m². 14. 96 m³. 15. £180.

Unit 29

29.2   *1.*   (a) 11 cm; (b) 44 cm; (c) 22 cm; (d) 66 cm; (e) 33 cm; (f) $37\frac{5}{7}$ cm; (g) $78\frac{4}{7}$ cm; (h) 88 cm; (i) $9\frac{3}{7}$ m; (j) 44 m.

   2.   (a) $25\frac{1}{7}$ cm; (b) 44 m; (c) 88 m; (d) 2 m 64 cm; (e) 2 m 20 cm; (f) 66 m; (g) 132 m; (h) 308 m; (i) 352 m; (j) $377\frac{1}{7}$ m.

   3.   3 956.4 m.

   4.   32 970 m.

   5.   474.768 km.

29.4   *1.*   (a) 154 cm²; (b) 616 cm²; (c) 2 464 cm²; (d) 7 546 cm²; (e) 38.5 cm²; (f) $314\frac{2}{7}$ cm²; (g) 1 386 cm²; (h) £1 $964\frac{2}{7}$ cm²; (i) 5 544 cm²; (j) 1 m² 2 474 cm².

   2.   (a) 154 cm²; (b) $962\frac{1}{2}$ m²; (c) $254\frac{4}{7}$ cm²; (d) 1 386 m²; (e) 2 464 cm²; (f) $346\frac{1}{2}$ m²; (g) $113\frac{1}{7}$ cm²; (h) 9 856 m²; (i) $38\frac{1}{2}$ cm²; (j) 5 hectares 8 $558\frac{1}{2}$ m².

29.7   *1.*   (a) $103\frac{5}{7}$ cm²; (b) 66 cm²; (c) $226\frac{2}{7}$ cm²; (d) $402\frac{2}{7}$ cm²; (e) $628\frac{4}{7}$ cm².

   2.   (a) 175.84 m²; (b) 178.98 m²; (c) 75.36 m²; (d) 678.24 m²; (e) 854.08 m².

   3.   (a) 169.56 cm³; (b) 628 cm³; (c) 1 538.6 cm³; (d) 4 559.28 cm³; (e) 9 231.6 cm³.

   4.   (a) 1 570 m³; (b) 3 165.12 m³; (c) 5 626.88 m³; (d) 17 584 m³; (e) 39 564 m³.

29.8   *1.* 4 146. *2.* 51.1. *3.* $1\frac{5}{16}$. *4.* £36.40. *5.* 600. *6.* 55 days. *7.* 8 500 000. *8.* 1 987. *9.* 480 cubes. *10.* £2 880. *11.* £57.60. *12.* £143.50. *13.* 154 cm², *14.* £267.50. *15.* 132 cm, or 1 m 32 cm.

Unit 30

30.4   *1.*   A, 180 hours; B, 290 hours; C, 210 hours; D, 100 hours; E, 600 hours; F, 240 hours; G, 410 hours; H, 430 hours; I, 90 hours; J, 440 hours.

   2.   Mr A, 17 years; Mr B, 19 years; Mr C, 20 years; Mr D, 27 years; Mr E, 24 years; Mr F, 45 years; Mr G, 19 years; Mr H, 20 years; Mr I, 24 years; Mr J, 17 years.

   3.

Males (over 18)	131 000	Females (over 18)	105 000
Males (14–18)	6 000	Females (14–18)	7 000
Males (under 14)	12 000	Females (under 14)	12 000

   4.   Monday 72 500 tonnes; Tuesday 74 300 tonnes; Wednesday 78 100 tonnes, Thursday 59 000 tonnes; Friday 49 800 tonnes; Saturday 84 300 tonnes; Sunday 56 500 tonnes.

   5.   A, 59 kg; B, 67 kg; C, 49 kg; D, 71 kg; E, 58 kg; F, 62 kg; G, 65 kg; H, 60 kg; I, 72 kg; J, 68 kg.

   6.   (a) 26 200; (b) 26 100; (c) 6 200; (d) 6 300.

30.6   *1.*   Total expenditure = £34 504m.

   2.   Sales in thousand tonnes: January 491; February 480; March 520; April 340; May 221; June 89; July 13; August —; September —; October 626; November 654; December 638.

   3.   6 970 000 tonnes.

   4.   Grand total = 3 911 tonnes.

30.7   *1.*   Number of voters, 28 258 272; number of MPs elected, 629.

   2.   Total housing starts, 1 113 000; total grants 1 283 000; total council house starts 411 000.

   3.   Coal, 62.5%; iron and steel, 25%; other traffic, $12\frac{1}{2}$%.

   4.   Total passes, 900; percentage results 2.8%, 4.4%, 14.4%, 29.4%, 48.9%.

   5.   Number of passengers, 50 000; percentages, 12%, 4%, 8%, 10%, 10%, 26%, 6%, 4%, 4%, 16%.

   6.   Other tenures: England 800 000, Scotland 120 000; percentages: England 52%, 28%, 15%, 5%; Scotland 30%, 52%, 11%, 7%.

7. Expenditure on other services: (1980–81) £1 898m, (1951–52) £49m; percentages: (1980–81) 55%, 11%, 6%, 9%, 19%; (1951–52) 69%, 8%, 2%, 9%,
12%. Changes 1951–1981, 1 956%, 3 575%, 6 989%, 2 416%, 3 873%.
Change in total expenditure 2 466%.

Unit 32

Answers to graphical problems are approximate and slightly different answers are ac-
ceptable.

32.4 *1.* (*a*) £115.20; (*b*) 56 hours.
2. (*a*) 405 km; (*b*) 3 hours 8 minutes; (*c*) 97.5 km.
3. (*a*) 270 km; (*b*) 3 hours 30 minutes; (*c*) 75 km.
4. (*a*) 60.5 lb; (*b*) 20 kg.
5. (*a*) £282.85; (*b*) 1 312.5 $.
32.6 *1.* (*a*) £102; (*b*) £18 000.
2. (*a*) 10° C; (*b*) 77° F.
3. (*a*) £79.20; (*b*) 13 hours; (*c*) £14.40.
4. 80 km/h.

Unit 33

33.4 *1.* (*a*) 396; (*b*) 3 534; (*c*) 45 713; (*d*) 528.75; (*e*) 62 902.75.
2. 27 years.
3. 63.06%.
4. (*a*) 4 020 m; (*b*) 1.48 m.
33.6 *1.* (*b*) 20 years.
2. 5 680 km.
3. 7 962 litres.
4. £484.
33.8 *1.* Jeans are *à la mode*.
2. 68 baskets.
3. 32 tonnes.
4. It is a bimodal series—beef and lamb are equally popular.
33.10 *1.* 25. *2.* 17. *3.* 17. *4.* 26. *5.* 45. *6.* 19.5. *7.* 5. *8.* 2 and 4. *9.* 231.
10. 12 803.

Index